Olga

Olga

Fernando Morais

Translated from the Portuguese by
Ellen Watson

GROVE WEIDENFELD

New York

Published by Grove Weidenfeld
A division of Grove Press, Inc.
841 Broadway
New York, NY 10003-4793

Published in Canada by General Publishing Company, Ltd.

First published in Portuguese in Brazil in 1985 by Editora Alfa-Omega, São Paulo.

The article on page 130 is copyright © 1936 by The New York Times Company.
Reprinted by permission.

Library of Congress Cataloging-in-Publication Data
    Morais, Fernando.
        [Olga. English]
        Olga / Fernando Morais : translated from the Portuguese by Ellen
    Watson.
            p.   cm.
        Translation of: Olga.
        Includes bibliographical references.
        ISBN 0-8021-1086-X
        1. Benario-Prestes, Olga, 1908–1942.   2. Communists—Germany—
    Biography.   3. Communists—Brazil—Biography.   4. Communism—
    Brazil—History—20th century.   I. Title.
    HX274.7.B46M6713   1990
    324.243′075′092—dc20
    [B]   90-40479
                                                                     CIP

Manufactured in the United States of America

Printed on acid-free paper

Designed by Irving Perkins Associates

First American Edition 1990

10   9   8   7   6   5   4   3   2   1

For Carlinhos Wagner,
with much affection

Contents

CONTENTS

Foreword

WHAT YOU ARE about to read is true and relates events that happened exactly as described here. The life story of Olga Benario Prestes has fascinated and tormented me since my adolescence when I heard my father refer to Filinto Müller as the man who sent Luís Carlos Prestes's wife, a Jewish Communist, who was seven months pregnant at the time, to Adolf Hitler as a "gift." Haunted by this image, I resolved to write about Olga, a project I jealously guarded during the black years of state-sponsored terrorism in Brazil, when it would have been unimaginable for such a story to get past the censors.

Three years ago, after beginning my research, I realized it would be much more difficult to compose a portrait of Olga than I had originally supposed. I found practically no information about her in Brazil and was surprised to discover that even the official historiography of the Brazilian workers' movement, commissioned by political parties or analyzed by Marxist scholars, invariably relegated her to the subordinate role of "Prestes's wife." I uncovered no more than a few vague and superficial paragraphs about her. There was another obstacle: Olga would have been seventy-four years old if she had been alive and, since she became a political activist at a precocious age, most of those with whom she had shared such turbulent times were already dead. The few surviving witnesses—

whether in Germany or in Brazil—were at least octogenarians, many without the memory or health to sift through the details of events that occurred half a century ago.

My first and obvious target was Luís Carlos Prestes. The Saturday afternoons I stole from him in Rio de Janeiro produced pages and pages of precious information, much of it previously unpublished. And in my struggle to break down the barriers he instinctively imposed to avoid discussing personal matters, I was often moved to see that the stern Communist, who projected an image of a man of action, didn't hide his emotions when revealing details of Olga's personality or recalling incidents in the short and dramatic life they had together.* A man of prodigious memory, Prestes was able to recall with great precision the time of a departure or the exact words of a conversation that had occurred fifty years earlier. Very rarely did information provided by him, when checked against official documents, turn out to be incorrect. After reviewing the tapes of our interviews, I began researching new facts and personalities involved in the Communist revolt of 1935. Meanwhile, a young lawyer and bibliographer, Antonio Sérgio Ribeiro (one of Brazil's foremost experts on Carmen Miranda), rummaged through stacks of newspapers and magazines, flight records, and reports on ship movements in and out of various ports.

The next step involved a trip to the German Democratic Republic, where, contrary to my experience in Brazil, I found a veritable gold mine of information. The memory of Olga, a national hero whose name graces dozens of schools and factories, was affectionately preserved by the Communists in her homeland. The Institute of Marxism-Leninism, the Committee of Anti-Fascist Resistance, and the small museums at the Ravensbrück concentration camp and the Bernburg extermination camp (both preserved as they were found by Allied troops) made available all documents and photographs in their files relating to Olga Benario. With the invaluable assistance of Alexandre Fischer and Katharina Schneider, interpreters assigned by the government of the GDR to help me with my research, I was able to select and reproduce the available material,

---

* Prestes and Olga never married officially. They tried to but circumstances prevented them.

as well as to interview those who I believe are the only surviving militants who had shared experiences with Olga in the Communist Youth during the twenties or, a decade later, in Nazi concentration camps. I will never forget the tears of Gabor Lewin, by then an elderly man, when we talked in his home, emptying a bottle of cognac while a ten-degrees-below-zero wind whistled outside. When I asked if he could confirm the legend that Olga had inspired burning passions in her comrades in the Communist Youth, Lewin began weeping. His wife, Herta, eased my discomfort, remarking with a smile, "Olga was the great passion of Gabor's life." In the modest apartment of Ruth Werner, honorary lieutenant-colonel in the Soviet Red Army and one of Germany's greatest writers, I obtained copies of interviews she had conducted during the fifties with the survivors of Neukölln, Barnimstrasse, Lichtenburg, and Ravensbrück and not used in her book *Olga Benario*.

My work in East Germany would have been infinitely more difficult without the help of Dario Canale, a young man of Italian, German, and Brazilian descent (and whom I had interviewed in Brazil in 1967 when he was incarcerated in prison, accused of "subversion"). Canale helped me locate and select material about Olga and Otto Braun, escorted me to West Berlin to see the Moabit Prison, and prompted his mother-in-law, Elfriede Bruning, to invite her friends, activist Communists since the turn of the century, to dinners at her home, where I waited, tape recorder in hand.

In addition to the documents obtained, interviews with Olga's contemporaries were invaluable in reconstructing her time in Brazil. During the years she spent at Barnimstrasse, Lichtenburg, and Ravensbrück, she told her fellow prisoners much about her Brazilian experience: her passion for Prestes, her fascination with Brazil, her expectations following the frustrated revolt, her deep admiration for the solidarity of her fellow inmates in the prison on Frei Caneca in Rio. Since the Brazilian chapters of her life were the most obscure part of the investigation, I pressed Olga's friends in Berlin to their limits with questions about every moment of her seventeen months in Rio—and in some cases came away with a flood of testimony.

From Berlin I went on to Milan, where I spent the entire time in the Archivo Storico del Movimento Operario Brasiliano (main-

tained by the Fundação Giangiacomo Feltrinelli and guarded tooth
and claw by José Luís del Roio), which contains a large portion of the
Brazilian worker and Communist memorabilia. My interviews and
investigations in Europe and Brazil led me to other sources, including the National Archives in Washington, D.C., and my first available congressional recess was dedicated to research in the United
States. With the assistance of Ralph Waddey, an Anglo-Brazilian
employee of the U.S. State Department, and the indefatigable
patience of Richard Gould, director of the Legislative and Diplomatic Department of the National Archives, I plunged into a fas-
cinating study of the wealth of documents located there, at the
modest cost of fifty cents per page photocopied. Above and beyond
the innumerable secret documents concerning the lives of my characters, there was abundant material concerning the suppression of
the 1935 Communist revolt in Brazil. Ironically, I found in the heart
of Washington copious reports of the torture inflicted by the Brazilian police on the German Communist leader Arthur Ewert,
unimpeachable information regarding the activities of spies among
the Communist leadership, and details about the unraveling of the
1935 revolt—all this written by an agent of the United States
government. To my surprise, I was able to examine internal documents of the Brazilian Communist Party unknown in Brazil and
which had mysteriously landed in the United States.

On my return to Brazil, I continued interviewing people, checking dates and facts with Prestes and others, and searching for additional survivors of 1935 who might give statements or at least assist
me in confirming the information already in my hands. It was during
this time that I recalled a favorite phrase of an old editor of mine—
"For a reporter, just as for a goalkeeper, doing it right is not
enough—you have to have luck." I did, many times over. It was
pure chance, for example, that led me to two characters in this
story, Tuba Schor and Celestino Paraventi. Tuba Schor's son was the
doctor who delivered my daughter Rita, and when he learned that I
was writing a book about Olga's life he put me in touch with his
mother. As for Paraventi—he discovered me: after seeing an interview with reporter Ney Goncalves Dias on TV Manchete about the
book, which was then in progress, he contacted his nephew, José
Gregori, my colleague in the state legislature, to offer his delicious
account of Olga's short visit to São Paulo.

In Rio, photographer and scholar Paulo César de Azevedo, who was already assisting me with research in public archives, took it upon himself to petition officially the Ministry of Foreign Affairs for authorization to consult documents concerning Olga's expulsion from Brazil. A year's wait and repeated complaints were not enough, however, to pry open the doors of the bureaucracy of Itamaraty, the Brazilian Ministry of Foreign Affairs. Professor Ricardo Maranhão had already provided copies of documents proving the complicity of Brazilian diplomats with the Gestapo, but I felt it was my right to obtain all correspondence on the subject through official channels. Chancellor Ramiro Saraiva Guerreiro's personal intervention was necessary to obtain finally the requested material, which had, of course, been previously censored.

In contrast to my treatment at Itamaraty before Saraiva Guerreiro's intervention, the Superior Military Tribunal granted me free access to their archives. My old friend Flavio Bierrenbach put me in touch with his nephew, Júlio de Sá Bierrenbach, president of the SMT, who made available all the court's files on the 1935 revolt, including unpublished documents that had been sealed since the closing of case No. 1 of the National Security Tribunal, an ad hoc tribunal created to judge the revolutionaries, thereafter disbanded. Vladimir Sacchetta, my great collaborator on the Brazilian section of this book, spent a week in Brasília poring over seventy volumes to select hundreds of documents and illustrations that, days later, Paulo César de Azevedo photographed and reproduced. In addition, Sacchetta had already arranged access to the files of his father, Hermínio Sacchetta, and all documentation on the subject in the Public Records Office in London.

With a limited amount of time and money for travel, I was reduced in some cases to the mail and/or telephone to confirm dates or follow up new information. Chief among those who helped me in this way were Professor Boris Koval of the Institute of the Workers' Movement in Moscow, the Yad Vashem Memorial in Israel, and, at least twice, Richard Gould of the National Archives. My telephone bill also swelled with phone calls all over Brazil to reconfirm dates or to try to pinpoint the exact words of a given conversation. Then there were the documents that mysteriously arrived in my mailbox, sent by anonymous Communist activists who had heard of my work in newspaper or TV reports and generously took the initiative to find me, interested in assisting with my project and at the same time enriching the archives from which I have reconstructed this story of love and intolerance with as much fidelity as possible.

This book is not *my* version of Olga Benario's life or the Communist revolt of 1935, but what I believe to be the *genuine recounting* of these events. Every single piece of information printed here has been submitted to the available test of confirmation. Any errors that may appear are the result of situations where it was impossible to find multiple sources. And certainly there will be mistakes; though I hope that most were caught along the way. There were times when I found myself pressing ahead with investigations based on apparently accurate information later proved false by new research or interviews. One example: I have a copy of a deposition given by a Ravensbrück survivor who swears she saw Olga executed by firing squad. The confident tone of her declaration leads me to believe that she did in fact see a woman shot and presumed it was Olga. The truth, however, is that Olga was *not* shot in Ravensbrück. Another example: an eminent Brazilian historian assured me that Paul Gruber was no more than a fictional character invented by the Comintern to confound the capitalist intelligence services. Facts, documents, and witnesses have, meanwhile, verified that Gruber not only existed but also played an important role in the outcome of the 1935 revolt. There were also instances where, faced with contradictory versions of a given episode, investigations and evidence led me to opt for one of those versions. The bibliography that appears at the end of this volume, which will be of interest to anyone who wants to learn more about the period, was useful not only for reference purposes but was also crucial to my efforts to immerse myself completely in the subject. In the end, the wealth of information at my disposal was such that I seldom had to "re-create" anything; in the rare instances where I did, it is the scene, not the facts themselves, that was re-created.

Before giving the manuscript to my publisher, I submitted my work to the eyes of three of the most brilliant and merciless journalists in Brazil—Luís Weis, Raimundo Rodrigues Pereira, and Ricardo Setti—and to the vigilant hand of Vladimir Sacchetta, indisputably one of the greatest authorities on the workers' movement in Brazil. And, finally, I received the help of the talented Claudio Marcondes, to whom my publisher Alfa-Omega assigned the job of preparing the text for the printer. Claudio was responsible for suggesting alterations to improve the book's clarity. I robbed him of precious hours of work and leisure—and I'm not sorry I did: after listening to his criticisms, observations, and objections, I sat down again at the typewriter to correct my errors.

Though I must bear sole responsibility for the contents of this book, I owe *Olga* to the generous collaboration of those interviewed (whose names are listed at the back), to all those whose names are mentioned in this foreword, and to Abelardo Blanco, Abel Cardoso Júnior, Alberto Dines, Alexandre Lobão, Ali Ahmad, Ana Maria de Castro, Beatriz Sardenberg, Bernd Wünning, Birgit Koyne, Bruno Kiesler, Célia Valente, Christiane Barckhausen, Daphne F. Rodger, Dieter Koyne, Edith Heise, Edmond Petit, Eric Nepomuceno, Flávio Kothe, Gerhard Desombre, Giocondo Dias, Heitor Ferreira Lima, Herbert Rösser, Horst Brasch, Inês Etienne Romeu, Jamile Salomão, Jasmina Barckhausen, John W. F. Dulles, José Antonio Penteado Vignolli, José Carlos Bruni, José Eduardo de Faro Freire, José Sebastião Witter, Karen Elsab Barbosa, Karl Burkert, Kerry Fraser, Leôncio Martins Rodrigues, Lothar Günther, Lutz Ellrodt, Manoel Moreira, Marco Aurélio Garcia, Marcia Madrigali, Maria Beatriz Paula Dias, Maria de Guia Santiago, Maria Vitória Menezes Camargo, Marisa Teixeira Pinto, Marisa Zanatta, Martina John, Moacir Werneck de Castro, Nicolau Tuma, Pedro Alves de Brito, Peter Skomroch, Régis Barbosa, Régis Fratti, Ricardo Gontijo, Ricardo Zarattini, Rita Magalhães Marques, Roberto Braga, Roberto Drumond, Samuel Krakowski, Samuel Soares, Sérgio Micelli, Siegfried Köllner, Silvia Oliva Araújo, Silvio Tendler, Suely Campos Cardoso, Susana Camargo, Tibério Canuto, Vera Maria Tude de Souza, Werner Bönecke, and Werner Thiele.

Fernando Morais
August 1985

Olga

Berlin,

APRIL 1928

IT ALL HAPPENED in less than a minute.

At precisely 9:00 A.M. on April 11, 1928, Gunnar Blemke, a guard, crossed the mahogany-paneled hearing room of the Moabit Prison in central Berlin leading the handcuffed Communist, Professor Otto Braun, aged twenty-eight, by the arm. Not that Otto was considered a dangerous prisoner; the handcuffs were a matter of form: he stood accused of "high treason against the fatherland" and had been imprisoned for a year and a half awaiting trial. The guard led him toward the table behind which sat the senior minister of justice, Ernst Schmidt, who was to interrogate him. At Schmidt's side, Rudolph Nekien, a clerk, was struggling against falling asleep over his typewriter. On the other side of the room, directly facing the table but separated by a wooden handrail, a small gallery intended for lawyers and spectators was occupied by half a dozen young men and women. "I thought they were law students," the guard would say later.

Blemke puffed up his chest in the face of authority and announced, "Presenting the prisoner, Otto Braun."

At that instant he felt something hard pressing against his neck. Turning his head, he saw a black pistol held by an attractive young woman with dark hair and blue eyes, who demanded in a steady voice, "Release the prisoner!"

3

Olga

The spectators fell into two groups and rushed Schmidt and Nekien, forcibly knocking them down. Schmidt lurched forward and managed to press an alarm button with the tip of one shoe—and received a blow to the head, administered by an enormous young man with a reddish beard and hair almost down to his shoulders. The girl who led the group kept her pistol pointed at the guard's head. After disarming him, she backed toward the door, shielding the prisoner with her body and shouting to her companions, "Let's get out! Let's get out! Anyone who moves gets it!"

The guard and the two officials were ordered to stand facing the wall. The girl gestured hurriedly for the group to leave. They were already moving toward the main entrance when her last shout echoed in the room: "The first one to move gets it!"

They disappeared into the hallway. Leaping down the steps, the group dispersed. The girl dropped her pistol into the woolen bag slung over her shoulder and dashed across Fritz-Schloss Park to the gymnasium on the far side, where she threw herself into a small green van that was waiting, doors open. At the wheel sat a young man with a large nose, and in the back, still handcuffed, slumped Otto Braun, in shock.

The dilapidated van threatened to fall apart as it raced through the streets of Berlin. They headed south, hurrying away from the immediate area of the prison, where alarm sirens could be heard blocks away. Avoiding the busiest streets, the van skirted the small Blucher Cemetery and crossed Schiffarts Canal. Once they had entered the Neukölln district they could finally breathe freely. Neukölln was home.

By midday, a special edition of *Berliner Zeitung am Mittag* was already providing details, under a scandalous headline, of what the writer referred to as a "daring feat, a scene straight out of the wild West," that had taken place that morning in Moabit Prison. The front page announced the name of the attractive young woman who had commanded the "Communist raid": Olga Benario.

"A daring feat . . ."

That evening, in the small apartment arranged as a hideout by the Communist Youth, Olga and Otto, her lover, read and reread the newspaper accounts, stopping each time at the same phrase. In

4

fact, "daring" was the only word to describe, not just her own actions that morning, but the very attitude that motivated the majority of the young Communists of the working-class district of Neukölln. Staring out at the street from behind curtains in the half-lit room, Olga observed another manifestation of the very same state of mind. Half an hour earlier police had thronged the area, plastering walls and lampposts with enormous posters, commissioned by the prosecutor general of Germany, offering a reward of five thousand marks to anyone providing information regarding the whereabouts of writer Otto Braun and typist Olga Benario. Now Olga gazed into the street below as her comrades, tiny Gabor Lewin and an agitated Emmy Handke, yanked down every single poster.

What word other than "daring" could aptly describe what was happening a few blocks away in the back room of the Müller beer hall? Indifferent to the fact that the police were gathering in Neukölln to capture the two, militants of the Red Front of the Communist Youth were planning a political action to commemorate Braun's liberation. First to speak was a girl with braids who announced to the hundreds of people crowded into the back room—young men and women, older workers with their wives and children—that everyone involved in Braun's liberation was safe. She drew applause when she revealed that the action had been carried out with unloaded weapons.

"We had no intention of hurting anyone. . . . If there had been any reaction from the Moabit fascists, we would no doubt at this very moment be trying to figure out how to liberate not only Professor Braun but the comrades who raided the prison as well. The truth is that the fascists responsible for the incarceration of thousands of German workers were brought to their knees by a band of kids with unloaded guns. . . ."

At 11:00 P.M. shock troops invaded the Müller beer hall with billy clubs and emptied the back room. From her room, Olga watched the tumult spill out onto Zieten Street. Otto slept beside her, indifferent to the excitement she felt. Reports from the almost inaudible radio only fueled her insomnia: all the late-night programs mentioned the raid on Moabit Prison. And they conveyed the same reassuring piece of information: of all the participants in the action, only Olga had been identified by the police.

There were, at most, only vague descriptions of the others. Rudi

König was referred to merely as "a well-built young man with short hair who grabbed Nekien, the clerk, by the throat"; Margot Ring was "a slightly overweight redheaded girl of no more than fifteen"; witnesses described Erich Jazosch as "a huge man with long hair who hit the minister of justice over the head"; a court employee described Erick Bombach as "a child less than five feet tall with a pistol in each hand"; and, as for Klara Seleheim, "no one has been able to say for sure whether the lanky one with the close-cropped hair was male or female," as one newscaster put it.

The police may not have known the identities of these young accomplices, but they knew all there was to know about Olga and Otto, which is why the next weeks were very tense. As the net tightened, the chance of arrest obviously increased, in spite of the great solidarity of the working-class families of Neukölln. The tranquil homes of metalworkers and bakers were transformed into safe houses where the young couple would hide for four or five days at a time. The Department of Security, a secret, semimilitarized section of the Communist Youth, was responsible for their safekeeping. Experienced in protecting the organization against terrorist attacks by right-wing groups or by the police, the Department of Security functioned like a clandestine cell within the legal Communist Youth. Its members were entrusted with arranging a succession of safe houses and for transferring Olga and Otto from one to the next when it was felt the police were getting too close.

Films showing in Berlin were regularly preceded by a slide of the poster bearing photographs of Olga and Otto and offering five thousand marks for information regarding their whereabouts. The audience would invariably break into applause for the two and, almost as invariably, the lights would come up and armed police stream into the theater. Once it was dark again, the air filled with boos, hisses, and balls of crumpled paper. What puzzled the police most was that no one came forward to claim a reward equivalent to two years' salary for a worker.

In early June, Judge Franz Vogt, the regional director of justice, summoned the press to his chambers in order to unveil a new poster-communiqué signed by the prosecutor general in which the five-thousand-mark reward was rescinded, because "according to information supplied by the police, the persons in question have managed to flee the country."

This time the police were right: just days earlier, accompanied by members of the Department of Security, Otto and Olga had traveled by car to the city of Stettin on the Polish frontier, where they boarded a train for Moscow. At the very moment Judge Vogt was addressing the group of reporters in Berlin, the couple was on a train at the Russian border, presenting false passports to a young Soviet soldier with oriental features and a white helmet bearing the red star. Thrilled to be "entering proletarian territory," Olga couldn't resist the temptation to give an affectionate nod to that "soldier of the people." To her disappointment, the soldier pretended not to notice. The train slowly gathered speed and headed on toward Moscow.

Buenos Aires,

·APRIL 1928

AFTER TWO WEEKS on the back of an ox slogging through the swampy Paraguayan Chaco, Luís Carlos Prestes, thirty years of age, found himself aboard a ferry approaching the port of Buenos Aires. A diminutive man, under five feet three, Prestes looked terrible after twelve months in the small, western Bolivian town of La Gaiba. A long, bushy beard concealed the lean face with protruding cheekbones, still sallow from repeated bouts of malaria. Prestes's arrival in the Argentine capital marked the end of an adventure that would remain forever etched in the history of Brazil.

A year earlier, wearing the stripes of a revolutionary general on his shoulders, with epic companion General Miguel Costa at his side, Prestes had led his army of 620 men to exile in Bolivia. He had turned over his arsenal—ninety Mauser rifles, four heavy-duty machine guns (one unused), two automatic decalibrated rifles, and some eight thousand bullets—to Major Carmona Rodó, a representative of the La Paz government. This voluntary laying down of arms, after which a brief document was signed by the Bolivian major and the two Brazilian soldiers, marked the end of a two-and-a-half-year-long campaign during which Prestes and his men had zigzagged through twelve states, on foot and burro, covering a total of twenty-five thousand kilometers. Now exiled and unarmed, still every single one of them knew they would go down in history, heads held high. Before the journey was over, that tattered army had become famous throughout the continent as "the invincible Prestes Column"—the rebel contingent that had confronted President Artur Bernardes's well-armed troops again and again without suffering a single defeat. To hundreds of thousands of Brazilians, whether from direct contact or merely from hearing tales of the Column, its leader, General Luís Carlos Prestes, was known as the "Knight of Hope." His fame became legendary and his influence was to prove long-lasting. Many of his followers later joined the army or became involved in politics, often returning their loyalty to him and his cause.

Artur da Silva Bernardes, from the state of Minas Gerais, had assumed the presidency of the Republic of Brazil in 1922 under a state of siege provoked by an uprising of lieutenants that took place at Fort Copacabana in Rio de Janeiro, and it was under a state of siege that he had governed the country for the duration of his four-year mandate. Authoritarian in the extreme, Bernardes stripped the discontented oligarchy of power and decreed federal intervention in the states of Bahia and Rio de Janeiro; his difficult relationship with the military led to an explosion of conspiracies throughout his administration. The repression of rebel movements was almost always a pretext for the adoption of further authoritarian measures such as the extraordinarily severe Press Act, better known as the Infamous Act, signed in November 1923, which restricted democratic freedoms across the board.

It was in this climate that the Column arose, though Prestes himself had not seen it born. When General Isidoro Dias Lopes and the then Major Miguel Costa assembled their troops in São Paulo on July 5, 1924, Prestes was an engineer serving as a captain in the Railroad Battalion of Santo Angelo, a small city near the Uruguayan border in Rio Grande do Sul. Lopes and Costa's plan was to march on the federal capital (then Rio de Janeiro), hoping for support from garrisons there, and to depose the Bernardes government. Cornered by federal troops in the state of São Paulo, they led their two thousand men southward instead, toward the Iguaçú Falls in Paraná, Argentina. In the early hours of October 29, Captain Prestes dashed off a short note of farewell to his mother, dona

Leocádia, and ordered his battalion to support the rebellious Paul-
istas, announcing simultaneously the insurrection of the Third Cavalry Regiment of the city of São Luís, some eighty kilometers
distant.

Alerted, the government managed to douse the flames spreading
through the state, aborting uprisings at the Uruguaiana, Alegrete,
and Cachoeira barracks and frustrating Prestes's plan to take all of
Rio Grande do Sul. Prestes continued on to São Luís, where he set
up general headquarters, and proceeded to occupy the cities of São
Nicolău, Santo Angelo, Santiago do Boqueirão, and São Borja.
Taking stock of the troops and weapons in his command, he recognized the fragility of a rebel force consisting of less than fifteen
hundred combatants, military and civilian, only half of them
equipped with weapons—eight hundred and six Mauser rifles and a
few machine guns. Already heading for São Luís to engage the
rebels were the government troops: fourteen thousand well-trained
and well-armed soldiers.

This disparity between forces provoked the first manifestation of
the military genius that was to be Prestes's hallmark throughout the
next two years. He managed to let fall into enemy hands the information that his outfit would be concentrated in São Luís, while at
that very moment dispatching them to the north. When federal
troops entered the city, they found not a single rebel soldier—
Prestes and his men were two hundred kilometers away wading
through the jungle of the Uruguay River. Cunning more than force
would be necessary to reach the Iguaçú Falls, where Prestes intended to join the Paulista insurgents; in order to economize on
ammunition, every shot, even in the midst of combat, had to be
authorized. Employing only traps and ambushes, and without los-
ing a single man, Prestes managed to inflict considerable losses on
government troops. His triumphant arrival at the Iguaçú Falls on
April 1, 1925, gave fresh vitality to the men quartered there, reduced by successive desertions to almost half the contingent that
had left São Paulo on July 5 the previous year.

Prestes and Miguel Costa, both now holding the rank of general,
joined forces and marched into the Brazilian wilderness in the hope
of putting an end to the despotism of the Bernardescos, as the
president's followers were dubbed. Advancing when it could, the

human serpent zigzagged through the countryside. Whenever they managed to round up herds of wild horses at some ranch, Prestes's soldiers had mounts for a few weeks or months. If they found no horses, they continued on foot. When there was food, they ate; more often they traveled for days with very little water and almost nothing to eat besides manioc flour and unrefined brown sugar. Time and again their stock of medical supplies was put to use attending to the wretched populace they met along the way. The pitiful living conditions they witnessed horrified the commanders, both of whom came from middle-class families. Though keenly aware of the poverty around them in the south as they were growing up, now they were coming face to face with a Brazil that was much more famished, miserable, and backward. The sight of children yanking roots out of the dirt to make what would be their only meal of the day crystallized Prestes's belief in the necessity to change the face of his country.

At each settlement the Column grew. The rigid discipline imposed by Prestes produced soldiers the people respected. Generally, the first measures taken after occupying a town were the liberation of prisoners and the burning of the civil registry files that "proved" land ownership by the few. With the exception of cases involving brutal crimes like rape and murder, prisoners were set free after a brief interview with officers of the Column. Much against Prestes's will, a contingent of fifty women, lovers of the Column soldiers, accompanied the march; the women's determination had been so strong that he was simply unable to prevent them from joining. Many gave birth along the way, having become pregnant before the journey began.

In spite of their military invincibility, the lack of a political program more definite than the overthrow of Artur Bernardes ate away at the rebels' morale. After almost two years and thousands of kilometers, the commanding officers knew—Prestes most of all—that even in victory the Column would not succeed in changing Brazil's social structure merely by doing away with a dictator. From the northeast, the Column made its way toward the southern Mato Grosso, practically repeating their initial trajectory. When they arrived in Bolivia to place in Major Carmona Rodó's hands what weapons they had remaining, Lourenço Moreira Lima—the Column's official historian—registered the exact numbers in his note-book: between São Luís, in Rio Grande do Sul, and San Matías, Bolivia, they had traveled 24,947 kilometers.

During the first months in Bolivia, Prestes attended to the concerns of his men, repatriating those soldiers who wished to return to Brazil and trying to find work for those who didn't want to or couldn't go home. Marx, Lenin, and the triumph of the Bolshevik revolution ten years earlier on the other side of the world were names and news items with little significance for the exiled Prestes, until, one day late in 1927, in Puerto Suárez, just a few kilometers from the Brazilian border, he received a visit from Astrojildo Pereira, one of the founders of the Brazilian Communist Party, or the Brazilian Section of the Communist International, as the organization was called at its inception in 1922. The amazing feats of the Column had caused a sensation among opposition groups in Brazil, including the Communists. Astrojildo's baggage was crammed with books, most of them French editions from the publisher L'Human-ité: the works of Marx and Lenin, the resolutions of the Communist International, texts by Engels, and odds and ends from the periodi-cal *Correspondance Internationale*, put out by the Comintern. After two days of conversation with Prestes, Astrojildo left him with a pile of books and a sly invitation: "In these volumes you will find something of the science that will solve the problems of our time: Marxism."

Prestes made no commitments to the Party. First he wanted to become familiar with the theory of communism, and he made use of what scant free time he had in the first months of 1928 to plunge into the rich array of literature left with him. It was during this period that he began to think about leaving Bolivia to find a better place for his men, and decided to move to neighboring Argentina. There, they would be closer to Rio Grande do Sul—and the effer-vescence of Brazilian politics—as well as being in a more demo-cratic climate than Bolivia's. And, since Argentina was more highly developed economically, there would, of course, be better job opportunities for him and the rest of his men. By late 1928, the whole group was installed in Buenos Aires.

Prestes became the main attraction for visiting revolutionaries from various countries, who came to ask advice of the mythical commander of the invincible Column. Paraguayans, Chileans, Uruguayans, Bolivians, and—to Prestes's utter surprise—even Brazilian tourists appeared at his door, accompanied by their tour guides, to see the "phenomenon" in person. In addition, the house (where he lived with his mother and his four sisters) continued to be a center for the conspiracy to overthrow the Brazilian government.

Prestes became friends with journalist Rodolfo Ghioldi, a director of the Argentine Communist Party and the Comintern. At one of the many gatherings at Ghioldi's home on Calle Mexico, Prestes met a man named Kleiner, also known as Bumpkin—both code names for Augusto Guralsky, a special envoy of the Comintern sent to Argentina specifically to contact the man whose political work had caught the attention of the Soviet leadership. Prestes's contacts with the Brazilian CP also became more frequent, and his prestige in Brazil was such that in 1929 the Party invited him to run for president of the republic the following year. He agreed to discuss the invitation, however, only if his candidacy was a result of consensus among the Column's lieutenants. There was no such consensus, and the plan fell through: a good number of them were already supporters of a new figure rising on the political scene, Getúlio Vargas.

In March 1930, Júlio Prestes (no relation) of São Paulo was elected to succeed Washington Luís as president of Brazil in a campaign typical of the Old Republic, with nonsecret ballots, extensive fraud, and an extremely restricted voting list. But he never took office. An insurrection, erupting spontaneously in Paraíba and directed nationally by the Liberal Alliance, brought Getúlio Vargas to Catete Palace. Luís Carlos Prestes immediately felt the consequences of the change in Brazil; he was arrested briefly, and then released, in Buenos Aires. He went into exile in Montevideo with his mother and sisters and from Uruguay requested affiliation with the CP. But the Party that had courted him only months before responded by refusing him membership. It was the directorate of the Brazilian CP—which shortly before had dismissed General Secretary Astrojildo Pereira, accusing him of opposing the "workerism" proposed by the Comintern—that prevented Prestes's acceptance.

President Getúlio Vargas tried to co-opt the "Knight of Hope," offering to restore the army rank of captain, which he had lost when he abandoned his post in Rio Grande do Sul to join the Column. Prestes rejected the overture, preferring to keep the honorary rank of general that his men had given him.

With each day that passed, his conviction grew that only a popular revolution could change Brazil's fate, and with this belief in mind he accepted an invitation from the Comintern to move with his family to the Soviet Union. Clean-shaven, wearing a discreet gray suit and carrying an elegant felt hat, Luís Carlos Prestes set sail on the *Eubee* from the port of Montevideo on October 1, 1931, bound for Moscow.

1

Inside the Red Fort

OLGA AND OTTO arrived at the Hotel Desna in Moscow, exhausted after seventy-two hours on the train. In contrast to the Hotel Lux, designed for illustrious foreigners, the Desna wasn't the least bit ostentatious, though it was, on the other hand, clean and discreet. As she registered, Olga noticed the curious coincidence that five years ago to the day she had first joined a Communist organization.

That had been in the summer of 1923, in her native city of Munich, just a few months before her fifteenth birthday. Banned by the police, the Communist Youth had gone underground. Its most militant members—eighteen years old and under—had created the Schwabing Group, which met once a week in an old sawmill in the suburbs of the Bavarian capital. One afternoon the meeting was interrupted by suspicious noises outside. Those in charge of security investigated, fearing the arrival of the police. Instead they found a tall, lanky girl with dark braids who demanded to become a member. Once inside the sawmill, Olga was closely questioned by the group's leader. When asked her address and her parents' names, she responded, "My father is Leo Benario, a lawyer. But that's not my fault."

15

For the majority of German Communists, the Right was not the only enemy. Social Democrats were placed in the same category and treated with the same disdain—and Benario was a Social Democrat. So, for the Schwabing Group, Olga's was an unexpected presence. Never until then had a young person from the conservative Bavarian bourgeoisie knocked at the door.

Their prejudice was unjustified. Though one of the most respected jurists in the state and an influential personality in the local Social Democrat Party, Jewish lawyer Leo Benario was a liberal with progressive ideas. Olga herself would one day say that her own conversion to communism had not been the result of reading Marxist theory but of thumbing through the cases of those working-class clients her father represented. "In those files, I saw close up the poverty and injustice that I was only superficially acquainted with from books," she would say.

In contrast to the considerable respect she had for her father, Olga's infrequent comments about her mother were marked by coolness and brevity. The product of a well-to-do Jewish family, Eugenie Gutmann Benario was an elegant high-society lady who regarded with horror the prospect of her daughter becoming a Communist. Olga's maternal grandmother was an even less important presence in her life. All Olga remembered of her was the bantam hen her grandmother presented her with during the depression that accompanied the Great War—a prosaic but useful gift in a time when eggs were rationed—and the question that was the old woman's response to any news of the world brought to her by her granddaughter, as if a prediction of the tragedy to befall Germany: "Just tell me—is it good or bad for Jews?"

Olga never concealed the affection she felt for her father. He was a middle-class Social Democrat—but with an important difference. Workers who wanted to make judicial claims against their employers but couldn't afford the services of a lawyer invariably came to Benario for help. He accepted whatever they could pay him and worked free for those who could pay him nothing. "Even more diligently than for the paying customers," Olga recalled. Observing the clientele that frequented the family's elegant home on Karlplatz, Olga grew more and more interested in their plight. The stream of people who passed through her father's office every day—

often discussing their problems in front of the young girl—ran the gamut from the wealthiest to the most poverty-stricken inhabitants of Munich. "The class struggle visited me daily," she joked.

There certainly was no lack of clients, many of whom were badly affected by the dramatic economic situation that had been eating away at Germany since the end of World War I. The brutal inflationary spiral had reached such an extreme that the dollar, which in mid-1922 was worth a thousand marks, cost 350 million marks just one year later. Diligent working-class Germans were on the brink of destitution and the middle class was rapidly becoming the proletariat. The apparent lack of a solution to the crisis had led labor unions, the majority of which were controlled by Communists and Social Democrats, to lose power along with the working-class population. Olga believed that she had found the answer, at least her own personal answer: she dedicated herself more and more fully to the Communist cause. In the first job assigned to her during that summer of 1923, she demonstrated to the young people of Schwabing that their newest member was no bored bourgeois teenager. As part of a clandestine crew putting up posters, Olga proved to be the most efficient of the team, which included older and stronger members. Efficient and daring: for the first time, not only the suburbs of Munich but the center as well woke to find their streets blanketed with posters. Olga had covered even the busiest areas, where the police presence frightened off the most experienced of militants. "Fear and caution are simply not in her vocabulary," said her new friends the following day.

Before long Olga was an integral part of Schwabing. Along with courage and determination, she brought from her upbringing something the sons and daughters of the working class lacked—an excellent education. She had actually read many of the Marxist classics that the majority of them had only heard about in lectures. They soon noticed another vivid characteristic—one that those most resistant to her presence in Schwabing attributed to the "radicalism peculiar to products of the bourgeoisie": intolerance of anyone who wasn't a militant Communist. She was warned innumerable times by older members to avoid behavior that was little more than childish provocation, such as walking down the street brazenly sporting a red brooch bearing the hammer and sickle.

Olga first heard of Professor Otto Braun toward the end of 1923, when she was working as an assistant in Georg Müller's bookshop. She began fantasizing about him just from his description— especially as reported by women—weaving a myth about young, handsome, intelligent Otto, who, it was whispered, worked secretly as a Soviet agent. When, finally, a mutual friend arranged for the two to meet, Olga was surprised. Her picture of Otto had been a caricature of a revolutionary: a ragged beard, fatigues, and long, disheveled hair. The Otto that sat across from her in the café smoking a pipe was actually quite polished: tie meticulously straight, hair neatly parted and fixed in place with hair tonic, crisply creased trousers, and brushed suede boots.

Though only twenty-two, seven years older than she, Otto was an experienced militant, even in the area that most fascinated Olga: armed action. During the frustrated popular revolution of 1919 (an attempt to repeat the Russian phenomenon of two years earlier), the Party had sent him on a secret mission to intercept a convoy of troops dispatched by the central government to retake Munich, then capital of the "Republic of Bavaria." The mission itself was a success and Munich resisted for more than a month longer, with Otto at the head of a group of combatants. The government, however, sent wave after wave of reinforcements to battle with the insurgents and finally retook the city. In spite of the outcome, Otto prided himself on having wiped out so many "right-wing Social Democrats." The battle of Munich ended with Otto in prison—his first and shortest incarceration.

Otto and Olga began seeing each other, their mutual fascination growing by the day. She imagined she had found the perfect man, someone who managed to combine a solid theoretical background with military experience. Not to mention the fact that he was very handsome. And Otto was clearly charmed by the half-girl, half-woman who thirsted for both theory and action like no one he'd ever met. Half an hour before her duties at the bookshop were over, he would appear with his pipe and elegant scarf, ready for conversation that stretched into the small hours of the morning.

Otto began to direct Olga's reading and to suggest, in addition to the theoretical works indispensable to her understanding of communism, various magazines and journals published by Marxist groups in Berlin. He was amazed by her insistent requests for manuals on military strategy, written statements by great generals, and reports of famous battles. The militant behind those soft blue eyes would emerge at Schwabing meetings, frequently criticizing the group's lack of interest in military techniques and the absence of regular training for all militants. Olga's quarrels with the young men in the group only became really serious, though, when she realized that on the basis of gender she was being assigned secondary duties. At the end of one such disagreement, she grumbled for all to hear: "I want you to know that at times like this it's a pain to be a woman."

The more she pored over the Marxist classics and the more she militated at Schwabing, the firmer became Olga's conviction that she should leave Munich for Berlin. The refined and perfumed clientele at Müller's bookshop, the arguments with her parents, her very home itself were becoming unbearable. News of political turmoil reported in Berlin newspapers inflamed her imagination. Olga's fantasy of life in the capital had a name: Neukölln, the working-class district in Berlin known by the German Left as "the Red Fort." After months of insistently badgering Otto, she finally got her way. It was late one afternoon, as they walked hand in hand in a park outside Munich. He himself seemed unsure of the arrangements.

"I've consulted the Party and it looks feasible for us to move to Berlin. But what about your family? How will you persuade your father to accept the idea?"

The question made her furious.

"I'm on my way the minute the Party gives us the go-ahead!"

In fact, it was not just politics that were pushing Olga toward Berlin. She was in love with Otto. Weekends spent together in snow-covered cabins had revealed the sweet, tender, patient man behind the sober professor of Marxism. The idea of spending her days among the young Communist workers of Neukölln and her nights with Otto was everything that Olga Gutmann Benario desired at that time.

Only after she had the second-class train ticket in her hand and her small suitcase packed and ready did she inform her parents that she was leaving that very evening. Dinner was silent. Her mother chose to stay upstairs. Olga valiantly tried to avoid a fight with her father. After three hours of discussion, she got up to leave. Leo's good-bye kiss at the door told her that deep inside, he knew that in her place he might be doing the same thing.

Twenty-four hours later, from the window of her room in the attic of a small two-story house, Olga gazed down at Weser Street: so, she was really here, in the heart of Neukölln. To someone who had spent her childhood and adolescence in the comfortable Benario home on Karlplatz, this tiny room hardly deserved to be called an apartment. Three strides of her long legs were enough to send her crashing into the opposite wall. There were two beds, a small corner table, a chair, and a chest of drawers. Planks of wood supported by cement blocks swayed under the weight of books and papers. This would be home to Olga and Otto for some time.

Noticing his lover's surprise at the modesty of the accommodations, Otto quipped, "This place is a real bargain—to begin with, we'll save what we would have had to spend on an alarm clock."

The trolley car began its route at 6:00 A.M., passing right below their window and making a noise loud enough to wake the dead. That first morning in Berlin, Olga learned that she had changed more than her address. At breakfast—a bottle of milk and a few crackers—Otto explained that his clandestine work for the Party demanded certain precautions that would involve both of them. He opened a leather briefcase and removed several sets of identity papers.

"From now on, you will have two identities, just as I do. My official documents are in the name Arthur Behrendt, traveling salesman born in Augsburg, September 28, 1898. And, as of yesterday, you are my wife, Frieda Wolf Behrendt, born September 27, 1903, in Erfurt. Here are your identity papers and a document certifying that we live at 11 Erhardtstrasse, in Leipzig. Be very careful and the best of luck, Mrs. Behrendt."

There was more: Otto's illegal work would probably keep him away for weeks, sometimes months, at a time. "Which means that although we'll be living together, it will be a while before I'll be able to marry you," he said tenderly.

Olga's reaction was brusque. "Well, I think you should know that I have no intention of getting married."

It didn't take long for Olga to leave behind the adolescent from

Munich and to become a woman. She made rapid progress within the Communist Youth of Neukölln, and a few months after arriving in Berlin she became secretary for agitation and propaganda in the most important workers' base of the German CP—Neukölln. By day, there were meetings, protests, and street activities. At night, interminable assemblies in the depths of the old building on Zieten Street that housed the Müller family beer hall. The same large room that hosted a stream of local workers for their quick sausage-potato-and-beer midday meal became, in the early evening, head-quarters for the district's Communist Youth. No password was required for entry. Since the majority of the group was still under the drinking age, Müller reacted mechanically whenever some new young face appeared at the battered marble bar. His eyes narrowing between an enormous mustache and a rapidly receding hairline, he would simply say, "The Youth? Down that hallway, as far as you can go."

Before coming to Berlin, Olga had heard many stories about the beer hall and its owners—Wilhelm Müller, his wife, and daughter. She knew the very corner in which Rosa Luxemburg and Karl Liebknecht—two outstanding leaders of the German CP assassi-nated in 1919—had hatched their political schemes. Whenever the Müller family finances took a turn for the worse, the news would spread through Neukölln and beyond; the other beer houses in the area would stand empty as business increased dramatically at the Müllers' for several weeks, until the family was back on its feet again. And twice a week, from 8:30 to 11:30 P.M., the back room that usually hosted political assemblies and clandestine meetings was transformed into a classroom. Every other Tuesday, Olga taught the rudiments of Marxist theory to a group of her comrades. Somehow they managed to juggle four or five different activities in the room simultaneously. There were times when Olga had to be gruff and request that someone come back another time to run off pamphlets on the mimeograph machine set up in one corner.

Work was relentless: pamphleting the Görlitzer railway station, demonstrations of support for strikes at neighborhood factories, protests against the imposition of extra working hours. And all of it had to fit in around the eight-to-six job that brought in the few marks she and Otto needed to live on. The Party had arranged for

Olga to work as a typist for the Soviet Trade Bureau, and though the work was tedious compared with her activities with the Youth, she was proud of working "side by side with the revolutionaries." While she knew it was probably just a fantasy, Olga saw "a Bolshevik of steel" in every one of those placid bureaucrats in jacket and tie.

Time for all these feverish activities had to be stolen from somewhere, and occasionally the couple's love life seemed to suffer. The few hours a week they managed to be together—usually late at night—were usually spent working. After much insistence, Olga had finally convinced Otto that she should be his secretary, not only so that she would have more time with him, but also for the political apprenticeship it offered. It was she, then, who typed the voluminous theoretical texts he either dictated or left on the bed in handwritten form. And it was through this work that she began to understand more completely the approaching struggle in Germany, revolutionary developments in other countries, and of course the internal structure of the German Communist Party.

The mutual love and admiration of Olga and Otto did not diminish; on the contrary, it was growing stronger. At the same time, the political activity and the passion for militancy they also shared reduced to minutes the time they could spend as lovers. When they argued, it was not over political differences but over something that irritated Olga more and more: the jealousy Otto felt toward the young men in the Communist Youth. Justifiable jealousy, any one of her sixty comrades in Agitation and Propaganda might say, for Olga was becoming more attractive. Even her gangly walk gave her a certain special charm. And the one characteristic that really kindled their interest was her independence. Olga was her own boss and did only what she believed to be important, both in politics and in her personal life.

Fortunately, this independence didn't prevent her from learning a great deal from Otto, and he taught her more than the theories of Marx, Lenin, Engels, and Karl Liebknecht. Advice that, coming from a woman friend, would have met with profanity, sounded different from Otto's mouth. It wasn't just the experienced Communist in him speaking. In patient, homeopathic doses, Otto convinced her that a militant need not be unkempt and poorly dressed—the few bottles of cologne and perfume on the couple's

small, improvised dressing table beside the sink belonged to him.
As a result of their long, late-night talks in bed, Olga grew more
tolerant of non-Communists and, more important, began little by
little to give up her moral prejudices against comrades who
smoked, drank, or spent their scant free time dancing on Saturday
nights. As time went on, she herself began to feel attracted to the
group's various entertainments.

There was one notion, however, that even Otto was unable to
shake loose, and that was her horror of formal, legally sanctioned
marriage. Olga associated the idea of marriage with what she considered the worst of bourgeois deformities—the economic depen-
dence of women, obligatory love, forced intimacy. When people
asked why she and Otto—apparently very happy living together—
didn't get married, Olga had a ready answer. "That's exactly why we
won't marry—because we're happy, because we love each other. I
will never allow myself to become another person's property."

But this way of looking at male-female relations didn't presup-
pose other sorts of liberal ideas; Olga was very upset whenever she
heard a girlfriend boast about how many men she'd gone to bed
with. At such moments, an intolerant, almost puritanical Olga
emerged. "You should know that giving in to your instincts is
tantamount to contributing to the bourgeois brothel. And that's not
just me talking; it's Lenin."

Who could argue with Lenin? If a member of the group was guilty
of behavior Olga considered "immoral," she didn't hesitate to bring
up the problem for discussion with the leadership—and all this in
the progressive Berlin of the twenties.

This rigid side of Olga didn't discourage the young men of Neukölln from falling in love with her. A girl named Ruth, for example,
insisted that her boyfriend, Martin Weiser, a young apprentice
jeweler, should quit the Marxist study group taught by Olga in a
Berlin suburb.

Kurt Seibt, another boy from the same group, who worked as a
typesetter and had managed to join the printers' union, also fell
under her spell. Olga had inspired him to join the Communist
Youth, and he became a sort of teaching assistant to her. Kurt
believed, along with Olga, that the natural step following theoretical course work and the recruitment of young people in working-

23

class neighborhoods was the clandestine militarization of the group. Under Olga's guidance, he took on the task of organizing young militia in each city block of Kreuzberg, a neighborhood near Neu-kölln. Despite its importance, this new post had the distinct disadvantage of separating him from his attractive mentor.

The first time he saw Olga after assuming his new mission, Kurt requested authorization to organize a brigade for the specific purpose of forcefully subduing a group of young Nazis who had been disrupting the Youth's work in Kreuzberg. He argued that their taunts, interruptions of classes, throwing bags of excrement through meeting-room windows, etc., could not be stopped without a skirmish. Olga firmly resisted this idea, insisting that instead of resorting to violence he should be trying to attract the young Nazis to the group. But once she saw that indoctrination was getting her nowhere, she decided to take part in the action herself. A single thrashing, administered by Youth of both sexes, and the Nazis disappeared.

2
In Jail

EARLY IN 1926 the Communist Party formally recognized Olga's work in Neukölln, promoting her to the post of secretary of agitation and propaganda of the Communist Youth in the entire German capital. Along with Günter Erxleben, a boy much younger than she, student Dora Mantay, and other Youth leaders, Olga spent her evenings organizing groups to hang posters, hand out pamphlets, and picket factories in support of workers' movements.

Operations planned by Olga were always marked by ingenuity and imagination; it was especially important to find creative ways of tricking the police in order to avoid heavy repression. When the cabdrivers went on strike in Berlin that year and street demonstrations were prohibited, the Youth nevertheless decided to organize a protest expressing solidarity with the strikers. They couldn't leave the Müller beer hall as a group or they would be picked up before reaching the center of town, so Olga came up with a plan. At 3:00 P.M., when the area was at its busiest, dozens of young lovers flooded into central Berlin, standing on street corners, looking in shop windows, pausing outside bars and ice-cream parlors. Suddenly there was a loud whistle and the couples stormed into the street and staged an instantaneous protest, dispersed minutes later by billy clubs, mounted police, and blasts of water cannon from police carts. In the meantime, the windows of shops and office buildings filled with red banners bearing the hammer and sickle in support of the young Communists as often as the Nazis' black swastika in support of the police.

Scuffles like this occurred frequently in Berlin. The activity of the opposition grew in direct proportion to the organization of the Right. The National Socialist German Workers' Party—the Nazi Party—was stepping up its recruitment in both middle- and working-class sectors. The Communists fought back by seeking to multiply their cells. Though the Russian Revolution had triumphed less than ten years earlier, the political isolation and physical distance of the newborn Union of Soviet Socialist Republics aided the growth of the German Communist Party, conspiring to make Berlin not only the capital of German, or European, communism, but a mecca for social insurrection in general.

The degree of organization of the Communist Party in society was comparable to that of a state. With hundreds of thousands of militants scattered throughout the country, the Party maintained publishing houses (not always officially linked to the Communists) in all the major cities, printing various weekly magazines and dozens of daily newspapers, both regional and national, many of them on paper manufactured in Party factories. In fact, the circulation of official and nonofficial Communist publications far outnumbered that of the independent press and other political parties combined. Innumerable clubs and associations of women, young people, and intellectuals—almost all of them "fronts," without overt ties to the organization—functioned with guidance from the Party or, just as often, directly from the cupola of the Third International—the Comintern—in Moscow.

The internal structure of the German CP also resembled that of a government, with its own mail service, political and industrial espionage sectors, and graphic arts divisions dedicated exclusively to the production of false documents. A sort of defense ministry in miniature was responsible for the security of Party leaders, documents, and headquarters. For each area of production, whether it be industry, agriculture, transportation, or energy, there was a corresponding department, with experts in every field. Two divisions received particular attention from the leadership of the Party and from the Comintern: the section responsible for dealing with the Social Democrats and the section that supervised the activities of the Communist Youth.

Within the CY, the operations carried out by the Neukölln group were held up as models of efficiency and dedication to the Communist cause. And Neukölln's brightest star, Olga Benario, was of the greatest current concern to the Party leadership. Fearing that the police were suspicious of Otto's double identity and would try to get to him through his girlfriend, security was stepped up around Olga. Her activities were cut back and she was forbidden to participate in risky operations. "If they get their hands on you," she was warned, "Otto will be next in line." Besides, Olga too had become a police target just a few weeks earlier, when she was chosen to be the political secretary of the directorate of the Communist Youth in Neukölln, the most important post after general secretary.

The suspicion that Olga would be used as bait did not materialize. In early October 1926, Olga left a meeting at the beer hall later than usual. Though it was already past midnight, she walked home to her tiny apartment at 25 Jung Street. She went upstairs and left her coat on until the heater took the chill off the room. When she heard knocking at around 2:00 A.M., Olga imagined that Otto had forgotten his key. She opened the door to find two policemen, the older of whom flashed an official-looking document and asked, "Is your name Olga Gutmann Benario?"

"Yes," she replied, dumbfounded.

"You are under arrest by order of the regional director of justice, Judge Vogt. Please come with us."

In the police car Olga read the order to take her into custody. On the basis of the Law for the Protection of the Republic, she had been arrested on suspicion of having committed various crimes: "conspiracy to undertake highly traitorous acts," "attempting to alter the lawful constitution by violent means," and "participation in an organization which is illegal, hostile to the state, and dedicated to undermining the republican form of government." Despite the threatening tone of the charges, which under the then-current law could lead to her rotting in jail for a number of years, Olga realized, from listening to the guards, that she had not been their primary target. The person they really wanted to put behind bars had been taken into custody that morning: Otto Braun.

From the outset of her first interrogation, it was clear to Olga that what the police wanted from her was information about Braun's activities and that the charge hanging over him was greater than she had supposed: "suspicion of high treason."

Olga was kept incommunicado in Moabit Prison for two weeks and subjected to interrogation from dawn until late at night, with short interruptions for what were called meals. Her cool, calm denials of all charges, both true and false, provoked impatience and irritation in the police who took turns questioning her. The first news from the outside world came from Munich: Olga's father sent a message through two lawyers who worked for the Investigation Department. With her consent, he would come to the capital to defend her in court and, providing that she was not too deeply involved, believed he would be able to arrange her release through influential friends in the Social Democrat Party. Olga realized that her father meant well and that he was deeply concerned for her, but she politely refused his help.

As soon as she was out of solitary confinement, she received her first visitor. The Communist Youth of Neukölln had taken a collection among Olga's fellow militants, sympathizers, and friends and elected Gabor Lewin, one of the members of the directorate, to visit her and deliver a sumptuous bundle of treats. The package, which was minutely examined at the entrance to Moabit Prison, contained sweets, biscuits, fruit, crackers, and jam from the best shop in the city. During the short visit, Olga was given a disconcerting report on the activities of the Youth and the measures being taken to protest the two arrests. Whispering, she summarized the charges and the hazards not only of her situation but, more important, of Otto's. The guard stepped out of the room; she knew at any moment he would stick his head back in to keep an eye on things. Olga quickly scribbled a note to the young Party members, which would be read that night at an assembly in Karl Liebknecht House, headquarters for official public functions of the German CP.

By early December, Olga began to fear that something more serious was going on than she had originally imagined. The total absence of news about the progress of her case and, worse, Otto's began to make her extremely apprehensive. But on the morning of December 2, exactly two months after her arrest, a guard opened the door to her cell and announced, "You can gather your things. You are being released by order of the prosecutor of the Federal Court of Justice."

Olga grabbed the two changes of clothes that lay folded in a corner, scrawled her signature at the bottom of the order for her release, and, in less than five minutes, found herself out on the street. Heading straight home, she saw as she walked through the apartment door that the two months had given the police more than enough time to search shelves, the bureau, every nook and cranny of the place. Otto's manuscripts and books, her own notes, all had been confiscated.

She lay down and slept for almost twenty-four hours. The next morning she was awakened, alarmed, by a pounding on the door. But when she drew back the bolt, more than twenty friends from the Communist Youth streamed into the apartment. Olga splashed some cold water over her face and talked for hours, describing the two months she had spent in Moabit.

Days went by without news of Otto. Every night before falling asleep, Olga felt a tightness in her chest as her eyes fell on her lover's belongings—pipes, tobacco pouch, two pairs of boots, a silk scarf hanging on the bathroom doorknob. This was a different kind of absence from the ones before, when she knew at any moment he might walk in, silently embrace her, and lead her to bed—and only much later would the two find the voice to exchange news. This time she felt a strong foreboding that she would be without him for a long, long while.

In the meantime, political activity was the best cure for anxiety and heartache. She threw herself into the struggle, concentrating on a task that wouldn't involve the risk of new arrest: preparation for Youth meetings outside Berlin. Even so, her longing and worry were so great that two weeks after being released she decided to take a chance. She picked up the phone and called the office of Judge Vogt. When the secretary said that in a moment the judge would speak to her, Olga held her hand over the receiver and said to her friend Frieda, "I must have become important. Fascist Vogt is going to talk to me!"

If, deigning to take a call from someone regarded as subversive, Vogt expected some important information regarding Otto's case, he was very mistaken. Olga wanted authorization to visit her companion at least once a month, she demanded the right to bring him special food regularly, and, lastly, she requested permission for an extra visit at Christmas, which was fast approaching. Irritated by the ex-prisoner's impudence, Vogt crisply informed her that she should put her request in writing and deliver it to the prison reception desk, and then he hung up. A typed request was handed in that very afternoon by Olga herself. The next morning's mail brought a final ruling signed not by Vogt but by his subordinate, Commissioner Kling. Otto Braun was not a political prisoner, but rather stood accused of high treason, and as such would not be permitted to receive special food on a regular basis; he did have the right by law, just as any common prisoner, to receive visitors and up to five kilos of food at Christmas; as for the request for monthly visits, that was flatly denied. Frustration turned to fury as Olga read the official letter. She crumpled up the paper, threw it in the trash, and said out loud, "Well, it looks like the only way Otto will get out of there is if we spring him."

Olga knew that the year 1927 promised to be a tumultuous one. Even though the Communist Party was still legal, the government was closing in. The jails were crammed with hundreds of political prisoners, and despite the country's overall economic growth since the crisis of four years earlier, poverty was intensifying in working-class neighborhoods. There was great national and international sympathy for those who had been arrested, but it was simply not possible to provide for the many families who had been deprived of their wage earners.

For Olga, the worst of it was that she didn't have Otto to help her work out political solutions to the crisis that threatened the country. On the two occasions when "fascist Vogt" had authorized visits, they were hardly able to talk. Presuming that there might be important information to be gleaned from the meeting, the judge posted guards just inches away from the couple, listening ostentatiously to every word they whispered.

The new year began badly for both of them. The government organ responsible for intelligence—Department I of the Interior

Ministry—informed the federal police of their suspicion that Frieda Wolf Behrendt and Arthur Behrendt were, in fact, Olga Gutmann Benario and Otto Braun, "lovers and accomplices in a case of high treason" pending in the German courts. The information services requested more precise data regarding "both couples," such as photographs, verification of addresses, and copies of all identity documents. It was recommended that all investigations be conducted "in absolute secrecy."

The response from the police, a concise report by Commissioner Heinz Junghans, left no doubt as to the truth of the Interior Ministry's suspicions. In addition, the police commissioner reported that the address listed when the couple had registered their fake documents—11 Erhardtstrasse, in Leipzig—did not exist. Finally, Junghans warned that the excellent quality of Braun's and Benario's forged identity papers indicated that they had access to some very sophisticated printing equipment, perhaps even capable of producing passports and currency. Until then, Otto had been the only one up to his ears in trouble; from that moment on Olga ceased to appear in the official records as merely his "secretary" or "girlfriend."

When news of the increasing seriousness of his daughter's legal situation reached Leo Benario in Munich, he decided to act, this time without consulting her. In a formal petition addressed to Attorney Neumann, chief public prosecutor of the Federal Court of Justice, Benario lodged a moving appeal for the separation of his daughter's case from the suit against Otto Braun.

Claiming to be "responsible before the law and lawyer for my daughter, a minor," Olga's father insisted that if she had in fact participated in the alleged crime, certainly she had not been aware of the gravity of her actions, since she was not even eighteen at the time. "Out of a sort of romantic solicitude for the working class, this youngster, completely inexperienced in political and economic life," he wrote, "was merely trying to be of assistance in some way to that social class, especially the youth." Benario explained that Olga had left the family home in Munich not to be an activist in the Communist Party in Berlin but on account of the job they had promised her there. He had not tried to force her to stay in Munich because "nowadays such methods are useless with young people, and the application of force would probably have led to the opposite result." At the end of the petition, Benario reiterated the request that his daughter's case be separated from Otto's, closing with a subtle irony: "If in fact Olga colluded with Otto at all, it was only at the typewriter and, even so, she was not aware of what she was doing."

The chief prosecutor's dry response made it clear that the German judiciary had not been moved by Benario's paternal appeal. The lawyer's last hopes of extricating his daughter from her predicament were summarily dashed by a ruling of only a few lines: "The judicial inquiry against your daughter having already been opened, there are no provisions for suspending this process," wrote Prosecutor Neumann.

Months passed without another word from the courts. As the year drew to a close, Olga read in the paper that the Superior Court had finally set a date in May to try Otto Braun for his role as "leader in a case of high treason against the nation." No longer mincing words, they explicitly referred to him as "a spy in the service of the Soviet Union." Olga was terrified; there was no way this would be a fair trial. With the appointment of a man from the extreme Right like Vogt as presiding judge, the government had proclaimed its intention to bury the Communists once and for all. The trial would be used to compromise the CP in the eyes of the public, ascribing to the organization acts of treason against Germany and espionage on behalf of the Soviet Union. "All the lawyers in the world, working together day and night, won't be able to stop them from giving Otto twenty years," she said to herself as she wandered the city, hands stuffed in the pockets of her woolen jacket, the newspaper announcing the forthcoming trial under her arm. "And if his conviction is a foregone conclusion, there's only one way out: Otto cannot be allowed to go to trial," she concluded. The idea alone cheered her. She pressed on toward the Müller beer hall. "That's it. Otto will not be judged by a fascist court."

Olga was well aware how much fantasy lay beneath this reasoning; she knew that the whole concept was the product of an inner mechanism to stave off the panic she felt at the thought of Otto's imminent conviction. After all, Moabit was not just any jail, but a virtual fortress occupying an entire block in central Berlin. Looking at the building from the street, a visitor would hardly imagine the elegant and compact construction with Gothic windows was a high-security prison, but it was. In addition to the dozen or so cells in the basement and on the west side of the building protected by brick walls, Moabit contained half a dozen legal training and hearing rooms on the ground floor facing Turmstrasse, where the main entrance to the prison complex was located. To prevent prisoners, escorted to this area for inquests or interrogation, from circulating in the section open to lawyers and the public, small cubicles were constructed outside the hearing rooms, linked to the cells by underground passageways. Though the security system was rigorous, Olga knew that if there was any chance at all of getting Otto out of Moabit it would be during the few moments when he was being transferred from the waiting room to the main chamber. And this would happen in a few weeks, at Otto's last pretrial hearing.

Olga walked the streets dreaming up schemes, plots, kidnappings, astonished by the world's indifference to her distress. "I can't believe it, Dora," she complained to one of the young women she worked with. "It's as if they're anesthetized. A revolutionary writer is in danger of spending decades in an ice-cold jail cell for the crime of trying to free his countrymen, and these people walking by have probably never even heard of his name." From the minute she woke up in the morning until returning home late at night, she thought of nothing else: Otto must not stay in Moabit and go on trial.

Olga didn't know it yet, but she wasn't the only one who felt that way; fantasy or no, other comrades had the same plan in mind. More than once it had been said, "Olga and the Party seem to think with one mind," and now the idea was to be confirmed. During the last week in March she was summoned to Party headquarters by a clerk from the counterespionage section. After pacing the hall for a few minutes, Olga was ushered into the office of the *Parteischutzgruppen*, the Party directorate's security unit. There she was instructed to select half a dozen militants from the Department of Security of the CY and to prepare them for a dangerous and delicate mission, which she was to direct personally on April 11, two weeks later: an armed attack on Moabit Prison to free Otto Braun.

3

Enter the Knight of Hope

A FEW DAYS AFTER checking into the Hotel Desna, Olga and Otto were moved to the apartment building reserved for young foreigners in Moscow working for KIM (*Kommunisti Internationali Molodoi*), a branch of the Comintern for the Communist Youth International. Though more modest than the hotel, this accommodation had the obvious advantage of bringing them into contact with young people from different countries, giving them a palpable sense of the international nature of the Russian Revolution. Dozens of languages and dialects mingled in the babble of Slavs, Latins, Africans, and Orientals hailing from the diverse Soviet republics and the four corners of the earth.

The couple was assigned a small room with a bath, closet, and bureau. They had hardly settled in when they received word that, due to the severe strain of the time spent underground in Berlin and the trip to Moscow, they were being given three weeks' holiday on the Black Sea. The departure date was up to them, but before traveling they were to have complete medical checkups, especially Otto, who was thought to be anemic.

It was clear within a few days of moving into KIM housing that nearly all the students knew who they were, knew, in fact, every detail of the story of the young German girl who had stormed Moabit Prison to rescue her lover, an important young Communist leader. Olga and Otto were amused whenever they overheard someone in the dining hall telling their tale, each version adding more fantastic touches.

Two weeks after they arrived in Moscow, their guide took them to the closing ceremonies of one of the political lecture courses sponsored by KIM. Walking into the crowded auditorium, Olga imagined it must have been a luxurious theater during the time of the czar; the place was so sumptuous, with gleaming marble, thick carpets, and blue velvet curtains. Every seat was taken, so the three joined those squeezed into side aisles. As the program drew to a close, the girl on the podium requested silence so that she could make an important announcement. She then proceeded to call to the stage "our comrade Olga Sinek"—Olga's code name during her stay in the USSR—"recently arrived from Berlin, where she masterminded the escape of Professor Otto Braun." The announcement of Olga's presence brought the house down. She took the podium to the applause of hundreds of young people and, nervously at first, briefly recounted the events of April 1. Unaffected by the outbursts of applause as she spoke, Olga concluded with a confession: "I must tell you that I did what I did for two reasons: loyalty to the Party and loyalty to my heart."

It was the crowning touch. From that day on, there was hardly enough time to retell the story of Moabit to all the people who asked to hear it. Held up by the leaders of KIM as an example of the ideal young Communist, Olga tirelessly attended to the many commitments arranged for her by the directorate, including speaking engagements at factories, farm cooperatives, schools, and radio stations. The holiday on the Black Sea kept being postponed, and two months after arriving in the Soviet Union Olga heard that she had been elected to the Central Committee of the Communist Youth International. This new post brought with it additional obligations, the first of which was to attend intensive courses in English and French and, in her free time, to work on improving her Russian.

Olga hardly had a minute left for Otto. When finally, one evening, he told her that his medical tests were complete and suggested that they leave for their holiday as soon as possible, she surprised him with her refusal. "I think you're going to have to go by yourself. I'm so busy with KIM right now that I can't, and don't even want to, leave Moscow for a minute."

Much to Olga's amazement, Otto's response was an explosion of jealousy. Indignant, she told him once more that she would never be anyone's property, no matter who he was. Otto raged and fumed, demanding to know who the young man was who had obviously turned her head and what country he was from. Before walking out and shutting the door behind her, Olga paused, furious, to point scornfully to the bust of Lenin on the table:

"He's Russian, and long dead, you idiot!"

Whenever Otto had one of his fits of jealousy, Olga would walk the streets of Moscow, longing for the early days of their relationship in Munich and Berlin. She scanned the newspaper kiosks on Gorki Street looking for a back copy of the official publication of the German CP, trying to forget Otto's tantrums. The *Red Flag*, which occasionally appeared on newsstands or at political meetings in Moscow, was the only source of news from Germany and, in particular, Neukölln, and news from her fondly remembered "red fort" generally consisted of increasingly serious battles between the CY and the "fascist police," almost always resulting in the injury or arrest of some of her friends. Every time she read about such incidents, Olga was even more convinced she had been right to insist that the CY develop a militarized section. As certain as ever that the struggle would be more than just political, she requested authorization from KIM to enroll in paramilitary courses in addition to theoretical classes.

Olga hounded her superiors so insistently that within months she was invited to Borisoglebsk—five hundred kilometers south of Moscow, near the Caspian Sea—where, as part of a regular unit of the Red Army, she was instructed in the use of light and heavy weapons and in horsemanship. Ten weeks later, she came home to find an angry letter from Otto, once more complaining how little time they managed to spend together. Though Olga felt that she still loved him, living together was becoming more difficult. Otto was a wonderful man, unquestionably a true Communist, but when it came to personal relationships he behaved like a real "petit bourgeois."

Early in 1931, during one of these crises in their relationship, Olga had a wonderful surprise. Her old and dear friend from the CY in Neukölln, Gabor Lewin, who had headed the patrols that pulled down the Wanted posters after Moabit, decided he could no longer resist the temptation to visit her in Moscow. His chances of locating her were pretty slim: he spoke not a word of Russian and for an address had only the vague information that she was living "in a building near the Moscow River." Nevertheless, he arrived in Moscow confident and determined to find his great platonic love. Lewin wandered through the city, looking for passersby with Jewish features. "After all," he reasoned, "Yiddish is close enough to German that we should be able to exchange a few words." On the fourth day of his pilgrimage, he caught sight of a cabdriver who "had a certain air of Jewishness and a nose as big as mine." He ran over to the man and, using gestures and a mixture of German and Yiddish, tried without success to make himself understood. The passenger who had just climbed into the taxi, however, was an official in the Red Army who happened to speak German. Minutes later, Gabor Lewin was knocking on Olga's door at the KIM housing. Olga admired her friend's perseverance and was able to arrange room and board for him for ten days. They talked endlessly, he bringing her up to date on the Youth's activities in Neukölln and she recounting the whirlwind that her life had become in Moscow.

Gabor's visit and the news from Berlin aroused Olga's curiosity regarding her own legal status in Germany. After her friend had gone home, she devised a scheme whereby she would learn how things stood. Her passport had expired a few weeks earlier, so she simply presented herself at the German embassy in Moscow to ask that it be renewed. The German consul, Von Twardowski, requested instructions from the Chancellery in Berlin and took advantage of the situation to transmit information about her to the German police. He said it was impossible to tell from the expired passport how she had entered the USSR (she told the consulate that her Soviet entry visa was on a separate sheet and had been handed in at immigration on arrival) and that she carried an "authorization for residency of foreigners," which meant that she had not become a naturalized Soviet citizen. He realized that Olga obviously had excellent lawyers in Moscow, because she had arrived at the embassy armed with a copy of the August 1928 Certificate of Amnesty, by which Germany had granted pardons to some accused of political crimes. While Olga was not among those named, still she hoped to benefit. Finally, she claimed to work as a secretary at the Marx-Engels Institute in the Soviet capital.

The reply from Berlin indicated that her political file had fattened substantially since 1928. The German courts had arbitrarily transferred to her all the charges that had landed Braun in prison including that of "high treason against the nation." She was told that the 1928 amnesty applied neither to her nor to Otto Braun. But the pile of documents sent to the consulate went on to say that, even though she was considered a "wanted Communist" and a "highly dangerous person," she had neither renounced nor been stripped of her German citizenship. A month after her visit to the embassy, Olga was sent a new German passport.

Late in 1931, Olga was given her first international mission: to intercede, in KIM's name, with the French Communist Youth, and to help select the new directors of the Executive Committee of the Communist Youth in Paris in order that the organization have a less sectarian focus. The news that Olga was leaving the USSR for an indefinite period was the last straw for Otto. Though they still shared an apartment, it was not uncommon for two months to pass without their seeing each other. When Olga suggested they separate, Otto agreed and added that he was already becoming involved with another woman in Moscow. It was arranged that by the time Olga returned from France, Otto would have moved out. As they said good-bye, Olga realized that she was experiencing for the first time the feeling she had so condemned in her companion: jealousy.

Brooding on her jealousy, under the false name of Eva Kruger she boarded the train that would eventually deliver her to France. At the railway station Olga ran into Ilze Unger, a comrade from the Neukölln CY. They discovered they would be traveling on the same train, though with different destinations and missions. Walter Ulbricht, the director of the German CP exiled in Moscow, had entrusted to Ilze some secret documents containing instructions from the Comintern to the Party in Berlin, which she was carrying in her bra. The two women decided not to sit together. As a part of her cover, Ilze flirted with the guards at the Polish border. One of them looked at her suspiciously and said, "Aren't you Olga Benario? Let me see your papers."

There was indeed a resemblance: both were tall, with blue eyes and dark hair, and they were about the same age. Ilze showed her papers and informed the soldier that she most certainly was not Olga Benario.

"Hardly. Neither I nor my fiancé, who lives in Moscow, have any affection for the Communists."

Five rows back, Olga listened to the entire exchange and sank a little lower behind the book she was pretending to read.

Once in France, Olga did not limit herself to the role of messenger-mediator from KIM but participated in street demonstrations as well, until finally being detained. Released, she was arrested again weeks later and deposited by the police at the Belgian border. With the help of Belgian Communists she traveled to London, only to be arrested there during a protest. A file on her was opened by the police, and the fingerprints taken would, years later, lead to a portfolio crammed with accusations much weightier than demonstrating in a public park.

Returning to Moscow, Olga was met with the news that the Fifth Congress of the Communist Youth International had just elected her a member of the Presidium, the highest level in the hierarchy of a Communist organization. Her name had been unanimously ratified in the final assembly of a congressional body composed of young people from more than fifty nations. The reward for this promotion was quick to follow: Olga was selected by the Comintern from among hundreds of candidates to take a course in piloting and parachuting at the Zhukovski Academy. Registered under the name of Olga Sinek, she was assigned to a mixed group of first-year students. As discreet as ever, Olga revealed nothing about herself or her past to her new colleagues, not even to her best friend in the course, Tamara Kojevnikova, a girl from Soviet Georgia four years younger than she, who affectionately called her Olya or Olguinha.

Only Olga's accent gave her away as German. At the academy she met young people who had come from various parts of the world to dedicate themselves exclusively to military training.

After a simulated flight lesson and over tea with a group of fellow trainees in the officer's cafeteria, Olga listened to a young South American recount in hesitant Russian a story he'd read in a newspaper at home about a revolutionary adventure there. It was the tale of a battalion just over a thousand strong, which had covered more than twenty-five thousand kilometers on foot, skirmishing with the regular troops of a dictatorial government. The story, related in great detail, full of heroic moments and bloody battles, ended with the guerrillas failing in their attempt to overthrow the government, but without having suffered a single defeat during their long struggle. The battalion was called the Prestes Column, after its leader, a young captain named Luís Carlos Prestes. Olga was intrigued, but skeptical.

"Are you sure they actually walked twenty-five thousand kilometers? That adds up to almost ten round-trips between Moscow and Berlin . . . and on foot!"

When the pilot insisted that the events he'd recounted were absolutely true, had taken place in Brazil, and could be confirmed by any Latin American in Moscow, Olga could hardly contain herself: "Can you imagine being there, being part of that invincible battalion?"

What neither Olga nor any of her colleagues at the academy knew was that the legendary commander of the unbeaten battalion was right there in Moscow, in an apartment on Sadova Boulevard, only a few blocks from where they were having tea.

The Prestes family—dona Leocádia, a widow, and her five grown children, Luís Carlos, Clotilde, Heloísa, Lúcia, and Lígia, all single —had come to Moscow months before, in November 1931. Luís Carlos arrived on November 7, during the commemoration of the fourteenth anniversary of the Bolshevik revolution, and was followed a few days later by his mother and sisters. The family had split up in Montevideo in order to throw off the police, Luís Carlos setting sail on the *Eubee* and the others, two days later, on the

Monte Sarmiento. In spite of having shaved his beard and mustache, Prestes did not manage to pass unnoticed during the ship's two ports of call in Brazil. Journalist Oscar Pedroso Horta recognized him after boarding the *Eubee* in Santos, but kept the discovery to himself. Then, when the *Monte Sarmiento* docked in Brazil, the police stormed the Prestes women's cabins, after a tip from someone who had noticed the presence on the passenger list of that surname so hated by the government. But it was too late: the *Eubee* had already weighed anchor with the famous captain aboard, carrying a passport that identified him as a Paraguayan painter.

In the Soviet Union, Prestes was immediately hired as an engineer for *Tzentralnij Soiuzstroy*, the organization responsible for inspecting the nation's civil constructions, and was shocked to discover the degree of sabotage perpetrated by technicians and engineers against the revolutionary government. Life in Moscow was somewhat difficult for the Prestes family. Luís Carlos had refused the special privileges offered to him as a visiting technician (such as a salary in dollars and permission to shop in the stores restricted to foreigners), preferring to be paid in rubles and live like the millions of Russians around him.

It wasn't easy. The Five-Year Plan had been in effect since 1928, and in order to maintain economic stability, nearly everything was rationed. One winter in Moscow was enough to give the family a very concrete idea of the problems the country faced: Heloísa, a tiny woman with very small feet, had to endure temperatures up to fifty degrees below zero wearing enormous boots, the only size available. But hardships like these only served to inspire dona Leocádia (who came from a wealthy family) to develop a passion for the Russian people, referring to them as "the true Soviet bulwark." To her mind, no enemy, however powerful, could ever conquer a people whose workers received a daily meal ration of two hundred grams of black bread and still toiled away enthusiastically. Countless times, and in freezing temperatures, she saw workers at the nearby factory reduced to drinking hot water because even tea was rationed.

For his part, her son Luís Carlos was witness to the grim proceedings that took place at public assemblies in factories and other places of work. Each member of the local directorate had to go to the rostrum and undertake what was called self-criticism. During the purges that followed, in which nearly a million active members were expelled from the Party, Prestes observed terrible scenes in which white-haired military men sat on the platform and wept through the entire ordeal. Politics. Politics that would lead to the so-called Moscow Trials, through which the old-guard Bolsheviks would be eliminated. In his free time Prestes attended Party meetings or conferences for Latin American Communist leaders. It was at one of these meetings at the Comintern headquarters that Party Secretary Dmitri Manuilski and veteran Elena Stasova, a member of the Central Committee of the CP since the time of Lenin, first spoke to Prestes of a young German named Olga Sinek, who was making meteoric progress in the Communist Youth International.

Whether because of lack of time or the difficulties imposed by rationing, the Prestes family rarely entertained. But late in 1934, Secretary Manuilski himself directed that a gathering be organized at the Prestes home, under the pretext of commemorating Luís Carlos's affiliation in August of that year with the Brazilian Communist Party. The Party that had first courted Prestes and then rejected him had finally been obliged to grant him admission after receiving a curt telegram from Moscow signed by Manuilski. The celebration was arranged for November 7, the anniversary of the revolution and the day that marked the end of Prestes's third year in Moscow. The small apartment in the Sadova Boulevard district was packed with friends, and the Prestes sisters were dressed up for the occasion. At one point in the festivities, the guests were treated to the amazing spectacle of Manuilski, the leader of the Communist world, practicing samba steps as carnival music was played on the gramophone. Of all the people present, only he and Luís Carlos Prestes knew that the gathering was in fact less an anniversary celebration than a farewell party: in three weeks the host would be returning to Brazil. As the first guests began to leave, Manuilski asked dona Leocádia to propose a toast, which she graciously did, raising her glass and proclaiming for all to hear: "I only hope that one day my son Carlos is as complete a Bolshevik as Comrade Manuilski."

Neither dona Leocádia nor her daughters had ever heard of Olga Benario (or Olga Sinek or Eva Kruger), but five days later she was to become part of their life. By the summer of 1934, when only twenty-six years old, Olga was considered by her superiors to be what dona Leocádia had wished for her son in that toast. Fluent in four languages, thoroughly conversant in Marxist-Leninist theory, she knew how to shoot, ride a horse, pilot an airplane, and sky-dive, and had given undeniable proof of her courage and determination. Even so, Olga was surprised when a messenger handed her a sealed envelope with a note from Dmitri Manuilski summoning her to the Comintern headquarters. She imagined that, finally, she was to be sent to lead the young Communists in Berlin in their struggle against Hitler's Nazis, now in power. To make a good impression, Olga dusted off the uniform she had been given at the Air Force Academy and wore it to the meeting.

When she arrived at the imposing Comintern building at 36 Mokovaia Street, Olga was immediately taken to the secretary. Gazing into the distance, as if concentrating more intently on the snow falling outside than on the subject at hand, Dmitri Manuilski immediately dispelled Olga's thoughts of returning to Germany. Yes, he was referring to the prospect of a popular revolution, but one in Latin America, not in Germany.

"One of the most courageous Communists we know is insisting on returning to his country. He and his friends in the Party have convinced us that this is the moment for a revolution there. After hesitating for some time, the international directorate has finally decided to authorize his return."

Manuilski walked around the room slowly, like a professor giving a minutely detailed lecture.

"We have accepted his plan, on the condition that the Comintern be responsible for his personal safety. After much discussion, during which dozens of names were considered, we have concluded that you are the one person who can escort him back to his country in absolute safety. Don't answer now. I want you to think it over and come back tomorrow at the same time with your answer. For security reasons, the only additional information we can give you at the moment is this: if you accept the job, the two of you will leave for Latin America within the next few days."

Olga's impulse was to announce right then and there that she was ready and willing to go. But she was disciplined: if Manuilski wanted her to have a day to think about it, she would postpone her yes until then. She returned the following day an hour early. Manu-ilski arrived to find her seated in the anteroom, and once they had gone into his office he got right down to business. "So? Has our comrade Olga Sinek made up her mind?"

"I have known since yesterday, comrade. I am ready to go."

The secretary proceeded to fill her in on the plans. Before the end of the month she would leave for Brazil, charged with the personal safety of Captain Luís Carlos Prestes, who would attempt to mount a popular insurrection in his country. The story of the invincible battalion flashed through her mind. When Manuilski had Prestes brought in, Olga remained expressionless, but later confessed to being a little disappointed. As thrilled as she was to meet the "Knight of Hope," she thought he looked a bit frail for someone who had led an army a distance of twenty-five thousand kilometers.

4

Honeymoon in New York

WHEN LUÍS CARLOS PRESTES left his apartment on the evening of December 29, 1934, his youngest sister, Lígia, walked with him to the door downstairs. Prestes embraced her and asked her to take care of their mother. Returning to the apartment, Lígia saw that dona Leocádia was extremely upset and asked why. Her mother was blunt. "I have the feeling that I'm never going to see my son again."

At midnight, Pedro Fernandez, a Spaniard, and Russian student Olga Sinek—Prestes's and Olga's new identities—settled into their carriage on a train bound for Leningrad. Arriving at eight the following morning, they bought tickets for the next leg of their journey, spent the day wandering the city, and then boarded another midnight train that would deposit them in Helsinki. This was not, of course, the shortest route to Paris, but it was unquestionably the safest. Taking a more direct path through Poland, Czechoslovakia, and Germany would have been tantamount to asking to be detained—much too great a risk, especially for Olga, whose photograph had been circulated to all German border posts.

From Helsinki, the couple boarded a ship for Stockholm, and at midnight on December 31 were standing on deck above the icy waters of the Baltic Sea toasting the arrival of the New Year. Prestes raised his glass of punch:

"May 1935 be the year of revolution in Brazil!"

Though their destination was Paris, Olga was concerned with the poor quality of their passports and decided they should spend a few days in Amsterdam, where a contact would be able to arrange more convincing papers. So they crossed southern Sweden by train, took a boat from Copenhagen to the east coast of England, and then immediately sailed back across the North Sea to Amsterdam. Olga and Prestes spent three weeks there waiting for word from the contact, but none came. Worried about the risks involved in staying in one place for so long, Olga finally decided they should leave for Brussels at once, despite their crudely forged passports.

The first weeks of the trip gave the two a chance to get to know each other. Prestes was surprised to find that the young woman Manuilski had described as a strict and disciplined Communist spent her spare time on board ship or train or at night in their hotel making delicate pieces of crochet work. Speaking in French—the language of the engineering texts Prestes had devoured in military school and of the political tracts Astrojildo Pereira had left him in Bolivia—they spent hour after hour recounting their respective adventures. Passionately interested in military strategy, Olga wanted to hear about every maneuver of the invincible Column, every ambush, every troop movement. On dining-car napkins and in the margins of tourist pamphlets, Prestes sketched maps, rivers, and bivouacs. The only point Olga had a hard time accepting was the inconclusiveness of the Brazilian enterprise. Why hadn't they tried to take power? Why hadn't they marched on Rio de Janeiro on their way south from Piauí?

In turn, Olga recalled the arguments with her parents, described joining the Schwabing Group in Munich, leaving home, the street demonstrations in Berlin, police repression, fights with the Nazis. And, in great detail, the daring operation to liberate Otto Braun from Moabit Prison, life underground, the escape to Moscow, her rapid rise in the Communist Youth International, her military training. Prestes interrupted Olga's story several times to confess shyly that he had never met anyone so much like his own mother.

"You have so many of the same qualities," he said. "It's not a physical resemblance, but a way of thinking and talking that's very close to hers. That is really strange, considering that you come from a culture completely different from that of my mother, who was born and lived practically her entire life in Brazil."

Had Olga known how passionately devoted Prestes was to dona Leocádia, she would have understood these words as a poorly disguised, or perhaps unconscious, declaration of love.

The general crisis in Europe at that time had made tourism—especially long sojourns—practically nonexistent. Those who did travel were often suspected of being spies, either for the Nazis or for the Comintern. Once more, fear of discovery convinced Olga it was time to leave town; in Brussels, a relatively small city, they were very exposed. Since the logistics of the trip were her responsibility, it was she who decided they would travel by train to Paris, their last stop in Europe. Starting in Paris, they were to use the cover created by the Comintern for their safe passage to Brazil: Olga and Prestes were to pose as a rich young couple on their honeymoon, and would have to behave as such. Accordingly, they would have luxury accommodations—the Grand Hôtel du Louvre, a majestic six-story turn-of-the-century construction with windows inspired by Roman porticoes, on the square of the Palais Royal across from the Comédie-Française, in the heart of Paris.

The contact Olga had been hoping to meet in Amsterdam and Brussels finally appeared in Paris and directed them to take a train to Rouen. There they met the Portuguese consul, Israel Abrahão Anahory, who, though he was not a militant Communist, held opinions considered progressive and had past connections with anarchist groups in Lisbon. The fact that he was the diplomatic representative of the right-wing government of Antônio Oliveira Salazar, who had taken power three years earlier, dispelled any suspicion of his clandestine activities in France. On March 8, 1935, Olga and Prestes changed their names once more, assuming the identities on the Portuguese passport they would use for the remainder of their journey. He became Antônio Vilar, a forty-year-old businessman from Lisbon, son of José Vilar and Angela Glória Vilar, and she became Maria Bergner Vilar, his wife. The passport was valid for one year of travel in South America, and another year to cover their return trip to France. Eighteen months later, the discovery of the help given by Anahory to Olga and Prestes cost him his diplomatic career and several months in a Lisbon prison.

Appropriate touches were needed to fill out the newlyweds' cover, for which Paris was the ideal city. Antônio Vilar was supposedly a wealthy businessman leaving Paris to honeymoon with his wife. The couple spent several days visiting the famous Parisian dressmakers to assemble wardrobes befitting the well-heeled characters they were portraying. Accompanying Olga to the elegant fashion houses, Prestes lent added realism to the farce by playing the jealous type, full of suggestions about which dresses to buy and complaints about low necklines or short skirts. To complete his own disguise, he purchased impeccable suits, fedoras, and formal evening attire for the parties and banquets they would need to attend en route. In order to ensure the success of the mission, sufficient funds had been provided to pay for all this finery.

Though the passport obtained in Rouen looked perfect, Olga was determined to add one more layer to the appearance of legality. She concluded that there was no better way to do this than to have it stamped with an entry and exit visa from the United States. The U.S. embassy in Paris granted an open-ended tourist visa with no questions asked, since the final destination of their honeymoon trip was Lima, Peru. Prestes relished filling out the visa application, on which he was obliged to state that he was not a Communist—an eccentricity of American law. And he was greatly amused by the final warning: "Any false answer to the above questions constitutes a crime for which the applicant is subject to the full penalties of the law." Every single bit of information he had given was false, starting with his name.

The newlyweds' cover was reinforced by two other false documents furnished by Olga's French contact. The first was a letter typed on the letterhead of an imaginary "Compagnie Générale d'Électricité Ateliers d'Orléans," addressed to Monsieur Antônio Vilar—and delivered to the desk of the Grand Hôtel du Louvre—in which the firm's director named Vilar, "as per previous agreement," official representative of the company's products in South America. The second ghost letter, from "Martin Zellermayer & Co." of Vienna, authorized Vilar to sell its engines in South America. These letters, above and beyond confirming Prestes's cover, would be helpful if it became necessary to explain the origin of the small fortune in cash the couple was carrying.

By the third week in March, Olga and Prestes were ready to leave Paris. They had booked a luxurious first-class suite on the passenger ship *Ville de Paris*, which set sail from Brest, south of Le Havre. The first night out from port, a basket of flowers with a charming note inviting them to have dinner in the captain's quarters was delivered to the Vilar stateroom. Prestes was worried that the captain might be a French secret agent and, indeed, found himself in a tight spot at several points during the dinner party—the captain had lived in Lisbon and knew the city well. Every time the subject came up, Olga broke in and threw him off the track. Luckily, the captain was much more interested in talking to the beautiful "Maria" than to her husband.

Olga and Prestes's cover story inevitably demanded certain intimacies. Here were two good-looking young people thrown together night and day. Their intellectual and political affinity was growing daily as they stood on the threshold of the revolution they were about to create.

At thirty-seven, Prestes had a sizable fund of political experience: he had led a military uprising, conspired against governments, been arrested and exiled, and found himself on intimate terms with the most important Communist leaders in the Soviet Union. But his rigor, discipline, and dedication to the cause had cost him dearly— Prestes had reached the age of thirty-seven without having been with a woman.

When he was only ten, he lost his father and became head of the family. What little free time he had outside military school was devoted to his studies. His mother refused to allow him to get a job; she preferred to work herself, insisting that he bury his nose in his books and be top of the class. Life was so difficult for the family in suburban Rio de Janeiro that Prestes had to request special permission to wear his uniform outside military school—he had nothing else to wear. As leader of the Column, he had felt obliged to be an example to his men, and unlike many of the younger officers he resisted getting involved with the women who accompanied them on the march. Politics and his concern for the education of his four sisters had taken up all his time. And now here he was, in a luxurious stateroom on the high seas, with an utterly beautiful woman—there couldn't have been a more propitious moment. By the time the *Ville de Paris* docked in New York on March 26, 1935, what had begun as a fiction arranged by the Comintern had become reality: just like the characters they were playing, Prestes and Olga were, to all intents and purposes, husband and wife.

Very much in love, the two really did have a honeymoon in New York. They went to concerts and films and, when the weather was mild, took long strolls through Central Park. As the only reason for their visit to the United States was to obtain entry and exit stamps on their passport, the lovers' time was theirs alone.

The contact in Paris had recommended that they send their heavy luggage on to Américo Dias Leite in Rio de Janeiro. Leite was a Communist Party sympathizer who, traveling in France some years earlier, had written to Prestes in Moscow asking his help in securing an entry visa to the Soviet Union. At the Wagons-lits Cook travel agency where they arranged to have the luggage shipped to Rio, Prestes and Olga purchased tickets for the remainder of their journey—first class all the way. Five days after docking in New York, the couple checked out of the elegant Hotel Pennsylvania on Seventh Avenue. At the last minute, Prestes removed several sheets of hotel letterhead from the desk in their suite and placed them carefully between two pieces of light cardboard in the bottom of his shoulder bag. Hours later the couple was on a train to Miami, where they would catch a plane to Brazil, via Santiago and Buenos Aires.

In those days the trip from Miami to Santiago was long and exhausting. Passenger planes did not fly at night, so their Pan American four-engine Sikorsky made overnight stops in Cuba, Panama, Ecuador, and Peru. Since they had no entry visa for Chile, Olga and Prestes had to offer American dollars to employees of the Chilean consulate in Callao to guarantee that the paperwork would come through before takeoff. Arriving in Santiago on April 5, they stayed only long enough to buy a ticket to Argentina. This time the plane was a small Panagra Airways Triford, requiring stops in Mendoza and Córdoba before landing in Buenos Aires.

Their stay in Argentina was to be longer and involved special precautions, for it was here that they would apply for entry visas to

Brazil. Through various intermediaries, Prestes had devised a way of securing visas that depended on the help of the vice-consul of Brazil in Buenos Aires, Manuel Paranhos, a childhood friend. As soon as they arrived, Prestes contacted the Brazilian embassy and learned that, to their good fortune, Paranhos had been designated acting consul general, allowing him even greater leeway. But a misunderstanding almost thwarted their plans. Prestes notified the diplomat that a "tall brunette" would meet him in a café to present the passport. Paranhos took "brunette" to mean dark-haired and dark-skinned and assumed that Olga, with brown hair, blue eyes, and fair skin, was not the person in question. Since she was the only unaccompanied woman in the café at the appointed time, however, he finally decided to risk approaching her. Paranhos's justification, should it be needed later, for having granted visas to the "Portuguese honeymooners" was a letter Olga handed him together with the passport. The letter, ostensibly from a Portuguese diplomat in New York requesting special assistance in obtaining visas for the Vilars, had been carefully typed on stationery from the Hotel Pennsylvania.

With the problem of visas solved, all that remained was to decide on the safest way of crossing the border into Brazil. After proceeding to Montevideo to get advice from their Comintern contacts in Uruguay, they decided to travel by air. The only airline that flew to Brazil at the time was a French company called Latécoère, the predecessor of Air France, which had a monthly flight following the route Santiago–Buenos Aires–Montevideo–São Paulo–Natal–Dakar–Casablanca–Paris. Though it was only a postal airline, whenever the aircraft did not have a full load of cargo Latécoère would sell tickets for the two existing seats on board. Prestes and Olga were in luck. Within days a plane would be coming through Montevideo and the seats were available. Since the May flight had been canceled, if they had missed this flight it would have meant waiting two months.

As a postal airline, Latécoère was authorized to fly at night. So, in the small hours of April 15, Olga and Prestes boarded the *Santos Dumont*, a four-engine hydroplane, for the six-hour trip to Praia Grande on the coast of the state of São Paulo. By daybreak the plane was flying low along the coast near the Rio Grande do Sul–Santa

Catarina state line. The *Santos Dumont* didn't have normal windows, so Olga had her first marvelous glimpse of Brazil through tiny portholes. Accustomed to the light and colors of Europe, what she saw seemed unimaginably luminous—brilliant sunlight throbbing on the deep green of hillsides; the blue of the sea slashed by an endless white line of sand. At midmorning, the navigator came back to inform them that the plane would make an unexpected brief landing on one of the beaches of Florianópolis and then take off again within minutes.

Olga, who had already made friends and distributed souvenirs from New York among the five-member crew, whispered to Prestes, "What a stroke of luck. If any of the intelligence services are aware of our route, they'll be waiting at Praia Grande. Let's see if we can get off in Florianópolis."

She went forward to talk to the captain, explaining that the couple's destination was northern Paraná, where they were to visit relatives of hers. Since they were carrying only hand luggage, she wondered if they might get off during the stop at Florianópolis and thereby cut several hours off their trip. The French pilot had no objection.

The maritime hangar where the hydroplane tied up was deserted. There was no inspection of luggage or papers. And when someone finally did appear, a few dollars was enough to arrange for a car to take them into town. They stayed the night in Florianópolis and the following day took a taxi north to Curitiba. After a further night's rest they hired another taxi to take them to São Paulo. It was dusk as they approached the capital. As they turned off the main highway, Olga was impressed by the height of the Martinelli Building, a skyscraper that was still miles away. By nightfall, Antônio and Maria Vilar were settled into a comfortable hotel on the Largo do Arouche.

A few blocks away, on Rua XV Novembro, a new machine was being tried out in the Café Paraventi, a machine as extravagant as the café's proprietor. Celestino Paraventi had replaced the familiar gold coffee urn with a steam-operated coffee maker imported from Italy, the first in Brazil. From that moment on, the poets, actresses, and Communists who gathered at the marble tables to sip coffee and watch passersby no longer asked for *cafezinhos*, but instead raised an index finger and said, "Espresso, please!"

Celestino Paraventi, an eccentric thirty-five-year-old millionaire, was a rare bird. In addition to the café, he had inherited from his father dozens of pieces of land scattered around the city as well as a coffee-roasting company where he had begun to produce another European novelty: vacuum-packed coffee, which could last for months without spoiling. Paraventi offered a safe haven to poor intellectuals, unemployed actors, and artists, who turned to him when in financial distress, earning him the nickname "Savior." There wasn't an opposition newspaper or pamphlet he didn't support. For as long as it lasted, every single issue of Oswald de Andrade and Patrícia Galvão's anarchist journal *O Homem do Povo*, for example, carried an advertisement for the Café Paraventi. But Paraventi was especially generous when it came to helping the Communists. He rented houses for clandestine printing operations, gave fat monthly contributions to Party coffers, and supported the families of imprisoned militants. When asked if he maintained an official connection to the CP, he would respond with a burst of laughter, "I'm not connected to the Party—the Party's connected to me!"

Paraventi's fascination with Prestes had begun during the days of the Column. Avidly devouring reports in the press or in underground pamphlets, he followed every troop movement, every victory over government forces. When the Column disappeared into the jungles of Bolivia, Paraventi was deeply disappointed. And he nearly drove his family to institutionalize him when he had the coffee-roasting factory and cannery appraised, declaring that he was planning to send the proceeds of the sale to Prestes, exiled in Buenos Aires, "so that he can reassemble the Column and return to overthrow the government." Paraventi sent word to Prestes in Argentina, and some weeks later the messenger returned with a response. Prestes expressed his gratitude for the offer but advised him not to go ahead with the plan. If Paraventi wanted to help, he could make regular shipments of coffee to Buenos Aires; Prestes, Lieutenant Siqueira Campos, and Orlando Leite Ribeiro, ex-members of the Column, would sell the coffee for export and the profit from the venture would be sufficient to support them in exile. Though he had never met Prestes, Paraventi often said that the captain's communism "had a lot of Christianity in it."

"A man like Prestes, with that kind of vocation, a man who

53

renounces everything to destroy the oligarchy, to destroy those who would take everything for themselves, leaving nothing for anyone else—a man like that certainly has some Christianity in him. Maybe he doesn't even know it, but it's there."

One Saturday evening, Paraventi had just returned from exercising one of his eccentricities—singing Italian songs on Nicolau Tuma's radio show *Tea on the Airwaves* on Rádio Difusora—when Olga Benario walked into the café. He'd been advised by Party leaders that he might receive a visit from some "very important people" in the coming weeks, but he had no inkling of what was to come when an attractive, elegantly dressed woman, who spoke heavily accented Portuguese, approached his table. Olga carried in her handbag a short note from Prestes saying that he was in São Paulo and that the bearer would know where to find him. Soon afterward, Paraventi had safely installed Olga, Prestes, and their luggage in his Lincoln Continental and was heading for his country house in Santo Amaro, on the shores of the Guarapiranga Reservoir. The next day, a messenger arrived in Rio de Janeiro to inform the general secretary of the Brazilian CP, Antônio Maciel Bonfim, better known as "Miranda," that Luís Carlos Prestes was back in Brazil.

5

Destination Rio

SEVERAL UNFOUNDED REPORTS that Prestes would be returning to Brazil, published in newspapers of both the Right and Left in late 1934 and early 1935, had provoked the excitement and vigilance of the police. The footprints left by the Prestes Column were still visible on the nation's political landscape, and a national veneration of the "Knight of Hope" had grown, compelling President Getúlio Vargas to demand rigorous and redoubled precautions on the part of the security forces.

They weren't the only ones anxiously awaiting Prestes's return. From the moment Moscow had given his trip the go-ahead, a small, select group of foreigners had begun their own discreet and sinuous journeys to the very same destination: Rio de Janeiro. Some came accompanied by their wives, many traveled under assumed names, and those who were not yet acquainted had at least heard of each other. They had this in common—all were Communists, professional revolutionaries in the service of the Comintern, and they came to Brazil to start a revolution.

Arthur Ernst Ewert and his wife, Elise, both German nationals carrying U.S. papers bearing the names Harry Berger and Machla Lenczycki, came from Shanghai to be political advisers, with a brief stop in Moscow en route. Rodolfo Ghioldi and his wife, Carmen, also political advisers, came from Buenos Aires via Montevideo, she under her own name and he as Luciano Busteros. Wireless operator and radio communications technician Victor Allen Barron arrived from the United States with authentic documentation. From Europe, also with genuine papers, came Belgians Alphonsine and Léon-Jules Vallée, who would be responsible for the operation's finances. And the mysterious Franz Paul Gruber and his wife, Erika, came from Germany to be explosives expert and typist/driver, respectively. When Prestes and Olga first touched down on Brazilian soil, this entire group was already in Rio, and had been since the beginning of the year, integrated into the life of the city and living in rented houses or apartments in the elegant southern section.

At least one member of the team—the highest-ranking and most experienced of all, in fact—was well known to Olga. During the time she spent as one of the few women enrolled in the political course of study in the International Division of the People's University in Moscow, she had taken a six-week seminar instructed by a stout and good-humored man whose photographs had been widely published in everything from the *Estrela Vermelha* (the *Red Star*) to the mainstream press of Berlin. This was Arthur Ernst Ewert, now one of the most respected international political figures of the Comintern.

Ewert was born in Heinrichswalde, eastern Prussia. Before World War I, at the age of twenty, he emigrated to the United States with his sweetheart, Elise Saborowski, known affectionately as Sabo. He purposely chose Detroit as his destination because, as industrialization had made the city a strong magnet for workers, it had also become a center of political agitation. Ewert worked for a year in a leather factory, saving as much of his earnings as possible. Then he left his job and for the next six months spent half his time reading in the public library and the other half engaged in political activities on behalf of unions.

In 1917 the couple moved to Toronto, but it wasn't until two years later that Ewert's name first hit the news when, in an attempt to prevent the organization of a Communist Party in Canada, the police raided the "subversive hideout" that was home to Arthur Brown and Annie Bancourt (the Ewerts' code names at that time), arresting the occupants and confiscating weapons and Marxist literature. After several months in prison as "aliens with irregular immigration status," they were deported to the United States, returning to Detroit to resume their Communist and anarchist activities. Years later, in Berlin, Ewert became officially affiliated with the German Communist Party. The combination of his international experience and the knowledge he had acquired reading in U.S. libraries led to his rapid promotion to the directorate; by 1923 he was already a member of the Secretariat. Ewert's budding career did not go unnoticed by the Soviet leadership, and soon he was invited to Moscow to work directly with the Comintern. Married by this time to Elise, Ewert spent four years as a high-level instructor at various centers for the "development of teams," training leaders not only for the Soviet CP but for parties worldwide.

Ewert's career continued to flourish. The all-powerful Joseph Stalin gave him unlimited authority to intervene in the Fifth Congress of the U.S. Communist Party, convened in August 1927 in New York, to ensure the choice of Jay Lovestone rather than Earl Browder or William Foster for the U.S. directorate. Ewert arrived in New York in early August, and by the closing ceremonies on September 8 Stalin's will had been done, though Ewert's heavy-handed interference caused some damage to his public image. The *Militant*, published by a Trotskyite faction of the U.S. CP, ran a notice accusing Ewert of having been sent by Moscow to "steal and divide the Party convention with the express objective of aiding the Lovestone group." To Ewert's mind, however, the opinion of an opposition rag meant little. What mattered was the opinion of Stalin, who was so effusive about the success of the mission in New York that on Ewert's return to the Soviet Union he was made a member of the Executive Committee of the Third International. Soon after, he was elected deputy to the Reichstag by the German CP.

Ewert's career began to founder, however—when the Comintern became embroiled in a profound disagreement on tactics, Ewert found himself in the thick of it. Arriving at the Sixth Congress of the Communist International in Moscow in the summer of 1928, he stood accused of being a "conciliator." His sin was to have opposed, as did his friend Gerhardt Eisler—another active, militant, international Communist—the line defended by Ernst Thaelmann, of the inner circle of the German CP, which held that the Social Democrats were the principal enemy. Under Stalin's leadership, the Sixth International reiterated and reinforced the crucial objective of laying siege to the Social Democrats, dubbing them "Social Fascists." The voluminous annals of the congress register a single, solitary voice of dissension. Alone in his open resistance, though scores of those present silently agreed, Arthur Ewert stubbornly maintained that, yes, the German CP would have to break with the Social Democrats ideologically, but that it should preserve strategic unity between the parties. His understanding was that it was a tactically necessary alliance. Accused of persisting in a deviation that had already dragged down more than half the German leadership, Ewert fell into disgrace, together with Eisler. They suffered a further blow when Nikolai Bukharin, their supporter— and one of the leaders of the October Revolution and now of the Comintern—himself lost favor with Stalin as he had not speedily imposed Party discipline on these "conciliators." Bukharin was first expelled from the Comintern and then from the Soviet Politburo.

The electoral victory of Hitler in 1933 proved Ewert to be correct; the division between the Communists and the Social Democrats had opened the way for the Nazis. But this was still four years away when Ewert's ostracism was decreed by Stalin before the full Party membership in a 1929 speech menacingly entitled "On the Rightist Deviation in the Communist Party of the USSR." Citing Ewert by name, Stalin pronounced him a "conciliator acting without the consent of the Central Committee of the Third International." Punishment for these grave crimes was quick to follow, in the form of his removal from both the Comintern and the German CP.

Ewert spent a year in total obscurity, until February 1930, when *Imprecorr,* an international periodical reporting on the activities of the Comintern, published the complete text of his "self-criticism." Those personally acquainted with Ewert knew that this recognition of political "guilt" was not sincere. Accustomed to life within the Party machine, he felt politically abandoned; if the price of readmission was self-criticism, so be it.

As his first duty after rehabilitation, Ewert was dispatched by the Comintern to Montevideo in 1931, where Yuamtorg, a commercial legation of the Soviet Union, was operating as a cover for the Latin American activities of the Communist International. His task was to evaluate the information gathered by Augusto Guralsky—nicknamed Bumpkin—on Prestes, whose name had been suggested for a visit to the USSR. On returning to Moscow, Ewert was even more enthusiastic than Guralsky had been: Prestes was a great political figure who was showing interest in Marxism and the CI should definitely not miss the chance to bring him into the fold.

Ewert's next assignment, this time with Elise, was a long stint in Shanghai—mecca of international agents, Communist and capitalist alike—where he became part of the leadership of the clandestine Chinese Communist Party, which controlled several "liberated" areas in the interior of the country.

The tens of thousands of White Russians who emigrated there after the triumph of the Soviet revolution had given this important Chinese port an even more cosmopolitan appearance than before. An international enclave located in the center of the city, governed and policed by French, U.S., Japanese, and Chinese forces, was turning Shanghai into something between a Far Eastern city and a Western European country. Drug traffickers and high-priced prostitutes of widely diverse nationalities, spies working for various major powers (sometimes for more than one at a time), exiles, conspirators, and foreign correspondents representing all the great news agencies gave the city a color and rhythm unique in all Asia.

Arthur and Elise Ewert arrived in Shanghai with an assignment similar to the one they had had in New York, in that it would demand both political dexterity and an extremely firm hand: they were to "guide" the reaction of the Chinese CP to the pact Stalin was about to sign with Chiang Kai-shek, head of the Kuomintang, the ruling party in China then engaged in a ferocious battle with Mao Tse-tung's Communist insurgents. Ewert would later attribute a good part of the brilliance and efficiency with which the mission was carried out to a fellow German known by the code name Li Teh, who had been in China for fifteen months and had also been sent by the Comintern—none other than Otto Braun.

Soon after his affair with Olga ended, Otto had been sent to China, initially to establish contact with Richard Sorge, an agent who would later gain worldwide notoriety as the chief of the Soviet spy network in Japan. Charged also with insinuating himself into the leadership of the Chinese CP, Braun published political articles under the name Hua Fu in the Communist journal *Revolution and War* and, as Li Teh, acted as military adviser to the Chinese Central Committee. Li Teh traveled to Jui-chin, capital of the "Sovietized" area of Kiangsi, to assist Mao Tse-tung and Chu Teh in planning the Long March. At the Party congress in Tsunyi, which gave formal approval to Mao's leadership, the chair designated for Stalin was occupied by Comrade Li Teh. And "Professor Albert List," codirector of the Chinese CP's Military Academy of Yenan, was also one Otto Braun.

During the three years he spent in Shanghai, Ewert's most consistent activity was to mobilize intellectuals in the creation of anti-Japanese propaganda. He was greatly impressed by the rapid progress of the revolution in China, more than once proclaiming the degree of communization of the country to be so advanced and irreversible as to render superfluous propaganda work by the agents of the Comintern. Of the Ewerts' many varied assignments in China, only one has been obscured by time; it will never be known whether or not they were successful in luring to espionage work for the Comintern their good friend Roger Hollis, who was head of MI-5 from 1956 to 1965. The last information recorded by the Shanghai police on the Ewerts—who had by that time adopted the names Harry Berger and Machla Lenczycki—was that they had left Shanghai on July 19, 1934, on board the SS *Yingchow,* bound for Vladivostok. From there they began the long voyage that was to end months later in a hotel on Rua Marquês de Abrantes in Rio de Janeiro.

In Montevideo, the last stop before Rio, Ewert was given the name of a contact in Brazil: Luciano Busteros (the code name of Argentine journalist Rodolfo Ghioldi). A member of the Executive Committee of the Comintern and secretary of the Latin American Bureau of the Third International, Ghioldi was also director of the Argentine CP. Ghioldi, who had met both Prestes and Ewert in Montevideo in 1931, had been to Brazil once before, thirteen years earlier. When

he was living in Moscow, the leadership of the International decided to send him to the Brazilian capital, where a group of Communists was planning to found a party and request affiliation with
the CI. Ghioldi was to advise whether or not to grant affiliation to
the fledgling party.

He spent three weeks with the Brazilian group, which he judged
to be "extremely interesting," becoming closest to two members in
particular, journalist Astrojildo Pereira and pharmacist Otávio Bran-
dão. Both men's roots were in the anarchist movement, which was
very influential among the Brazilian working class, but they had
reexamined their ideas and theories in the light of the Russian
Revolution and become Communists. Following Ghioldi's favorable
report, the Brazilians went to Moscow; months later the bylaws of
the Brazilian Section of the Communist International were distributed discreetly in various Brazilian states. Rodolfo and his wife,
Carmen Alfaya de Ghioldi—inexplicably traveling under her real
name even though her husband's surname was well known to the
political police—returned to Rio and settled into an apartment in
the Leblon section to await the event that would mark the beginning of the conspiracy: the arrival of Prestes and Olga.

The youngest of the team—which by now also included the
Bergers, the Vallées, and the Grubers—was twenty-seven-year-old
American Victor Allen Barron. Tall and thin, with something of the
film star about him, Barron had been introduced to the history of
workers' struggles and Communist militance by his father, Harrison
George, to whom he was very close. Listed by United States authorities as "one of the most important secret agents of the international
Communist movement," Harrison George was the representative
in the United States of the International Red Labor Union, the
section of the Comintern dealing with labor activities. He had
traveled to Latin America in 1926 as a delegate to the Second
Dockworkers' Conference of the Western Hemisphere in Montevideo, when the Latin American Federation of Unions was
founded with headquarters in the Uruguayan capital. Harrison
George and his wife, Edna Hill, were divorced when their son
Victor was still an infant, and though he was given the name of his
mother's second husband, C. N. Barron, the boy was to become
much closer to his father.

As an adolescent, Barron picked fruit for a company in Yakima, Washington, but he soon moved to New York to be near his father and the political militancy of a big city. And it was thanks to Harrison George's influence in the U.S. Communist Party that Victor was able to travel to the Soviet Union, where he studied electronics, specializing in radiotelegraphy. Toward the end of 1934, when the Comintern decided to support the Brazilian insurrection, Barron was chosen to set up a clandestine radio transmitter for communication with the rebels scattered throughout Brazil. The installation was to be powerful enough to reach Moscow as well, so that the Comintern could follow the unfolding events in Rio.

For months, the directorate of the Comintern had resisted approving the insurrection in Brazil, remaining skeptical in spite of the dozens of triumphant intelligence analyses and reports received from "Miranda," general secretary of the Brazilian CP. But in the end, the prospect of seeing a country the size of Brazil—in an area of influence increasingly coveted by the United States—transformed into a popular socialist republic was seductive enough to overrule their reluctance. "Miranda's" optimism for what he imagined to be prerevolutionary conditions was so great that it managed to cut through the doubts of the general secretary of the Comintern, Dmitri Manuilski, who was sufficiently enthusiastic by late 1934 to cover his office wall with a gigantic map of Brazil, complete with colored pins indicating the places where—according to reports from the Brazilian CP—the revolution would first explode. The most eloquent proof that "Miranda" had overcome Moscow's doubts was the broad experience of the team sent to Brazil. The Soviet Union would not have sent a pioneer of the international Communist revolution—Arthur Ewert, fully rehabilitated and his difficulties with Stalin now in the past—to take part in a minor escapade.

6

The Conspiracy Begins

OLGA AND PRESTES'S HOLIDAY in the comfortable Paraventi home on the shores of Guarapiranga Reservoir did not last
long. In less than a week a messenger was back with the green light
from "Miranda" for the couple to come to Rio. Celestino Paraventi,
who had showered them with every kind of hospitality, insisted that
the best way for them to get there would be with him, in his
expensive new car. "The police wouldn't dream a limousine like that
was chauffeuring a couple of Communists," he said. Paraventi had
even gone so far in his wild planning as to have a trusted mechanic
drill five breathing holes in the trunk, in case it became necessary to
transport Olga and Prestes that way. But his guests were firm; they
would travel the next leg of their journey as discreetly as they had
arrived in São Paulo—by cab.

This decision was almost their downfall. In the middle of the
night they were stopped at a routine police checkpoint on the state
border between São Paulo and Rio. Olga's excessive anxiety about
her handbag attracted the attention of one of the guards, prompting
a more thorough search. Inside he found a tiny ivory-handled
revolver. Prestes tried to defuse the situation, offering money and
chatting up the guard, but to no avail. Finally the policeman de-

cided to informally "confiscate" the revolver. Though this caused him to forget to check their documents, it also meant that they were forced to continue to Rio with only one weapon in their possession: the pistol Prestes always had at his side.

As they entered the city and headed for their hotel in the Botafogo district, Olga was dazzled by what she saw. With only a million and a half inhabitants, Rio was far from a cosmopolitan metropolis like New York or Berlin; but it was without a doubt the most beautiful city she had ever seen. The view from Praça Paris was lush: to the right, mountains blanketed with vegetation, to the left, miles of dazzling white sandy beaches. Tucked in between was the city, with its colonial mansions, well-tended gardens imitating Versailles, and countless churches of every size and style. And framing the whole celestial vision was the profile of Sugarloaf Mountain rising out of the sea. Leaving the beach, the car turned into a row of houses and followed Rua Marquês de Abrantes, a narrow street lined with towering palm trees, to the small hotel where a suite had been reserved for the Vilars.

Arthur and Elise Ewert had stayed in the same hotel, poring over advertisements for houses and apartments to rent. They had chosen a house on Rua Paul Redfern in Ipanema, only a few steps from the beach. With a map of the city in her hand, Olga suggested that she and Prestes look for a place nearby. It didn't take long. The *Jornal do Brasil* listed a two-story house on Rua Barão da Torre, only two blocks from the Ewerts. Owned by a Swiss, Eurisch Sommer, the house had been rented to a chemical engineer from Germany who worked for Bayer Laboratories. Like many of his countrymen, he was returning home—Hitler was gathering Germany's best technicians from around the world in anticipation of the war effort. The German engineer wanted to transfer his rental agreement to the new tenants and leave everything in the house, even the live-in maid. Beyond all this, there was the advantage that the departing tenant was not a Brazilian. As far as the neighbors were concerned it would be merely a matter of one family of foreigners being replaced by another.

The fact that the Vilars were not Brazilian wouldn't in principle be a major cause for concern, in any case. During the twelve months before their arrival, over 15,000 immigrants had arrived in

Rio, 11,000 of them from Europe. Olga and Prestes would be able to blend in easily with the 1,700 Germans and 5,000 Portuguese who had exchanged a Europe in crisis for a Rio de Janeiro where opportunities seemed more encouraging. In addition, the Copacabana area of the city, which included Ipanema, counted among its 30,000 inhabitants a disproportionate number of tourists and immigrants from all over the world, which would certainly help cover the activities of the Comintern's representatives.

Settled into the house on Rua Barão da Torre, Olga and Prestes met the rest of the team at the Ewerts' home for the first time in order to assign initial duties. Paul Gruber, the explosives expert, was instructed to install a violent alarm system in the small safe at Prestes and Olga's house to protect their money and secret papers. Victor Barron announced that he had been hard at work on his assignment since his arrival. After a painstaking survey of stores specializing in electrical equipment in Rio and neighboring towns he had started to build the radio transmitter, purchasing each piece from a different source. He was assembling the apparatus in a room meant to be the maid's quarters in his Copacabana apartment. As a cover, he passed himself off as a millionaire playboy on permanent holiday in Brazil, always dressed in well-cut white linen suits and imported hats and ties. The finishing touch to his disguise was his mode of transportation—the ultra-chic car of the year, a Graham Page limousine. Barron played at representing a United States machine-manufacturing company as well, and in his free time dabbled in journalism.

In spite of the group's apparent security, they decided to take action to discourage once and for all the suspicion of the public and the police that Prestes was in Brazil. Early in May, a standing-room-only crowd packed the Hall of the Workers in São Paulo for a formal meeting of the recently founded National Liberation Alliance (ANL). As soon as official business had been completed, the Communist historian Caio Prado Júnior yielded the floor to Lieutenant Timótheo Ribeiro da Silva, so that he could read "an important document" that Commander Hercolino Cascardo, president of the Provisional Commission of the National Liberation Alliance, had "just received from Spain." That document was a long letter from Prestes, dated April 25 and "written in Barcelona," in which he announced his affiliation with the ANL. Though the letter's date and place of origin were false—Prestes was right there in Brazil by then—its contents were absolutely authentic.

Prestes wrote that he had been following newspaper accounts of the formation of that mass movement and expressed regret for his delay in responding to his being named honorary president of the ANL at the March 30 session. The letter's style was unmistakable; tough and aggressive as always, it stifled any suspicion that it might have been apocryphal. "Not personally acquainted with the founders of the movement, and well aware of the shameless use of my name by Brazilian demagogues in their efforts to dupe the masses, I was waiting for more complete information before setting pen to paper," he began. "I have today in my possession more dependable data regarding the new organization, including confirmation that my name truly did arise spontaneously from the hearts of the people, who evidently wanted, in this way, to endow the ANL with an anti-imperialist, combative, revolutionary character." After a lengthy analysis of the Brazilian political situation, Prestes described his experiences of three years in the Soviet Union "helping to construct socialism" and then addressed himself "to the people of Brazil, to all the adherents of the ANL, to workers, peasants, soldiers, and students, to honest intellectuals and the urban middle class, in short, to all those who suffer more every day as a result of the poverty and hunger so widespread in Brazil." Interrupted by applause at the end of each paragraph, Lieutenant da Silva finally came to the triumphant declaration: "I hereby join the ANL. As a member, I hope to fight side by side with all those who, having refused to sell themselves to imperialism, are committed to the struggle for the national liberation of Brazil, all those who want to destroy the feudal regime under which we now vegetate, and to defend the democratic rights being crushed by fascist barbarism."

Just under a month old, the National Liberation Alliance was an unquestionable success. A gathering similar to the one in the Hall of the Workers was also held in Rio's Brazil Stadium, where one of the founders of the ANL, journalist Benjamin Cabello, read Prestes's letter to an audience many times larger than the one in São Paulo. The first political movement of national scope to emerge since the revolution of 1930, the ANL attracted diverse social and political groups united by a common objective: to struggle against fascism, imperialism, underdevelopment, and big landowners. This veritable crusade united Communists, socialists, liberals, Christians, workers, professionals, and a great number of military men who had been involved in the revolts of 1922 and 1924.

From the moment it was publicly launched in late March at the João Caetano Theatre in Rio, where journalist Carlos Lacerda proposed that Prestes be named its honorary president, the ANL had set the nation ablaze. Tens of thousands of people knocked on the doors of local headquarters, asking to join the organization and to participate in the public demonstrations taking place in parks and plazas all over Brazil. Hundreds of small groups sprang up in various states, the most euphoric estimates placing total membership at over a million. At least three thousand new members signed on every day. The charismatic, mythological figure of Prestes in the role of honorary president stimulated much of the ANL excitement, though most of the activists joining up knew him only from drawings and photos that almost always depicted him with the black beard and high-topped boots from the days of the Column.

The men chosen as national directors of the movement—Commander Roberto Sissón of the navy, fellow naval officer Hercolino Cascardo (veteran of the rebellions of 1924 and 1930, and acting governor of the state of Rio Grande do Sul in 1931), journalist Benjamin Cabello, physician Manuel Venâncio Campos da Paz, and lawyer Francisco Mangabeira—were all linked in some way to the Communist Party. The leadership in São Paulo fell to Miguel Costa, cocommander of the Column with Prestes, historian Caio Prado Júnior, and intellectual Abguar Bastos. In Rio Grande do Sul, physician and writer Dyonélio Machado and Captain Agildo Barata of the army, both Communists, were elected. The Northeastern Alliance was also placed in the hands of militants from the CP: Sylo Meirelles, a member of the Party's Central Committee, Agliberto Vieira de Azevedo, student at the Realengo Military School, and peasant leader Gregório Bezerra. Though it did include workers and peasants like Bezerra, the ANL leadership was fundamentally made up of militants from the middle class—so much so that Commander Sissón once referred to the bourgeoisie as "the revolutionary troops of the National Liberation Alliance." Other leaders, such as Caio Prado Júnior, saw the close relationship between the ANL and the CP as a way for the Party to accomplish its goal of reaching the working masses. Before long, the ANL was productive in another sense; various fledgling groups emerged from it, including the Modern Culture Club, the Popular Culture Defense League, and the Women's Association of Brazil. The Alliance's platform and, more important, its street activities were made public in the local daily newspapers.

As the Alliance worked inside and outside Brazil, the Communist Party was busy infiltrating the barracks. The amnesty of 1934 permitted young officers who had participated in previous rebellions to return to active duty, and many of them were CP militants. The leadership recognized that, paradoxically, it was easier to build the Party from inside the barracks than from inside the factories, and they acted on it. Taking advantage of the factionalism and weakening of discipline provoked by the 1930 revolution, the Communists were able to count support in almost all the most important garrisons. One underground Communist publication or other was placed on every commander's desk daily. In the army it was *União de Ferro* (Iron Union), in the air force *Asas Vermellias* (Red Wings), in the navy *Triângulo Vermelho* (Red Triangle). The overriding impulse of the young officers, however, was to be overwhelmed by the excitement of all this agitation instead of calmly developing support among the rest of the men for their dream of a popular revolution. Olga and Prestes, in their daily discussions at home or among the group that met at the Ewerts', voiced their concern that in Brazil, practice was threatening to contradict both revolutionary theory and experience; instead of the vanguard of the revolution being made up of workers, here it was drawn from middle-class military men. And not all the young officers were pledged to the revolution. When Lieutenant Lauro Fontoura of the Reserve Officer Training Center (CPOR) attempted to win over First Lieutenant Sílvo Frota (who during the seventies would serve as secretary of the army and try to assume the presidency by force), what had begun as a peaceful conversation almost ended in a gunfight. Frota's response to being invited to join a leftist organization was to unbutton his holster and slap his hand on his pistol. "Look, Fontoura, communism is a matter of life and death with me. You try to get something going here in CPOR, and I'll answer with lead. Communists in the CPOR—over my dead body!"

When such episodes were related to the group, Rodolfo Ghioldi expressed his concern over the ever-growing preponderance of military men in the Alliance. "We have to give the military their due, as men of great conscience, but unless the proletariat has a much greater role, I don't see much of a future for us as a popular organization, or for the revolution." Ghioldi recognized, however, that the degree of barracks' involvement spurred by the ANL was unprecedented in South America.

Accustomed to a certain level of discipline in political work, Ghioldi was rather taken aback by the Alliance's heterogeneity and its eclectic style of militancy. At each meeting, the Communist leadership was treated to yet another of the humorous incidents he had witnessed or heard about. One day it was the story of a militant spiritualist in Rio Grande do Norte, a valiant man, veteran of the Column, who had taken an entire provincial city by force in an attempt to ensure radical agrarian reform. At a meeting with Ghioldi, he had pulled a stack of blurry snapshots out of his pocket, swearing they were photographs of the souls of friends who were long dead . . . pictures he was very proud of having taken himself. Another time, Ghioldi related how, during a local rally, he had had to be careful not to yield the floor to a certain member of the Alliance, a fiery speechmaker who ended all his declamations with "Long live the petite bourgeoisie!"

The ANL's growth and outreach began to alarm the government. The pretext President Getúlio Vargas needed to clamp down on antiadministration opposition materialized sooner than expected. Early in June, the São Paulo ANL was responsible for preventing, by force, a rally planned by the *Ação Integralista Brasileira*, a fascist organization led by Plínio Salgado. Days later, Alliance members in Petrópolis, in the state of Rio, organized a march on the local headquarters of the *integralistas*. The skirmish between the two groups ended in the death of blue-collar Alliance member Leonardo Candu, and the city was paralyzed by a subsequent general strike. On July 5, 1935, during festivities to mark the thirteenth anniversary of the 1922 lieutenants' uprising at Fort Copacabana, word got out that Luís Carlos Prestes had sent a letter commemorating the event "from Paris or Barcelona." The leaders of the ANL had tried to rent the Brazil Stadium, where the first Prestes letter had been read, but Vargas succeeded in preventing its use, as well as the Feira de Amostras auditorium. The incredible power of the Alliance to mobilize Rio resulted in tens of thousands of people streaming from the stadium to the auditorium and then to ANL headquarters a few blocks away, in search of a place to hear the letter from the "Knight of Hope."

At home, Olga and Prestes followed the crowd's movements by listening to the radio and to reports from Party members. In the middle of the afternoon, the order came for the demonstrators to assemble at the Chamber of Deputies, where the representative from Paraná, Otávio da Silveira, who had first announced the foundation of the Alliance to Congress, would take the rostrum and read Prestes's manifesto. As the city seethed with soldiers and police spies, demonstrators filled the streets and alleys surrounding the building.

Prestes's message was uncompromising. He denounced the "decay of the Vargas administration, as well as its supporters on the state level," and said that the opponents in the current struggle for Brazil were "on the one hand, those who would liberate the country and, on the other, those who would betray it in the service of imperialism." Pronouncing the ANL heir apparent to the lieutenants of 1922, Prestes proposed that the masses be organized and actively prepared "for the moment of attack," proclaiming a "state of war, in which everyone should be at his post." The packed hall and the multitude listening from the street went wild when Deputy Silveira read the last lines of the document: "Down with fascism! Down with the hateful Vargas regime! Power to a popular, national, revolutionary government! All power to the National Liberation Alliance!" Outside, 150,000 copies of the São Paulo Alliance journal *A Platéia*, carrying Prestes's manifesto in its entirety, were frenetically distributed. The human wave surged toward Alliance headquarters, where as many as could squeeze inside attended the unveiling of a photograph of Prestes.

The manifesto provided Vargas with the excuse he had been looking for to clamp down. On June 11, less than a week after the Prestes letter had been read publicly, the president made use of the recently enacted National Security Law to decree the nationwide illegality of the National Liberation Alliance.

It was a staggering blow to the movement. A good part of the liberal membership bowed to the official edict, abandoning the Alliance to form other parties or political groups. An attempt to hold a protest against the Vargas decree in São Paulo met with harsh repression from the police. By July, a new ANL, illegal and supported mainly by Communist revolutionaries, began its life underground.

Though technically living underground herself, Olga took advantage of the fact that she was unknown to the Brazilian police to circulate freely. Almost always accompanied by her friend Sabo, Olga made frequent visits to the beach at Ipanema, as well as to theaters and cinemas in Rio, a city she grew to love. The two women attended everything from sentimental films like *The Gay Divorcée*, with Ginger Rogers and Fred Astaire, to the dense plays of Oduvaldo Vianna. Every once in a while, Prestes would risk a walk along the beach with Olga, certain that the photos in police files showed him with a full beard and long hair parted in the middle.

On one of these occasions, however, he was almost recognized. Strolling past women bathers wearing the latest in Rio's beach fashion—strapless maillots displaying sensuous shoulders—they suddenly came face to face with Captain Paulo Kruger da Cunha Cruz, who, though he had spent some weeks with Prestes in the Column in Maranhão, was now back in the ranks of the army. But the captain walked on by without even noticing Prestes, who quipped, "Luckily, he was much more interested in looking at you!"

Dressed extravagantly to maintain her cover, her hair in a blunt cut just below the chin, Olga attracted lots of male attention as she stepped from theaters in up-to-the-minute, ankle-length Parisian dresses that showed off her slender and elegant figure. Young men in panama hats and driving sports cars slowed at the sight of her, calling out flirtatious remarks that she didn't always understand.

During their first weeks in Brazil, Olga had been forced to purchase an emergency wardrobe for both of them, because the trunks were late arriving from New York. Only Américo Dias Leite, the official addressee, was authorized to pick them up at the Rio office of Wagons-lits Cook; he and Olga made countless trips to the port before finally collecting the luggage. All correspondence from Europe was sent care of Leite as well, addressed to Antônio Vilar or to his wife, renamed "Yvone Vilar" for this operation.

Olga and Sabo's social excursions were suspended on Thursday and Sunday evenings, when the team, calling itself the General Staff of the Revolution, met at the Ewerts' home to discuss the progress of their work. Sabo would give the maid, Deolinda Elias, the night off so they could talk openly. Members invariably present included Ewert, Antônio Maciel Bonfim (general secretary of the Party, also known as "Miranda"), Rodolfo Ghioldi, and Prestes. Olga, who was fluent in four languages and managed to express herself fairly well in Portuguese, acted as simultaneous interpreter. The meetings began late in the afternoon, were adjourned before midnight, and were punctuated by light snacks and whiskey. On particularly hot evenings, Ewert toasted his companions with a cocktail of his own invention: German white wine mixed with pineapple juice.

At one of these meetings the decision was made to step up security around Prestes. Prestes lived an extremely discreet life, it was true, and in the event of a police raid the group's important documents would be protected by the diabolical security system Gruber had installed in the safe at the house on Rua Barão da Torre. Anyone attempting to deactivate the system would set off a tiny detonator attached to incendiary devices and a large quantity of dynamite and be blown sky-high with the contents of the safe as well as much of the rest of the apartment. As well, there was Olga, who accompanied Prestes everywhere he went, armed with an automatic.

Despite all these safeguards, there was still concern for his safety. Occasional newspaper reports insinuated that the police were suspicious of his whereabouts. Something had to be done, something along the lines of the letters he had ostensibly sent from abroad, to convince the authorities he was not on Brazilian territory. Arthur Ewert, like Olga one of the most concerned about the danger to Prestes, suggested that Rodolfo Ghioldi should book a seat on the *Graf Zeppelin*, moored in Rio, and travel to Moscow to discuss the question with the Comintern, but the idea was set aside. Weeks later, the group would discover that the Soviet party leadership shared its concern.

In early September, British Intelligence passed to Captain Filinto Müller, the much-feared chief of police of the Federal District, a copy of the August 25 edition of *Pravda*, which contained welcome news for the Brazilian authorities. Beneath a full-length photograph of Prestes—an old one, with full beard and long hair—the caption announced his presence in Moscow and noted that it was the first time a Latin American had been elected a full member of the Executive Committee of the Communist International. Prestes was taking his place in the inner sanctum of world communism beside Joseph Stalin, Dmitri Manuilski, Georgi Dimitrov, Mao Tse-tung, Dolores "La Pasionaria" Ibárruri, Palmiro Togliatti, and Bela Kuhn, among others. And if Prestes was in Moscow for the Seventh Congress of the Communist International at the end of August, the earliest he could possibly be back in Brazil, if that was the plan, was somewhere around the end of the year, because with all the intricate travel arrangements involved, a clandestine voyage from the Soviet Union to Brazil would take a minimum of two months. The article in *Pravda* dispelled the tension that had been gripping the Brazilian police. British Intelligence and Captain Müller had taken the bait.

7

Revolution in the Streets

OLGA WAS DETERMINED not to interfere with the internal affairs of the CP or the Alliance, but she couldn't help expressing to Prestes and Rodolfo Ghioldi her anxiety about several inexplicable facts. She was at a loss to understand, for example, how "Miranda"—whom Ghioldi had called "semi-illiterate with zero political background"—had managed to become general secretary of the Party, exercising influence and authority over so many intellectuals and militants with so much more experience. After only two years as a Party member, Miranda was the one calling the shots.

Vargas's June decree making the National Liberation Alliance illegal had transformed a mass movement of national scope into an underground operation controlled for all intents and purposes by the Communist Party. It was difficult to tell whether a given member was merely an *aliancista* or a Communist as well. Those who remained in the organization were instructed to work diligently toward the insurrection Miranda had so often predicted to the Soviet leadership. Prestes's job was to carry out, within the Alliance, decisions made by the Party.

The Party was gearing up in every sense of the word. A small but intricate intelligence service was mounted, which included an in-

74

dex of all the informers employed by the political police and all the police active in AIB, Brazilian Action, a Brazilian variant of European fascism. Since many of the participants in the Prestes Column had gone into police work on returning from exile, Communist infiltration was rich and abundant. A secret bulletin of personnel changes within the police was circulated sporadically among the revolutionary command, with updates regarding transfers, new members, and investigations being pursued by Filinto Müller and his right-hand man, Captain Miranda Correia, chief of security.

Material resources to keep the Party machine functioning were not a problem. In addition to the money Olga and Prestes had brought with them and the funds controlled by Léon-Jules Vallée, the group received via Argentina a large and regular influx of dollars that might or might not have been genuine, since the Comintern had at its disposal some of Germany's most talented counterfeiters. However, expenses were high: one balance sheet reveals that Party outlays for less than two months during the second quarter of 1935 amounted to seventy contos de réis—enough to buy fifteen luxury cars.

The dominance of the CP over the Alliance, together with the revolutionary line the movement had begun taking, caused Prestes to lose some of his most valuable allies. In August he received a letter from his old friend Miguel Costa, who had been codirector of the ANL in São Paulo. Costa presented an analysis of the political climate, criticizing Prestes for the July 5 manifesto and declaring himself opposed to the idea of insurrection:

> Then we have July 5, when you, little or badly informed, supposing Alliance support to be as deep as it was wide, penned your manifesto, your word of command: "All power to the ANL!" A subversive, revolutionary shout, only advisable immediately preceding action. A battle cry that, to ring true, must be answered by insurrection. . . . So the ANL was declared illegal and our supposedly popular movement didn't react, didn't even respond to the two strike calls. Our friends in the army and navy found themselves smack in the middle of the mess and were either arrested or transferred to the boondocks. ANL headquarters were locked up and its members forced to work illegally, making every operation slower, more difficult,

and much less efficient. Yes, we badly needed a word from you at that moment. But if instead of proclaiming the assault on the citadel you had recommended more fervent work to strengthen the Alliance, things wouldn't have happened the way they did. If the masses had been gradually conditioned to respond to orders, they would have answered the call to take power, later, when the leadership determined the time was right. But such an order should only be given once the government has been rendered physically incapable of reacting; otherwise it's like pitting an unarmed child against an elephant.

Costa closed by proposing to continue the struggle within legal limits through the creation of partisan organizations on a state level, with programs identical to those of the ANL, though with a different name, each duly registered with the Board of Elections. He suggested that these parties each maintain a secret division, in addition to the legal façade, "to prepare an effective mass response in the event of a fascist coup." Prestes's response did not come until mid-October. In a typewritten letter of two hundred lines, as courteous as Costa's, Prestes accepted some of the criticism, disagreed on other points, and invited Costa to remain in the ANL, even envisioning his friend as leader of the São Paulo state government under an Alliance administration. There was one issue, though, on which they remained divided. Prestes was intransigent in defending the idea of taking power:

> As for how much time we have left to prepare for the struggle to take power, the information I have from various sources around the country indicates that that critical point is drawing rapidly nearer. It would be frivolous to set a date, but objective conditions suggest that at any moment we could be faced with events on a scale that would demand the taking of power be our first priority. This is why joint action is so important, not only in military terms, but also for organizing the movement. And so I would ask that you continue to give support and assistance in every possible way.

Mindful of security, Prestes ended the letter with a red herring regarding his whereabouts:

Of course, once events begin to unfold we will have a chance to meet in person and define priorities, because the moment the struggle begins, or shortly before, I will arrive in Brazil. Please deliver revolutionary greetings to my comrades in São Paulo and warm embraces to our old friends from the Column.

There was obviously no doubt in Prestes's mind that the time for revolution was close. The weeks that followed, however, brought no sign that anything unusual was going on in the country. Curiously, reports in conservative newspapers claimed that Prestes was either somewhere in the northeast or in Três Rios or Barra do Piraí, in the interior of the state of Rio. These reports were planted by the police in order to preserve the fiction that they were not ignorant of his whereabouts. At each false alarm, the São Paulo paper *A Platéia*, which had survived the closing of the National Liberation Alliance, printed a denial: "It is common knowledge that Prestes is in Europe, his last letters to this country having been sent from Barcelona and Paris."

But not even Prestes could have imagined the rebellion would explode so early and in such a sudden way. At noon on November 23, 1935, the sergeants and troops of the Twenty-first Riflemen's Battalion of Natal, the capital of Rio Grande do Norte, tired of awaiting orders from Rio and seized the city's military garrison, taking prisoner the few officers on duty (it was Saturday) and entrusting command of the unit to Sergeant Dinis Henriques and Corporal Estevão. Governor Rafael Fernandes, his cabinet, the municipal police on duty, and the officers not in the barracks at the time fled. Some hid at the home of the honorary consul of Chile, some managed to get a seat on Latécoère Airline's *Croix du Sud*, which happened to be in the city at the time, and the rest chose to resist at the state police barracks. The captured officers were confined in ships anchored in the port.

A hastily assembled special edition of the Natal daily newspaper *Liberdade* proclaimed that power was in the hands of the National Liberation Alliance, which had installed a Popular Revolutionary Government headed by worker José Praxedes de Andrade, Sergeant Quintino de Barros, postman José Macedo, student João Galvão, and public official Lauro Lago.

Political rebellion and a spirit of carnival combined: masses of people joined the revolt, overran the occupied barracks, stole uniforms from the stores, and paraded through the streets dressed as soldiers. Urban transport was declared free by revolutionary decree. The safes of all the banks were broken open and the money expropriated and distributed among the people. The "liberated area" extended to half a dozen more municipalities in the interior.

The revolution was to last only five days. Federal troops and reinforcements from neighboring states soon recaptured the capital and other occupied towns, reinstated the governor, and arrested hundreds of rebels.

During those same five days, the government had to crush another military uprising carried out in the name of the ANL. On Sunday, November 24, Lieutenants Lamartine Coutinho and Sylo Meirelles seized command of the Twenty-ninth Riflemen's Battalion of Recife in Pernambuco, but after forty-eight hours they were finally surrounded and subdued by troops loyal to the government.

Back in Rio, Rodolfo Ghioldi blanched when he picked up the Sunday paper and saw the news from Natal. He hurried to see Prestes, who himself had only just heard about the uprising. Olga accompanied the two men to the Ewerts' home, where it was decided to get hold of Miranda so that the group could decide what measures to take. They were unable to locate him until late on Monday afternoon. Prestes already had his own ideas about what to do but, as a matter of Party discipline, did not want to act without first discussing the situation with the general secretary.

The meeting took place at the house on Rua Barão da Torre and lasted into the night. At first, Prestes was the only one to defend the idea of insurrection in Rio de Janeiro, insisting that they couldn't abandon their comrades in Natal and Recife. Ewert and Ghioldi merely listened and Miranda actively disagreed. As Prestes listed the garrisons prepared to join the rebellion—Vila Militar, the Military Academy, the School of Aviation—Miranda began to concede. Halfway through the meeting he was so convinced the revolution would triumph that he proposed a general strike in support of the military uprisings.

Finally Rodolfo Ghioldi broke his silence:

"I vote against the uprising and against the general strike. Everything about this situation says we are not in a position for either one to succeed. I've talked to a lot of our people and I know that much of this support exists only on paper."

Ewert nodded his head in agreement. This was when Prestes produced what Ghioldi would refer to as "his trump card." The "Knight of Hope" looked solemnly at his comrades and said, "The navy is on our side. If we go ahead with the insurrection, they will take power with us."

Ghioldi and Ewert were astonished by this news, and by the assurance with which it was delivered. Ghioldi asked Prestes to be kind enough to repeat what he had just said. Prestes did:

"I have assurances that the navy is pledged to take power with us."

Ghioldi and Ewert bowed to this argument and the Argentine said, "If that's the case, then let the revolution begin."

The plans for the revolution were spelled out then and there. Prestes would dispatch messages to all garrisons with officers expecting orders and to the navy, whose bases had pledged to support the uprising. Captain Agildo Barata would divide the Third Infantry Regiment into three columns: one would march on the Navy Arsenal to assist the Navy Battalion; the second would head for Catete Palace, the seat of the federal government, to arrest President Getúlio Vargas and whoever was with him; and the third would take Guanabara Palace, the president's official residence. Prestes scrawled a short note to Captain André Trifino Correia, the commander of a battalion in Ouro Prêto, in the state of Minas Gerais, and asked Miranda to arrange for a reliable person to deliver it.

> My dear Trifino,
>
> The revolution is before us. We cannot wait any longer. I'm counting on your spirit and determination to lead the revolution in Minas Gerais.
>
> Warmly,
> Prestes

Prestes gave orders with the fire of a born leader. He instructed Miranda to take care of a few things the next morning—a new safe house had to be arranged for him and Olga, this time in the northern suburbs. Once the rebellion was under way, it would also be important for him to have easy access to the Vila Militar, the most important garrison in the city. Miranda was told to advise Barron to put the radio in working order. Barron would then inform the Comintern in Morse code of the decision to go ahead with the revolution. Prestes chose the frequency on which they would operate, and by the next day they were in contact with Recife. Days later, they would be communicating with the Latin American Bureau of the Comintern in Montevideo.

News arriving in Rio on November 26 about the events in Recife was imprecise and contradictory. But there was no doubt about the success in Rio Grande do Norte: Natal and the cities in the interior continued to be held by the Popular Revolutionary Government. The only opposition came from a certain large landholder, "Colonel" Dinarte Mariz, who had personally armed his own squadron of thugs and attempted to oust the revolutionaries. On the morning of the twenty-sixth, the newspapers prominently announced the decision of President Vargas to counterattack. He decreed a state of siege for thirty days throughout the entire country, "so that the state can defend itself against the Communist insolence." Prestes and Olga spent the day in feverish activity. All Party contacts and sympathizers in the army, air force, and navy barracks had been advised of the decision to rebel. The presumed support of the navy, plus the spontaneous uprisings in Natal and Recife, must have weighed heavily in Prestes's decision, since only weeks earlier, responding to a letter from Commander Roberto Sissón, he had made it clear that he didn't believe the moment to take power had yet arrived. Sissón was very enthusiastic about a workers' strike in Petrópolis, but Prestes had wisely replied, "We're going to need many Petrópolises to create propitious conditions."

By the end of the afternoon, preparations had been completed. As night fell, Prestes and Olga left Ipanema on their way to the house Miranda had arranged for on Rua Correia de Oliveira, in Vila Isabel, halfway to Vila Militar. Only minutes after the rebels had taken the units, Prestes would be able to get to Vila Militar to take command of the nation. Before leaving Ipanema, he improvised a "safe-conduct" pass for Ewert, the very phrasing of which was an indication of his certainty that the uprising would be victorious.

Rio, 11/26/35

Safe-conduct:

The bearer, Mr. Harry Berger (nationality, North American), is a person for whom I demand the greatest respect and consideration.

Luís Carlos Prestes

One last task remained—the writing of the manifesto that was to be distributed to the population, a call to join the rebellion. In this manifesto, the Communist Party admitted for the first time that Prestes had come home.

PEOPLE OF BRAZIL!

. . . At this moment the welfare of Brazil and all her sons and daughters is being decided. No one can remain indifferent. This is not a question of a "Communist movement," as proclaimed by the press, which has sold out to imperialism and to Vargas's inner circle! The Popular Revolution for the National Liberation of Brazil has begun, under the direction of the National Liberation Alliance and its illustrious leader, Luís Carlos Prestes.

The Communist Party of Brazil . . . supports with all its strength, firmness, and decisiveness this heroic revolutionary movement!

People of Brazil! The hour of victory over the age-old oppressors and exploiters of our country is at hand!

Luís Carlos Prestes, anti-imperialist and antifeudal hero, beloved leader around whom all Brazilians come together, has returned to his homeland! He is here among us, planning the battles that will be decisive for the National Revolution of Liberation.

Communists and Party sympathizers! Man your action stations with diligence and determination. Everyone to the streets! To the struggle! To the barricades alongside the soldiers and sailors of Brazil!

. . . Transport workers, factory workers—join the strikes and street confrontations to win your just demands and the liberation of Brazil! Peasants, tenant farmers, farm workers—join the struggle against the big landowners to win your demands and the land that belongs to you! Soldiers and sailors of Brazil!

With the Brazilian people by your side, we will free our nation from the yoke of imperialism.

. . . Down with the traitorous Vargas regime and his clique of reactionaries!

Long live the National Revolution of Liberation!

Long live the Popular National Revolutionary Government and its glorious leader, Luís Carlos Prestes!

Bread, land, and liberty!

All power to the National Liberation Alliance!

> The Political Bureau of
> the Communist Party of Brazil
> (Section of the Communist International)

Acting purely on instinct, Prestes and Olga decided not to have Gruber's young wife, Erika, who until then had been their regular driver, deliver them to Vila Isabel. Instead, Prestes called an old friend, Major Vitor Cesar da Cunha Cruz, who was studying at the Officers' Training School of the army high command. Though not a Communist, Cunha Cruz was utterly trustworthy and, as an official of the army, would cut down the risk of being stopped by military patrols. The move went without a hitch.

That night, for the very first time, Victor Barron hooked up the enormous radio transmitter. It had taken him a year of combing dozens of supply shops in several cities to secure the necessary parts. When the tiny colored lights flickered on and the machine began to function, he checked his notes for the frequency that would synchronize with the Comintern's transmitter on the other side of the planet in Moscow. It didn't take long to transmit the coded message from the revolutionary command, informing Moscow that the rebellion was under way. The airwaves carried back to Rio a compliment, also in code, that filled him with pride. The leadership of the Comintern sent good wishes for the complete success of the mission and congratulations to "the great Bolshevik Victor Barron for his excellent work."

The Brazilian Communist revolution would begin at 3:00 A.M. the following day—November 27.

Olga Benario at sixteen—a Communist militant in the Schwabing Group of her native city of Munich. (IML)

Olga, seventeen, in a Berlin park at the beginning of her meteoric career in the German Communist Youth. (IML)

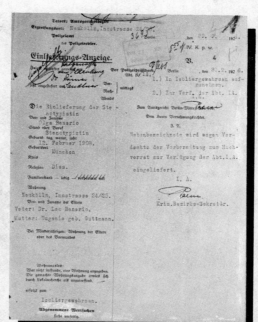

Olga's first arrest occurred in October 1926. The police suspected her and her boyfriend, Otto Braun, of "high treason." The arrest order notes that the prisoner is to be held incommunicado. (DCEG)

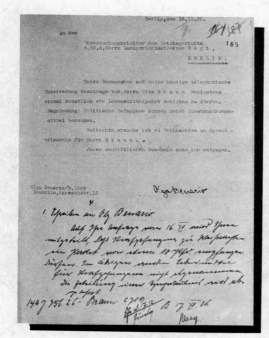

After her release, Olga asked Judge Vogt for permission to visit Braun in prison to bring him food, a privilege often granted to political prisoners. The judge turned her down. (DCEG)

Communist Youth activists from Berlin's Neukölln district setting out in horse-drawn carts for a street demonstration, Olga Benario among them. (NMO)

Minutes before the raid on Moabit Prison, Communist militants pose for a street photographer. Those identified: (1) Rudi König, (2) Olga, (3) Margot Ring, (4) Klara Seleheim, (5) Erick Bombach, (6) Erich Jazosch. (IML)

B·Z· am Mittag

Nr. 100 — 10 Pfennig

Berliner Zeitung
51. Jahrgang

Berlin
Mittwoch
11. April 1928

Mit Waffengewalt aus Moabit befreit

Untersuchungs-Gefangener Redakteur Braun entführt
Kommunistenüberfall im Zimmer des Untersuchungsrichters

Wegen Hochverrats
Seit 1½ Jahren in Untersuchungshaft

Amerika sendet 50 Millionen Dollar

Wildwest-Pistolen-Szene

Wie der Ueberfall ausgeführt wurde

"Hände hoch"

Verfolgung eingeleitet

Im Eigenheim von Moabit

Protest Japans in Moskau
Wegen Unterstützung der roten Verschwörung

Marx und Wirth Spitzenkandidaten des Zentrums

The front-page headline from the *Berliner Zeitung am Mittag* after the raid on Moabit: a "scene straight out of the wild West." (IML)

Defying police, militants of the Red Front of the Communist Youth
(above) celebrate Braun's liberation at the Müller beer hall. Months later,
the police rescinded the five-thousand-mark reward (below) for
information about Olga and Otto: they had fled to Moscow.
(IML; DCEG)

Bekanntmachung.

Die Auslobung vom 13. April 1928, durch die eine Belohnung bis zu
5000 Reichsmark ausgesetzt wurde für die Beihilfe bei der Ergreifung
des flüchtigen Schriftstellers

Otto Braun aus Berlin

und der flüchtigen Stenotypistin

Olga Benario aus Berlin

nehme ich zurück, da es nach hier eingegangenen Nachrichten den Genannten
gelungen ist, in das Ausland zu entkommen und damit die Erreichung des
mit der Auslobung verfolgten Zweckes, eine der Flucht auf dem Fuß
folgende Wiederergreifung zu erleichtern, unmöglich geworden ist.

Alle übrigen Fahndungsmaßnahmen gegen die Flüchtigen werden
aufrecht erhalten.

Leipzig, den 6. Juli 1928.   **Der Oberreichsanwalt.**

Wilhelm Müller and his wife and daughter, owners of the beer hall that served as an informal meeting place as well as the location for political rallies for the Communist Youth of Berlin-Neukölln. (IML)

Photographs taken in Moscow, where Olga lived in exile for six years . . . (IML)

. . . leaving several times to carry out political assignments in Western Europe. (IML)

Olga and a friend at a public bath in the Moscow area. (NMO)

Olga in Moscow, by now one of the leaders of KIM, the Communist Youth International. (IML)

On special occasions, Olga wore her Red Army uniform, which she received while training at the Air Force Academy. (IML)

Olga (circled) during military training in a cavalry regiment of the Red Army. (NMO)

The Prestes Column command in exile in Santo Corazón, Bolivia, in early 1927: Cordeiro de
Farias, Prestes, and Djalma Dutra. (CHB)

Prestes and Lourenço Moreira Lima (both circled) tried to find jobs for the exiled troops in the city of La Gaiba, Bolivia. (CHB)

October 1931: Prestes leaving Montevideo on his way to Moscow. (IML)

8

A Spy Among the Communists

THE REVOLUTION DID BEGIN at 3:00 A.M. and was over by 1:30 that afternoon.

None of the garrisons at Vila Militar rebelled. There was no insurrection at the Military Academy nor at the Navy Arsenal nor by the Navy Battalion. In police custody in Minas Gerais, Captain Trifino Correia never received Prestes's note—the messenger who was to deliver it met the same fate as the one carrying a note to Rio Grande do Sul: both were picked up by the police before leaving Rio de Janeiro.

Years later, full of melancholy, Rodolfo Ghioldi said, "The general strike Miranda envisioned didn't manage to paralyze a single person. And the promised support from the navy didn't even mobilize the passenger ferries."

The revolt was limited to the Third Infantry Regiment and the School of Aviation and was put down in a couple of hours. The Third Regiment barracks were located in the south of the city at Praia Vermelha, squeezed between three towering hills. The Communist

Party and the National Liberation Alliance had less than thirty men on the inside to subdue three hundred officers and nearly seventeen hundred soldiers. Command of the insurrection fell to the intrepid Communist Captain Agildo Barata, who had been sent to the Third Regiment less than a month before and was only there to serve a disciplinary sentence of twenty-five days for having tried to recruit for the ANL in the barracks of Rio Grande do Sul.

All federal troops stationed in Rio de Janeiro had been placed on full alert after news of the revolt in Natal reached the capital. A report that Prestes had been seen in the nearby city of Barra do Piraí prompted the command of the First Military Region to dispatch a company of the Second Infantry Regiment in that direction to prevent "any disturbance of civil order or upsurge of subversive movement." Meanwhile, at Praia Vermelha, the entire Third Regiment remained on alert throughout the night. The troops were allowed to stretch out on their beds but had to remain in full uniform, boots, weapons, and all. The officers, in a constant state of vigilance, paced the barracks, pistols at the ready, requiring the men to show authorization from a superior even to go to the bathroom. The extent and timing of these precautions raises the question of whether the government had been informed of exactly where and when the rebellion was to begin.

At the appointed time, Lieutenant Francisco Leivas Otero shot a burst of machine-gun fire into the air—this was the signal for each rebel to seize his company commander and loyalist officers and assume command of the troops. Agildo Barata, doing his bit in the officers' card room, captured Captain Luís Máximo, who went down in the history of the uprising as the first hostage and the first casualty—when a soldier attempted to help Barata disarm the captain, the loyalist officer's gun went off and shot him in the leg. After an intense half-hour gunfight, the revolutionaries won control of the Third Infantry Regiment, but victory was fleeting. By then, President Vargas had been informed of the events by his aide-de-camp, who had been awakened by a phone call from Lieutenant-Colonel Eduardo Gomes reporting the rebellion in the School of Aviation. Minutes later, as he was on his way to the Ministry of War, notice arrived that the Third Regiment had also rebelled.

General Eurico Gaspar Dutra, commander of the First Military

Region, ordered the barracks at Praia Vermelha, where the situation seemed most serious, to be completely surrounded. Within minutes, the area around the military unit was teeming with men from the Battalion of Guards, as well as a motorized company of machine guns and a howitzer group. Dutra also requisitioned the First Riflemen's Battalion from Petrópolis. At approximately 4:00 A.M. the rebels finally realized they were surrounded. When a patrol left the barracks to clear the street in front for the revolutionary troops, the heavy machine guns from the Battalion of Guards sprayed the building with bullets. Three or four further attempts to occupy the street were repelled by 155-millimeter howitzers. With the windows shot out and holes blown through the walls, civil police were able to lob tear gas canisters into the building.

A few meters away, General Dutra, protected by the cement overhang of a gas station, managed to telephone the barracks and communicate with Colonel Affonso Ferreira, one of the captured loyalist officers. Soon afterward, Dutra sent an emissary with a proposal for surrender addressed to Captain Barata, the rebel leader. His note was brief and formal.

11/27/35

Revolutionary Commander of the Third Regiment:

The Commanding General of the First Military Region— your commanding officer—urges you to lay down your arms immediately and surrender.

Your situation is untenable, and it would be advisable to avoid unnecessary casualties.

General Eurico Gaspar Dutra

Agildo Barata considered the proposal of unconditional surrender "insolent," but the tone of the note made it clear that the general already considered himself victorious. From what he had heard over the radio in the barracks, however, Barata knew there were "serious disturbances" in the School of Aviation at Campo dos Afonsos. The fact that the government had not brought in the air force to oust Barata's group from the Third Regiment could very well mean the school was in rebel hands. Better, then, to wait and

85

play for time. None of this "surrender" stuff. He delayed awhile before allowing General Dutra's messenger—a sergeant from the Battalion of Guards—to leave the barracks with his reply. Making use of an ambulance that removed the wounded from the building, the sergeant delivered the rebels' response to his commanding officer:

> General Dutra, Commander of the First Military Region:
>
> Regiment under our command will not surrender until corrupt Vargas regime overthrown.
>
> We urge esteemed comrade to save Brazil from being placed in foreign hands by Getúlio, Flores, and their thugs.
>
> Entire regiment with us. We hope and expect Commander First Military Region see our point of view, capable of freeing our nation from Getúlio's claws.
>
> Movement not Communist! but national, popular, revolutionary, with the most honorable of comrades at helm: Luís Carlos Prestes.
>
> > Captain Agildo Barata Ribeiro,
> > Commander Third Popular Revolutionary
> >   Infantry Regiment
> > Captain Alvaro Francisco de Souza,
> > Commander of the Third Infantry Regiment

Barata didn't know it then, but by the time the sun rose on November 27 the revolt at the School of Aviation had been crushed and its leaders, together with more than a hundred other officers and enlisted men, had been taken prisoner. As General Dutra was reading Barata's reply to his surrender proposal, President Vargas was inspecting the ruins of the School of Aviation, accompanied by Lieutenant Colonel Eduardo Gomes, who had survived the skirmish with a gunshot wound to the hand. Once the School of Aviation was back in their hands, the government could bring even greater force to bear on the Third Regiment. By 11:00 A.M., with one whole building devoured by flames, the rebels could see defeat written across the sky: military planes began buzzing threateningly over what was left of the barracks. Barata ordered a bugle to play "cease fire" in order to continue his dialogue with Dutra, but his two messengers were taken prisoner and disarmed. Minutes later the general himself walked in to receive the insurgents' surrender.

One of the officers accompanying Dutra was unable to contain his curiosity and irritation. "Who the hell is Agildo Barata?"

Furious, the revolutionary captain replied, "I am Agildo Barata! Who the hell are you?"

And so, the revolution came to a close with one swear word, two dozen dead, and hundreds of prisoners. The Communists, *aliancistas*, and sympathizers became victims of the biggest manhunt the country had ever seen. The defeated officers left the Third Regiment in a festive mood, arm in arm and shouting, "Long live the revolution." At police headquarters, where they were taken in buses lent to the army by the Canadian Light & Power Company, Agildo talked cheerfully with reporters, recounting details of the dawn gun battle. When journalists asked why he had led the uprising, Barata didn't hesitate to produce the note from Prestes spelling out when the revolt was to begin. Within minutes, this breezy interlude came to an end as officers, corporals, sergeants, and enlisted men were taken to the House of Detention, an enormous building on Rua Frei Caneca in Rio, which had been transformed into a political prison.

The state of siege declared by the president the previous night enabled the government to unleash total repression. Invested with absolute powers, the federal chief of police, Captain Filinto Müller, prohibited the carrying of arms in Rio de Janeiro and decreed that no one could leave the city without authorization. The files on "extremists," anarchists, Communists, socialists, Trotskyites, and members of (or mere sympathizers with) the National Liberation Alliance were transformed into arrest warrants. The most notorious agitators and those suspected of membership in the Communist Party were taken to the general barracks of the Security Police on Santo Antônio Hill. In just a few days, "going to Santo Antônio Hill" was synonymous with being subjected to the most brutal forms of torture. Filinto Müller intended to get to the bottom of the revolutionary plot, and no one was safe. Müller imposed a lighter punishment—the loss of his or her job—on those who were suspected of extremist ideas but who had not put them into practice.

The police requisitioned the *Dom Pedro I* from the shipping company Lloyd Brasileiro and transformed it into a floating prison in Guanabara Bay. Its first three lodgers were the directors of the *União Feminina Brasileira*, an organization aligned with the ANL and accused by the authorities of being a front for the Communist Party. The maelstrom of repression was so great that the ship was soon filled with prisoners, as were the corridors in the House of Detention, where prisoners and suspects sat waiting by the hundreds for formal charges to be brought against them. A fleet of buses brought four hundred soldiers from the House of Detention to Pharoux Pier, where they embarked for the Ilha das Flores, a nearby island, which received new shipments of prisoners every day. By the end of the month, thousands of people had been taken into custody all over the country.

Investigations profited from the collaboration of some important allies: agents from British Intelligence and, as was commented upon openly by the Rio police, from the terrifying Nazi Gestapo. A month into the crackdown, with the Communist leaders still at large, the state of siege was extended to permit investigations to continue. Christmas would find Brazil transformed into a war zone, immersed in terror.

On December 26 Pedro Nava, a young doctor, was going to work in an ambulance along Rua Prudente de Moraes when he remarked to the driver on the beauty of a young, foreign-looking woman walking down the street. When the woman came to the corner of Rua Paul Redfern, she suddenly turned and fled the way she had come, as if running away from someone. Nava craned his neck to see what had terrified her and saw that, halfway down the block, dozens of plainclothes policemen were dragging a couple, who were also foreign-looking, out of a house. The young woman was Olga Benario and the couple being taken away by Filinto Müller's men were Sabo and Arthur Ewert.

Olga and Prestes had returned to the house on Rua Barão da Torre in late November, as soon as news of the failure of the revolution reached them in Vila Isabel. The police had set up barricades on every street corner but concentrated their forces in the immediate neighborhood of Urca, near the Third Regiment. Because of this, Major Cunha Cruz, their trusted friend, was able to drive them back to Ipanema without incident. For the next thirty days Olga and Prestes went into hiding. Party militants who had not yet been identified were used as carrier pigeons between the Party leadership and the revolutionary command. Rigid security restrictions were imposed on the few face-to-face meetings that were arranged. Though his clean-shaven appearance had little in common with the photographs that appeared daily in the newspapers, Prestes knew he was being hunted down and could not risk going out. Olga too rarely left the house except to carry messages to the Ewerts, just around the corner. On very rare occasions, when Prestes was being guarded by someone absolutely reliable, she permitted herself the luxury of spending part of the morning swimming at Ipanema with Sabo.

On the morning of December 26, on her way to bring Ewert some of Prestes's notes on the current situation, Olga was terror-stricken when she turned the corner onto Rua Paul Redfern and saw the commotion in front of her friends' door. Ewert was shoved inside a van and several men piled in after him. Sabo was dragged off to another vehicle. Brandishing rifles and machine guns, the police pushed back curious onlookers who had gathered on the sidewalk. Olga stopped in her tracks, afraid that running would draw attention to herself but knowing that a second's delay could be fatal: if the police had discovered their address, the house on Rua Barão da Torre would be raided in minutes. She took the chance and ran. Once home, she flew up the stairs to the second floor, where Prestes was working, grabbed his hand, and cried in a mixture of German, Portuguese, and French, "We have to get out of here this minute! The police just picked up Sabo and Ewert and they could be on their way here right now."

There was no time to collect clothing, papers, or personal belongings. Prestes gathered up the papers before him on the table, threw them into the safe guarded by Gruber's explosives, and slammed it shut. Olga considered bringing her police dog, a gift from Prestes, but quickly thought better of it. The couple stepped out onto the street, trying to act naturally and yet still get out of the area as fast as possible. They hailed the first taxi that passed and headed for Victor Barron's apartment in Copacabana. There, in relative security, they could get in touch with the Party, which had arranged safe houses in various locations throughout the city. Both Prestes and Olga knew the address of the next locale reserved for them—a one-story house on the busy street of Rua Nossa Senhora de Copacabana—but, since they weren't sure how the police had found the Ewerts, they were afraid the hideout might already be compromised. It was only after nightfall, when they were assured that the police had not discovered the place, that they were willing to climb into Victor Barron's Graham Page. Barron drove around the block for a while to be sure they weren't being followed, then cruised past the new place several times checking for police lookouts, and finally left them at their hideaway, where they stayed for the next two weeks until another, more secure location could be arranged. With the morning papers came intriguing news: not a line appeared in the press about Sabo and Ewert's capture, which meant one of two things: either Filinto Müller was well aware of whom he had detained—and at that very moment was using his customary methods to extract information from Ewert, who would be exhibited to reporters only afterward—or else the police had been taken in by Ewert's cover story and were at a loss to establish a connection between Harry Berger and last month's frustrated insurrection.

Ewert himself dared to hope the police would not discover his true identity. Participation in the rebellion by Harry Berger, a supposed U.S. citizen, would not have serious consequences—the Brazilian government would no doubt treat him like so many other "undesirable aliens" and simply deport him. All hell would break loose, however, if they discovered they had in their hands a member of the Third International and the German Communist Party. In the van on the way to Special Police headquarters, Ewert's hopes were dashed.

At first, no one had asked either him or Sabo a single question. Dozens of police had raided their home, wielding a veritable arsenal of weapons: pistols, rifles, machine guns. While he and his wife were being dragged outside, four detectives and two others, whom he understood to be "witnesses," stayed in the house gathering up everything they could find. Once in the van, Ewert was seated on a metal bench, his hands cuffed to a steel bar behind his head. One of the four men who had climbed into the police van seemed to Ewert too blond and fair skinned to be Brazilian. Placing his machine gun on his lap, the man pulled a nutcracker from his coat pocket and began cracking and eating hazelnuts, which he removed one by one from his other pocket. As casually as he had been cracking nuts, he suddenly grabbed Ewert's left hand, placed the nutcracker around the thumb, and squeezed with all his might. Ewert didn't make a sound, but his face ran with sweat. Still impassively chewing bits of hazelnut, the cop leaned into Ewert's face and muttered, *"Du Kommunistischer Hurensohn . . ."*

This wasn't the first time he'd been called a Communist son of a bitch, and it certainly wouldn't be the last, but Ewert was terrified. The words had been spoken in perfect German, without a trace of an accent. If this man was with the German police, Ewert would be unlikely to get out of Brazil alive. And even if he did he would probably be deported to the Gestapo in Berlin. So the rumor was true—the Gestapo was indeed lending a helping hand to Filinto Müller.

When Müller had selected the agents to participate in the operation on Rua Paul Redfern, he knew very well who Harry Berger was. A week earlier, District Chief Antonio Canavarro Pereira, one of many policemen under Müller's authority, had brought to his office a deposition that merited the personal attention of the chief of police. Among the dozens of Communists in custody was one Josué Francisco de Campos, known by the code name "Bagé," who had made some very interesting declarations. Months earlier he had been invited by the Central Committee of the Communist Party to attend a meeting on a ranch in Jacarepaguá, outside Rio, at which a foreigner, apparently American, had given a lecture on the Chinese revolution. Speaking in English for nearly an hour, the foreigner had described to the small group of Brazilian Communists the course of Mao Tse-tung's Long March, pointing to a map of China hung on the wall beside him. Müller passed this information to the Intelligence Service in the hope that they could identify the mysterious lecturer of Jacarepaguá. In a matter of days a complete file arrived on his desk. The blond, stocky specialist in the Chinese revolution was an ex-deputy of the Reichstag and a member of the Comintern, Arthur Ernst Ewert, who also operated under the names Harry Berger and Arthur Brown.

British Intelligence had followed Ewert's movements since he had left Shanghai for Amsterdam, using a U.S. passport in the name of Harry Berger. From Amsterdam he had gone to Moscow (with a different passport), then returned to Amsterdam, and, once again Harry Berger, had gone on to Montevideo and Brazil, where he was joined by his wife. Though they managed to keep close tabs on him after he first arrived in Rio, and had even interrogated the owner of the truck that had transported his things from the port to the hotel on Rua Marquês de Abrantes, the British agents lost him after a few days. There was no doubt, however, that the man lecturing at the ranch in Jacarepaguá had been Arthur Ewert. With thousands of police occupying the city, with roads out of the city sealed and hundreds of Communists and sympathizers imprisoned, Müller did not have too much trouble tracking Ewert to the house on Rua Paul Redfern.

In addition to the mountain of papers, documents, manuscripts, manifestos, letters, and notes that fell into police hands when the Ewerts were captured, their maid, Deolinda, provided the police with information on the couple's most frequent visitors, including an address that would help them unravel another part of the story. Deolinda told them that one of the foreign couples who attended evening meetings at the house—the man had light hair and his wife had a slight limp—lived just up the street at the corner of Rua Paul Redfern and Rua Prudente de Moraes. Their names were Alphonsine and Léon-Jules Vallée. Also, a block and a half away, on Rua Barão da Torre, lived the Ewerts' closest friends. She described Prestes and Olga's house, which minutes later would be ransacked in an unusually blatant police operation. Seemingly aware they were in no danger, two of the investigators broke open the safe installed in the bedroom wall.

Neither the flashlight stuffed with dynamite nor the bomb containing a pound of TNT exploded: the police gained free and easy access to the money and all the documents, letters, pamphlets, maps, and notes on the failed revolution. Far from revealing Paul Gruber's incompetence, the failure of the explosive system—which police grandly termed an "infernal machine"—appeared to be deliberate, confirming something many members of the revolutionary command suspected but had never expressed. Though considered a trustworthy member of the German CP and of the Comintern (months before coming to Brazil, Gruber had been described in a Nazi court action as a "high-ranking functionary" of the German CP), he was actually a spy in the service of British Intelligence. Proof of this would only come to light four years later, and even then in the form of information to which very few had access. After arresting Gruber in late January 1940, Brazilian authorities threatened to deport him to his country of origin. When informed of the situation, British Intelligence was determined to save the skin of the agent who had infiltrated the Communist circle. A member of the British Foreign Office went to the Brazilian embassy in London and asked Ambassador Souza Leão to intervene on Gruber's behalf, "considering the services he rendered in denouncing the Communist movement of 1935." Leão immediately telegraphed the British appeal to the president of Brazil, thus saving Gruber from dying in a Nazi prison. A very painstaking double agent, Gruber had even managed to confound the U.S. authorities, diplomats, and police alike. Several days after Gruber's arrest, the first secretary of the American embassy in Brazil, William C. Burdett, transmitted to Secretary of State Cordell Hull "strictly confidential" information about Gruber, claiming proof that he had received "from U.S. sources" no less than forty thousand dollars to finance his activities in Brazil. When discreetly released from jail, Gruber disappeared as if he had never existed.

Though Müller was later informed by London of the details of Gruber's mission, neither he nor the British ever revealed precisely what "services" Gruber had "rendered."

9

Mr. Xanthaky Appears

EARLY IN THE AFTERNOON, Filinto Müller went to Ipanema to examine for himself the treasure that had fallen into the hands of the police and that was still being sorted and boxed by dozens of agents. It was unbelievable. In addition to U.S. dollars, Dutch guilders, French francs, and Argentine pesos, the police had seized maps and army instructions for "aviation combat exercises," "target shooting," and "organization of radio connections and field transmissions." The papers left in the safe by Prestes and Olga were sufficient to incriminate, or at least raise suspicion about, hundreds of people, some identified by code name only but many others by their full names and addresses. Müller triumphantly leafed through documents from the Comintern, secret papers of the Brazilian army, letters signed by "Vilar" or "Garoto" to leaders of the CP and the National Liberation Alliance all over the country, as well as drafts of letters from Prestes to Roberto Sissón, Hercolino Cascardo, and Agildo Barata with instructions for the rebellion. He found detailed diagrams of the workings of Communist cells, diagrams showing how to tune the radio transmitter set up by Barron, notes decoding the aliases of Communist leaders and other persons helpful to the Party, letters between Prestes and Miguel Costa, instructions for the working of state Party committees after the failed revolt, memos revealing that the mayor of the Federal District—Pedro Ernesto—was an ally of the rebels, and, finally, eight sheets of foolscap paper on which Prestes had practiced again and again the most natural-looking way to sign his new name: Antônio Vilar.

The haul from the Ewerts' home was no less rich. There were folders with directions to cell chiefs in workers' unions, letters between CP and ANL leaders, copies of instructions from the Party leadership, as well as posters and teaching materials on the Chinese revolution. Some of the documents were of special interest to the police: meticulous reports on the personal lives and activities of police chiefs (including details of all the meetings attended on a particular day by Captain Miranda Correia, district chief of the Security Police) and a small scrap of paper found in a drawer—the safe-conduct Prestes had given Ewert the night before the insurrection.

Before returning to his office, Filinto Müller visited Olga and Prestes's house once more and issued an enigmatic order to the investigators. "Before closing up the house, untie that dog outside and bring him to my office."

Back at headquarters, Müller contacted President Vargas and Vicente Rao, the minister of justice, with an official report on the results of the raid that morning.

Even though British Intelligence had sufficient information about the identity of Harry Berger, Müller decided to seek further confirmation from the U.S. State Department. He would need a formal pretext for this: until proven otherwise, the prisoners from Rua Paul Redfern were U.S. citizens, with legitimate passports issued in New York. As soon as he was contacted by Müller, the U.S. ambassador to Brazil, Hugh Gibson, sent a coded telegram to Secretary of State Cordell Hull requesting instructions. FBI Director J. Edgar Hoover could not be of much help; there was no FBI file under the name Harry Berger, and the one on Arthur Ernst Ewert was very slim, containing only a vague reference from five years earlier describing him as a "prominent German Communist." A document signed by Hoover himself even raised doubts about whether Ewert had visited New York for the American Communist Party convention in 1927.

Next, Cordell Hull instructed Raymond Geist, the U.S. consul in Berlin, to furnish as soon as possible "biographical data, physical description, and fingerprints" of the mysterious American (or German) in custody in Rio de Janeiro. Hugh Gibson's reference to Berger's familiarity with the Chinese revolution prompted Hull to send a top-secret telegram to Monnet Davis, the U.S. consul in Shanghai, also requesting information, photographs, and the fingerprints of Ewert/Berger.

While diplomats and secret agents scoured their files, Ewert and his wife, Elise, suffered a week of torture by Müller's police. The teams and their methods alternated every two hours, but they were consistent in not asking the couple anything, not even their names. The police wanted to break their prisoners' morale first and then begin the interrogation. Isolated in the prison on Santo Antônio Hill, Ewert and Sabo miraculously withstood the violence of the German and Brazilian police in incessant rotation. Ewert's body was covered with bruises from being beaten with billy clubs, his left hand was still swollen from the nutcracker, and his anus and penis were bruised from electric shocks and objects thrust into them. Elise's back, breasts, and legs were covered with tiny burns from cigarettes, and there were lacerations all over her body from the whippings administered by a young German policeman.

When finally the interrogation began, the violence increased— but to no avail. Nothing would coax information out of Ewert or Elise. The police decided to torture husband and wife in turn while the other was made to watch. Ewert saw Elise being raped by dozens of soldiers. He was "executed" by a firing squad shooting blanks. Elise was placed in a coffin and buried alive. All this without either one of them being allowed to sleep a single minute from the time they were arrested. When a night's torture session was interrupted at dawn so that a fresh team could take over, they were forced to remain standing with their eyes open. One night Ewert was caught dozing on his feet with his head slumped back and his eyes closed. The guard on duty became so furious that he carried a heavy typewriter from the prison office and tied it around Ewert's neck so that he would be forced to stand perfectly straight for the rest of the night. The slightest tilt forward or backward and the typewriter would have broken his neck.

The couple lost all sense of the time that had passed since their capture. The police were intrigued by their obstinance in saying absolutely nothing, especially since the seized documents revealed practically all their activities in Brazil. In early January, Ewert almost cracked when two policemen, one German and one Brazilian, stood him against the bars of the cell naked, his arms and legs open in an X. The German held up a piece of wire about twenty inches long and said: "Now we'll see if you talk, you commie son of a bitch. We're going to roast you from the inside out."

This said, he threaded a length of wire into Ewert's urethra. The prisoner remained stoical. Then the Brazilian appeared with a small welding torch, flames shooting from the tip. The German held Ewert's penis delicately, as a doctor would, and began heating the end of the wire. Ewert could no longer remain silent, but the only sound from his throat was a bellowing, like the cry of a bull. Then he collapsed, hanging from the bars by his wrists. The Brazilian looked almost happy to see someone so stubborn and laughed with amazement. He said to his Nazi colleague, "Well, doctor . . . it looks like we're really not going to get a thing out of your countryman here."

The interrogators convinced Müller and Correia that the couple was not going to talk. If their superiors wanted them to, the men could eliminate them, but it was clear that Ewert and Elise would die without giving a single name. Not even a name that the police already knew. On January 6, Müller decided to announce to the press the arrests made eleven days earlier. To fill out the story, he selected a few of the thirteen hundred documents seized at the house on Rua Paul Redfern and released them to reporters with detailed biographical information on the couple. The arrest was presented as a result of investigations by Brazilian authorities, while in fact the only thing the political police had done was to translate material sent to them by British Intelligence, the Gestapo, and the U.S. State Department. Ewert was described as "the organizer of Communist activity in Brazil and all South America." Since the police consistently denied that political prisoners were tortured, journalists were not permitted to see the couple. The photographs that appeared in the papers the next day were those taken just after the arrest and showed a ruddy-cheeked and robust Arthur Ewert in an elegant white suit.

That same day, by a stroke of luck, the police made another important arrest. Captain Correia had ordered undercover police to keep an apartment building on Avenida Paulo de Frontin under constant surveillance because it was suspected of being a safe house for Communist intellectuals—including a young Brazilian writer named Jorge Amado. One of the detectives assigned to watch the building noticed a tenant whose photograph he thought he had seen in police files; the man came and went nonchalantly with his young, beautiful wife. After the couple was brought in for questioning, the police discovered their prize was none other than the general secretary of the Communist Party, Antônio Maciel Bonfim, also known as Adalberto de Andrade Fernandes or "Miranda." Until then, no connection had been made between the Miranda cited in the confiscated documents and the Bonfim whose police file from five years earlier modestly characterized him as having been "identified as a criminal subversive/anarchist." The woman taken into custody with him was Elvira Cupelo Colônio, known also as "Garota." An illiterate, Elvira told the police that she had been a maid until meeting Bonfim on a Rio beach and falling in love with him. When she claimed she had come all the way to Rio from her home in Sorocaba on foot, the police were not sure whether they were dealing with a madwoman or an experienced militant trained by Moscow. Sorocaba is located in the interior of the state of São Paulo, some 480 kilometers away.

The material confiscated from their apartment, though less copious than the collection from the two houses in Ipanema, was equally promising: dozens of copies of letters sent by Miranda to regional Party committees; reports from all over the country and from abroad; questionnaires sent by Miranda to CP directors in various states, which had been duly filled out and returned; manuals for the manufacture of bombs and instructions on how to contact Red Aid International, an organization created by the Third International to help Communists in trouble. In the midst of this mountain of paperwork the police found the "filet mignon," as one detective put it: detailed balance sheets showing Communist Party finances. There were entries for all funds received by the Party and, in minute detail worthy of the most painstaking bookkeeper, all expenditures: from salaries paid to leaders, to money spent buying newspapers and clothing, to expenses for rent, water, and electricity at the safe houses.

News of Miranda and Elvira's arrest, made public four days after the fact, left Prestes and Olga even more apprehensive: the Party general secretary was one of the few people who knew the address of their present hiding place in Copacabana. It was time to move again. Since the arrests were multiplying, they needed to keep to a bare minimum the number of people who would know their new location. With this in mind they decided to find a new house themselves. Looking through the classified section of the *Jornal do Brasil*, Olga and Prestes found what they were looking for in the section called "Suburban Houses and Apartments":

House for rent: 220 mil réis per month. Clean. Waxed floors. Two bedrooms, two sitting rooms, gas stove, garden, yard with fruit trees, perfect for a good family. On Cachambi streetcar line in Meyer. Rua Honório, 279.

It sounded ideal. By all indications, the police had concentrated their investigations in the southern and central areas of the city. If so, what better than to trade Copacabana for Meyer, a working-class area of seventy thousand inhabitants—double the population of Copacabana and Ipanema combined. Manoel dos Santos, shoemaker and CP militant, was assigned to arrange the rental, told only that it was for "a comrade and his wife." It was a modest house, sufficiently discreet for their needs. Manoel and his wife, Júlia, were to live there with Olga and Prestes until the Party decided where the "Knight of Hope" would go next. Manoel went to see the owner, José Gomes, introducing himself as head of the light-bulb division of General Electric. Rather than involving a cosignatory or guarantor for the lease, he proposed to pay four months' rent in advance, and they agreed to a sum of eight hundred mil réis. Two days later he moved to Meyer and settled in to wait for the arrival of the new lodgers. If anyone asked, he and his wife were to say they had decided to save on rent by subletting one of the rooms to a couple, to whom they would also supply lunch and dinner.

Only one Party leader—whose name Prestes would never reveal —was informed that the Copacabana safe house was being traded for another "located in the neighborhood of Meyer." In mid-January Olga and Prestes asked Victor Barron, who had not been troubled by the police and whose presence in Brazil was apparently unknown to the authorities, to be their chauffeur once more. Barron waited until nightfall and discreetly delivered them in his Graham Page to a spot near the house on Rua Honório. Olga and Prestes brought precious little with them besides their identification papers in the names of Antônio and Maria Bergner Vilar—just a small overnight bag with half a dozen articles of clothing and a few Party documents. From that moment on, Prestes's contact with the Party leadership—Miranda's position had been filled by Lauro Reginaldo da Rocha, or "Bangu"—would take place only through messengers of his own choosing. His first recommendation was that the new leadership arrange yet another safe house for him and Olga. At the slightest hint that the police suspected their move to Meyer, they would have to leave immediately.

Under the pretext of tracing the origin of the U.S. passports used by Ewert and Elise, the U.S. government became deeply involved in the investigations of the "Brazilian connection" of the international Communist movement. Secretary of State Cordell Hull demanded that an American investigator be allowed to work with the Brazilian police. R. C. Bannerman, chief of the "Special Agents' Section" of the State Department (an investigative division exercising some of the functions assigned today to the CIA), contacted Ambassador Gibson in Rio. The "special agent" chosen was Theodore Xanthaky, a thirty-eight-year-old former bank functionary from New York, who had worked as a "clerk" in the U.S. embassy in Brazil between 1920 and 1922. Xanthaky spoke fluent Portuguese and Spanish.

His first task was to interrogate Ewert and Elise. Late in the afternoon of January 14, with the necessary papers from the American ambassador, Xanthaky went to see Captain Correia—"the man in charge of the entire anti-Communist department," as the agent said in his report to Washington—to arrange his visit to the prisoners. Probably in order to avoid the curiosity of reporters who hung around headquarters looking for news, Correia asked Xanthaky to come back at ten that evening. At the appointed time,

Francisco Jullien, one of Correia's men, took the American to Santo Antônio Hill. On the way, Jullien thought it best to warn Xanthaky of the state in which he would find the two prisoners.

"They've been kind of roughed up by the boys in interrogation, and they haven't been allowed to sleep for a couple of days. I don't know if it will do any good, though. Up till now neither of them has said a word. They won't even admit they're Communists."

At the entrance to the prison Xanthaky was met by José Torres Galvão, who introduced himself as the head jailer. Smiling, Galvão didn't hide his admiration for the Ewerts' physical endurance. "I've never seen anything like it in all my years of police work, Mr. Xanthaky. That German's had the crap beaten out of him nonstop for three weeks and still hasn't opened his trap. Same with his wife. I've got to take my hat off to him—this commie is something else. Fantastic. But they should be in good shape now. This afternoon Captain Correia told us to give it a rest until later tonight, on account of the illustrious visitor. Go right in, they're all fixed up."

Theodore Xanthaky was shocked by what he saw. The man he found sitting on a wooden crate didn't bear the slightest resemblance to the robust German whose photographs he had been shown at the embassy. Ewert was emaciated; his left thumb was purple and swollen, looking like a large fruit; the sores and scars all over his body left no doubt that Galvão had been telling the truth. The man had been beaten like an animal. Ewert raised his eyes and the visitor identified himself.

"The embassy received an anonymous call saying you wanted to speak to us. Since you're here in Brazil with an American passport, we used all the leverage we have with the Brazilian police to get them to let me come and listen to your story."

Arthur Ewert was direct, and he replied in English, as fluently as his mysterious interlocutor. "I didn't ask to see anyone from any embassy, but I have to admit it's good to see someone walk in here without a whip or a club in his hand. They haven't let me or my wife sleep for days, and we've been violently beaten the entire time. I welcome anyone who could intercede and put a stop to this brutality."

"We're concerned about your situation because you carry American passports. Are there friends or relatives in the States you'd like to contact?"

Ewert smiled for the first time. "Yes. I have a friend in the U.S. His name is Earl Browder."

"And you'd like the State Department to get in touch with Mr. Browder?"

The prisoner smiled again, ironic and suspicious. "I think maybe you didn't catch my friend's name. Earl Browder is the general secretary of the American Communist Party."

Xanthaky was a professional. He saw right away that Ewert realized as long as the visit lasted the torture would be suspended. And he was trying to take advantage of that fact. Xanthaky changed the subject, remarking on an interview published in *Harper's* magazine about the fire in the Reichstag in February 1933; he talked in general terms about irrelevant subjects. When he tried to slip in a few indiscreet questions, he found the prisoner was also a professional. In response to a query regarding his marriage to Elise and his acquisition of the passports, Ewert cut the conversation short with a dry, gruff question of his own.

"Are you trying to interrogate me?"

"No, of course not, and you're perfectly free to refuse to answer my questions. But if you'd like us to help you, we have to establish, beyond a shadow of a doubt, your and your wife's true identities."

Changing tactics, the American agent feigned sincerity and concocted a new story. "Look, we have information that your passport was obtained with a genuine birth certificate and so we're convinced you really are Harry Berger. The situation with the woman you claim is your wife is different, though. We have reason to believe that she is not Machla Lenczycki as her passport states."

Ewert lost his patience. Slowly and deliberately he said, "Mr. Xanthaky, my wife and I have been beaten senseless for several days now by Nazi police and White Russians on loan to the Brazilian authorities, and we have told them precisely nothing. They've been trying to get names and addresses out of us which neither of us will supply under any circumstances. Not to them. Much less to you."

"But if you open up to me, your situation here will improve."

"There's no reason in the world to open up to you. Both the Brazilian and German police know full well that my name is Arthur Ewert and that my wife is Elise Saborowski Ewert. They know my past. And the information they don't have—well, it won't be me or my wife who provides it."

"But who financed the movement here in Brazil?"

Ewert spoke carefully, trying to remember what information the police already had. "You know that as a rule the more powerful parties help the poorer, less established ones, but here in Brazil we didn't need a lot of money. Elise and I lived very modestly. You exaggerated enormously the role of Youamtorg [the Soviet Union's trading company in Montevideo] in the Latin American revolutions. In Brazil, the largest donations made to the National Liberation Alliance were by prominent Brazilians—one individual alone, for example, donated fifty contos de réis to the ANL."

Xanthaky wanted more information about the rebellion and the involvement of foreign Communists with the military. Ewert said nothing that wasn't already known by the authorities.

"The insurrection in the north was as big a surprise to me as it was to Prestes. I had no personal contact whatsoever with the Brazilian military. That was Prestes's job."

Xanthaky realized that Ewert was trying to close the conversation. As he stood up, the prisoner made a request. "If you can, talk to the police and ask that they transfer my wife into this cell. Though she is a member of the Communist Party, as I am, she had no active role here in Brazil. And if I'm to be deported and the American embassy can intervene at all, I'd like to avoid being sent to Germany. That would be like jumping from the frying pan into the fire. I'd prefer to be sent to some French port."

On his way out, Xanthaky asked a strange question. "Do you and your wife profess any religion?"

Ewert smiled as he said, "We were born Christians."

It was approaching dawn when Xanthaky moved on to his second mission of the night, simpler and less time-consuming than the first: interrogating Elise Ewert. It was obvious that she had also been beaten severely, though she seemed to be in better condition than her husband. Sabo politely repeated what her husband had told the American agent. He could not coax out of her with good manners what the Brazilian and Nazi police hadn't managed to beat out of her. Xanthaky insisted that he needed to know more about her activities in Brazil and about the couple's contacts with Communist leaders and the military. She repeated that she had nothing to say. "Even if I knew someone's name and wanted to reveal it to you, it wouldn't do you any good. Our contacts always used code names. If

I knew someone as Adalberto, for example, that certainly wasn't his real name, and he would have had half a dozen other names as well."

Xanthaky mentally filed the name Adalberto and returned to the task at hand. "British Intelligence informs us that you've used the names Kathe Gussfeld, Ethel Chilles, and Edith Braser. Is that true? We've also been told you were in the United States in 1926. Is that true?"

"No. None of it is true. I never used those names nor was I in the U.S. in 1926."

Xanthaky saw that he would get no new information from Elise. Before leaving, he told Galvão and Jullien about Ewert's request that his wife be transferred to his cell. Galvão replied, "We could give it a try. Roughing them up didn't get us anywhere—who knows if maybe we treat them nicely for a while they might talk? But if they think they're going to spend the night fooling around, they've got another think coming. We'll put six German cops in there with them, so there'll be no nooky and no napping."

In the car with Jullien on the way back to police headquarters, Xanthaky wrote in tiny letters on a cigarette pack: ADALBERTO. He mentioned the name to Captain Correia, who produced a file and pulled out a photograph of a man with a thin mustache who had been picked up a few days earlier.

"It wasn't mere chance she used that name as an example. We've already got her Adalberto under lock and key: he's Antônio Maciel Bonfim, the general secretary of the CP."

The American firmly demanded that all the information he passed on from his conversation with Ewert be kept secret. Correia agreed. "Don't worry about it, Mr. Xanthaky. I can assure you, you are the first and only outsider to have the privilege of talking to the prisoners. And you've got carte blanche to interrogate anyone you'd like."

"What about Prestes? Any news?"

"Well, Mr. Xanthaky, since you represent a government allied with us in the struggle against communism, I can give you firsthand information, confidentially of course. A few days ago we picked up a Belgian couple, Léon-Jules Vallée and his wife, Alphonsine. They were carrying a veritable fortune, the origin of which they couldn't explain. Our men believe that Léon will lead us to Prestes. I've ordered that the couple be released, and we have two men tailing them. I think within the next couple of days we'll finally get our hands on their top man. By the way, you're certainly free to take a look at the Vallée file, or others that interest you, for that matter. Jullien will make copies of anything you'd like."

Xanthaky wanted to know more. "What will happen to Prestes?"

"Our orders are not to take him alive."

The first light of day found Theodore Xanthaky seated beside a code operator in the American embassy, transmitting a detailed telegram to the State Department reporting his conversation with the Ewerts.

10

"Miranda" and Ghioldi Talk

ASSISTED BY THE GESTAPO, the intelligence service of the U.S. State Department, and British Intelligence, the Brazilian police were slowly closing in on Prestes and Olga. The mass of seized documents had been scrutinized and their contents confirmed by confessions extracted from people in Rio prisons through beatings and electric shocks. Two months after the insurrection, the government had a chart revealing the network of Communists and their military allies in Brazil. Only a few pieces were still missing from the puzzle. Numerous documents, including communications between Party leaders and members of the military who led the rebellion, were signed "G.I.N." The police knew these were the initials of the three most important leaders of the revolt: *G* for "Garoto," the code name for Prestes, *N* for "Negro," the code name for Arthur Ewert, and *I* for "Indio." But who was "Indio"? In one of her many depositions, the controversial Elvira, wife of the general secretary of the CP, said she believed "Indio" was a foreigner. In only one case could the police see a relation between code name and owner: Prestes was a small man, so it was natural that he came to be called "Garoto" (Portuguese for "boy"). Ewert's case was puzzling, on the other hand, since far from being "Negro" he was fair-haired and German. And who could this "Indio" be?

The information that led them to the third leader of the rebellion came in an unexpected way: a friend of District Chief Jullien told him he was suspicious of the behavior of a young Spanish-American couple who had recently moved into the apartment building across from him in the southern area of the city. The police learned from the doorman that the man in question was Luciano Busteros, a Uruguayan journalist who lived there with his wife, Carmen. Though the name Busteros did not appear in Brazilian, German, British, or American intelligence files, Jullien had the building watched and told his men to photograph the journalist at the first opportunity.

When a picture of the dark, black-haired Uruguayan in round wire-rimmed glasses was shown to Elvira Colônio, she said without hesitation, "That's the 'Indio' you're looking for."

Rodolfo Ghioldi and his wife, suspecting that their building was being watched, decided to flee on the night of January 22. Carrying only one small suitcase, they hailed a cab in front of their apartment building and went straight to the central railway station, where they bought tickets for the night train to São Paulo. As the train pulled away from the platform, the Ghioldis imagined they had managed to elude the Rio police. But during a middle-of-the-night stop in Jacareí, in the state of São Paulo, Jullien, who had been following them all along, arrested the couple as they stepped off the train to buy a snack. Rodolfo Ghioldi spent the rest of the night trying to convince Jullien that there had been some mistake: here was his passport proving that his name was not Rodolfo Ghioldi and neither was he Argentinian. However, when they reached São Paulo, one of Müller's men greeted them with Ghioldi's file in his hand. There was clearly no point in continuing the pretense.

The Ghioldis were escorted back to Rio and taken immediately to police headquarters, where they sat in the waiting room outside Correia's office alongside the other prisoners captured that day. From her chair in the waiting room, Carmen strained to see what was going on in the inner office. Suddenly her eyes widened, the color drained from her face, and she whispered to her husband, "Rodolfo, you won't believe who's in there—it's Miranda. And he's working for the police. I saw him point you out and tell them you're 'Indio.'"

"If Miranda is collaborating with the police," Ghioldi thought as he was led into the office to give his statement, "they must already know all about us." Perhaps it was this conclusion that led him to identify so readily the photo shown to him by Correia and Jullien. He said without blinking, "Yes, I know him. That's Léon-Jules Vallée, the man in charge of finances."

The hope that Vallée would lead the police to Prestes was never realized. Two weeks of rigorous surveillance produced only the address of a Dr. Balestre, who turned out to be a legitimate physician treating Alphonsine Vallée for phlebitis. On the evening of January 28, six days after Ghioldi's arrest, Léon-Jules Vallée and his wife were walking in the Lido section of Rio when he noticed they were being followed by two men. They headed for the center of town, where intense pedestrian traffic and a series of galleries and arcades between the streets might help them escape. When Vallée noticed a momentary lack of attention on the part of their pursuers, he and his wife ducked into one of the arcades and out again, jumped into a cab, and disappeared. The couple went straight to the safe house where Eduardo Ribeiro Xavier, a member of the CP leadership, was staying. Weeks later, Xavier (code name "Abóbora") would spirit them out of Brazil to Buenos Aires. When informed that the Vallées had managed to flee the country, Filinto Müller decided to take no more chances. He ordered the immediate arrest of an American living in Copacabana, whose address had been furnished by Ghioldi, and who had been under surveillance for six days. Minutes later, police raided 972 Rua Nossa Senhora de Copacabana and took into custody a slender young man over six feet tall: Victor Allen Barron.

For the U.S. embassy, the arrest of an American citizen was a gift from above, providing an indisputably legal pretext to become more deeply involved in the investigations of the Brazilian police. Despite his claim that he suffered from tuberculosis, Barron was beaten mercilessly by members of a Special Police battalion jeeringly nicknamed by the people the "tomato heads"—five hun-

dred professional fighters handpicked from the army and distin-
guishable from other troops by their red kepis. Dispatched by the
embassy to interrogate the American, Xanthaky found Barron in a
deplorable state—in spite of Müller's assurances that "no one had
laid a finger on the prisoner." Barron denied any link with the
insurrection, claiming that he was in Brazil as a commercial representative of John Reiner & Co., a New York motor manufacturer. He
had some difficulty in explaining how he could afford his elegant
apartment, natty wardrobe, and luxury car without having managed
to sell a single motor for the company he supposedly represented.
Another strike against him was the visas on his passport, which
Xanthaky considered clear evidence of political involvement: he
had retraced the traditional trajectory for agents of the Comintern,
with obligatory stops in Amsterdam and Montevideo, "important
centers of Communist activity," as Xanthaky stated in his report.

Though suspected of being a militant Communist, Barron was an
American citizen and, as such, deserved greater concern from the
embassy agent. In an extensive secret memo sent to Secretary of
State Cordell Hull and signed by Ambassador Gibson, Xanthaky
tried to exempt himself from any responsibility for Barron's fate at
the hands of the police:

> I have impressed upon the police the seriousness of manhandling
> American citizens and have received definite assurances that Barron
> will be subjected to no further rough treatment and that in the future
> American suspects will be interviewed by the embassy before being
> interrogated by the police and that there will be no third-degree
> measures in such cases. I have also been given assurances that Barron
> will be afforded good medical care. I am frankly troubled as to how to
> handle this case.

After witnessing the results of the treatment given the Ewerts,
Xanthaky apparently foresaw the risks of leaving in Filinto Müller's
hands someone who might have information about Prestes's whereabouts:

> The Communist pot is boiling here and if there is any way of
> establishing that Barron is not involved I think it urgent that we get
> him out of the picture. He is apparently either unwilling or unable to

help us; his story does not ring true and as matters now stand the police are justified in entertaining grave suspicions. He does not appear disposed to contribute to building up a case explaining his situation, and his general attitude is less a protestation of his innocence than a reiteration of the phrase "they have not got a thing on me."

Cordell Hull wired Ambassador Gibson within days of receiving the report, sending along the State Department file on Barron's background: he was the son of Communist leader Harrison George, who, Barron's mother claimed, must have financed the young man's trip to South America. The charge of setting up a clandestine radio transmitter echoed the procedure adopted by the Comintern in previous instances, including China, for example. As for Barron's high standard of living in Brazil, the Reiner Company steadfastly maintained that Barron hadn't managed to close a single deal in South America, lending credence to the suspicion that his contract with them was merely a cover for subversive activities. And neither Barron nor his family had the means to take luxury vacations. Probably because he was not acquainted with Filinto Müller's police, the U.S. secretary of state closed his telegram seemingly unworried about Barron's fate:

DEPARTMENT WILL TRANSMIT FURTHER INFORMATION
WHEN PRACTICABLE. ANY INFORMATION YOU MAY BE ABLE
TO OBTAIN FROM BARRON WITH REGARD TO HIS ACTIVITIES
IN THE INTERNATIONAL COMMUNIST MOVEMENT WILL BE
APPRECIATED. IN VIEW OF FOREGOING AND ALSO IN VIEW
OF ASSURANCES OF BRAZILIAN POLICE REGARDING FUTURE
TREATMENT OF BARRON THE DEPARTMENT FEELS THAT
THERE IS NO PRESENT NEED FOR INTERVENTION BY
EMBASSY ON HIS BEHALF.

One of Xanthaky's memos to Hull clearly indicated that Barron had been denounced by someone before his arrest. The police had informed the American agent that they had information on "a young American in charge of assembling a transmitter, and that he was the son of a certain Harrison George, who had been divorced several times." The report sent to Washington in early February 1936 indicated that Barron had adopted the same technique as the

Ewerts: he limited his discussion to facts already known to the police. Barron acknowledged that he had come to Brazil to set up a radio station to facilitate communications with the Comintern. This had been deactivated on November 27 and transferred to another safe house in the suburbs, the address of which he did not know. He said also that he had driven Prestes to a spot somewhere in the city. "That's it," he repeated dozens of times both to Xanthaky and to the police who beat him. "You won't get so much as another comma out of me."

Since the embassy seemed unconcerned about Barron, Xanthaky returned to his work with the Ewerts. As before, he arrived at police headquarters after dark and was taken by Jullien to Santo Antônio Hill. No longer particularly interested in the "Brazilian connection," Xanthaky was eager for information about the American Communist Party. After a brief visit to Elise, he was escorted to Ewert's cell, where he was obliged to go over the same ground for hours to obtain only a mere tidbit of information about an event that had taken place five years earlier in China. Ewert himself sounded almost discouraged when he said, "But the American authorities are already aware of that, Mr. Xanthaky. . . ."

Frustrated with the insignificant crop of information, Xanthaky was preparing to leave when Ewert said, "I heard from one of the cops that Laval, the French prime minister, has stepped down. Is it true?"

"Yes. He's been succeeded by Sarrault."

"And Daladier is a member of the new cabinet?"

"Why do you ask? Is Daladier a Communist?"

Ewert smiled. "No, he's not a Communist, but he has serious liberal leanings, which is better than nothing."

Ewert's refusal to talk in the face of police brutality was not, however, the general pattern of behavior among the prisoners. Miranda either simply crossed over to the enemy, as some of his comrades insisted, or caved in as a result of the torture sessions of his first days in custody. In any case, he told the police everything he knew. He talked during the electric shocks and beatings with a wire whip; he talked during the formal depositions; he confirmed and reconfirmed what the police already knew and what they wanted to know. He told them that "Bangu," his successor at the

helm of the Party, was Lauro Reginaldo da Rocha; that in addition to
"Garoto," Prestes also used the code name "Antônio," on such
occasions speaking only Spanish; that "Negro," Berger, and Arthur
Ewert were one and the same person—the representative of the
Comintern in Brazil, who chaired CP meetings and provided guid-
ance to the other leaders.

While he had boasted at the meeting just before the insurrection
of his capacity to "bring the nation to a halt in support of the
rebellion," at police headquarters he humbly said that the Party he
headed "could do little to back the revolution, since the support it
enjoyed was minimal." And he identified, one by one, the people
behind the code names mentioned in the papers confiscated during
police raids, adding each one's role in the Party. Every sheet of
paper the police put in front of him was translated, decoded, explained, and identified.

Rodolfo Ghioldi neither betrayed the Party in the same way nor
was he subjected to the same brutality as Miranda, but he too was
generous with his confessions. Years later, Ghioldi admitted that the
violence directed at him by the police was limited to "a lot of threats
and a few blows," but even so he identified the photograph of Léon-
Jules Vallée, without knowing whether or not Vallée was already in
police custody; he identified several manuscripts in police hands as
being written by Arthur Ewert; he revealed the link between the
mayor of the Federal District, Pedro Ernesto, and Luís Carlos
Prestes; he provided the address of Prestes's hideout on Rua Nossa
Senhora de Copacabana and said that Prestes would be leaving
there on January 19; he said that the owner of the safe houses on
Rua Sá Ferreira and Rua José Higyno was Benjamin Schneider. And
he presented to the police the gift of an entirely new piece of
information: Prestes, he claimed, was married to a light-haired
woman, probably a foreigner—she always spoke to him in
French—who was at his side at all times. Ghioldi didn't know her
last name, but he was absolutely sure she was called Olga.

11

In Pursuit of Olga

THE NUMBER OF PEOPLE arrested after the November 27
uprising was so great and the prisoners scattered so widely that the
police themselves were not always completely sure who was still at
large and who had already been captured. This undoubtedly explains why District Chief Pereira sent the following official letter to
Correia the day Rodolfo Ghioldi gave his deposition:

> His Excellency Captain Miranda Correia, Chief of Security:
>
> I would appreciate your cooperation in arranging for the
> woman referred to as Olga (surname unknown) in Rodolfo
> Ghioldi's statement to appear at this office on March 8 at 12:00
> to give a deposition. Best regards,
>
> District Chief Antonio Canavarro Pereira

Correia was not in his office when the letter arrived. He had gone
to São Paulo to witness a confrontation at the "Maria Zélia" prison
between two Communist leaders cited in various depositions given
by prisoners under his jurisdiction. Though the bulk of the repression was concentrated in Rio, the streets of São Paulo had also been

swept clean by the Security Police. With the jails overflowing, the police had transformed the old Maria Zélia factory in Brás into a gigantic prison where hundreds of Communists, *aliancistas*, and sympathizers were quartered. It was there that the long arms of Vargas's repression held Celestino Paraventi, who had been denounced anonymously for playing host to Olga and Luís Carlos Prestes on their arrival in Brazil. As Paraventi observed of the prisoners at Maria Zélia, "There were some who were up to their necks in the rebellion and others who didn't have the slightest idea why they'd been arrested." Far from being alarmed at his incarceration, Paraventi was enjoying himself. Every morning he added his gifted tenor to the throng of voices singing the National Liberation Alliance hymn and "The International."

In the midst of all the commotion, Paraventi gradually began to feel that "something smelled in all this Communist business." A romantic at heart, he could not understand how the Communists, all victims of the same adversity, could have split into so many different factions, "each ready to consume the next." He kept searching for "the fraternity and understanding Prestes said was inherent to communism." Devastated by his lack of success, he decided one day to eavesdrop on a Communist group meeting in a corner of the prison, "to find out which rival faction this one was knocking." When his intent became obvious, someone in the group turned to him and said, "This isn't a secret cell meeting, you know. It's a spiritualist session. You can join us if you'd like."

For lack of anything else to do, Paraventi sat down—though he was not himself a believer. At one point after the spirit had descended, the man he was speaking through tapped the young millionaire on the shoulder: "You are a very powerful medium. You will be very useful to spiritualism."

When he was freed, months later, Paraventi continued his work helping political activists but announced that he had "traded communism for spiritualism."

Correia suddenly had to leave the spiritualists and Communists of Maria Zélia behind and hurry back to Rio to have a look at Ghioldi's deposition. The news about Prestes surprised him. If the "Knight of

Hope" was married—and to a foreigner—Captain Filinto Müller should be informed right away. There was in fact a standing order to all detectives and department heads: any suspicion, information, or even the mere mention of Prestes's name in a deposition must be reported immediately to the chief of police.

Filinto Müller was pursuing Prestes for two reasons. First, as the dictatorship's feared and all-powerful chief of police, he was reminded daily by the president of the republic and his minister of justice, Vicente Rao, that his priority was to capture the commander of the fabled Column. Investigations had revealed Prestes to be the most important rebel leader, and he was the only big fish not yet in custody. Though the position of chief of police of the Federal District was in the lower echelons of the government hierarchy, the November insurrection had elevated Filinto Müller's power and importance to that of a prime minister. With his agents and spies placed in all government bureaus and ministries, he possessed information on the activities of all the influential people in the country. The rooting out of Moscow's Communists demanded weapons, manpower, equipment, and vehicles, and this turned the Rio police into a sinkhole of funds that Müller obtained personally from President Vargas and for which there were no limits. Every week the papers carried reports that the president had authorized thousands more contos de réis for "the battle against subversion." Filinto Müller was, really, part minister of war, part minister of justice, and part minister of information. And, without being minister of anything, he participated in cabinet meetings and talked on policy matters with the president. With the men, money, and information at Müller's disposal, only Vargas himself had more power than the chief of police of Rio de Janeiro.

Second, Filinto Müller was in pursuit of Prestes not as a policeman hunting a Communist, but as an ex-officer of the Prestes Column tracking down his former commander for a final settling of accounts. Almost eleven years before, on April 14, 1925, a revolutionary communiqué signed by General Miguel Costa, commander of the First Revolutionary Division, announced to the troops several promotions for "bravery, intelligence, and the capacity to command." The same decree that elevated Major Oswald Cordeiro de Farias to lieutenant colonel also promoted Captain Filinto Müller to the rank of major. Prestes justified Müller's promotion by arguing that it was necessary to have an officer in command of the available artillery: two seventy-five-millimeter cannons and two mountain cannons. And in addition, all the artillery troops and sergeants under Müller's command in the Osasco barracks in São Paulo had joined the Column.

Müller's promotion, as well as his very tenure in the Column, was short-lived, however. In just nine days Prestes realized he had chosen the wrong man. Müller wrote a letter to Miguel Costa, his immediate superior, announcing that he was on his way to Asunción, Paraguay, to visit his family, who lived in exile there, and promised to rejoin the Column in Mato Grosso. But he sent another letter as well, this one to the sergeants and troops who had been with him since the July 5 São Paulo uprising, proposing their collective desertion. He confessed that in his view it was all over; he had no hope for the success of the Column. The troops could do what they thought best, but as for him, from that point on he would no longer consider himself responsible for any of his subordinates. Filinto Müller never imagined that both letters would fall into Prestes's hands. By the time they did, though, the recently promoted major had fled to Argentina (not Paraguay, as he had announced), taking with him a hundred contos de réis of Column funds. Furious, Prestes demanded that General Costa immediately strip the deserter of his week-old promotion and issue a new communiqué expelling him from the Column. Before the day was out, Lourenço Moreira Lima, the field director of the Column, had in his hands the document Prestes had ordered.

Communiqué No. 5
Billet of Porto Mendes, State of Paraná
April 25, 1925

So that it be known to this division, and in execution of my duties, I hereby release the following Expulsion of an Officer:
Captain Filinto Müller is hereby excluded from active duty in the revolutionary forces for the cowardly act of crossing into Argentine territory, effectively abandoning the village of Foz do Iguaçú, which was under his guard, resulting in the loss of the enlisted men under his command who imitated him in this

shameful behavior, and took with them weapons and munitions that are property of the Revolution. I hope to God that this officer acquits himself in the eyes of his comrades, who still struggle in defense of the Republic, of this accusation which weighs heavily on the conscience of this son of our great nation.

> General Miguel Costa, Commander
> First Revolutionary Division

For eleven long years, Müller had fed his rage over the accusatory communiqué ordered by Prestes, which had called him cowardly, a deserter, and shameful. But fate had taken it upon herself to reverse their positions, and now, in February 1936, it was he who had the power, the men, the weapons. The chief of police had promised Vargas that he would deliver Prestes "in a matter of days." At a meeting with his division chiefs, Müller solemnly announced that whoever found Prestes first and brought him in—dead or alive—would receive a reward of one hundred contos de réis, to be paid by the captain himself. Ironically, this was the same amount that Müller had taken when he left the Column and went into exile in Argentina in 1925.

It was almost February, but Rio hardly seemed the "universal capital of gaiety and carnival," as some society editor had recently proclaimed. It had rained intermittently for weeks, draining the streets of the color and festivity of the carnival decorations. Laws counted for nothing: what mattered were the decrees Müller employed to make the 1936 carnival go down in history as the most dejected and joyless of all time. Early in January he had proclaimed that for the duration of the state of siege masks would be prohibited at public dances, carnival parties, and parades. People wore Hawaiian leis instead—which didn't have the same effect, but at least lent some color to the festivities. A few days before carnival came more decrees with more prohibitions: confetti fights would only be permitted at private clubs, with police authorization. Each club was allowed a maximum of three such fights. Not only were masks forbidden, but so were all costumes considered "offensive to family morals." Carnival parade rehearsals required authorization from

117

the chief of police and had to be over punctually at 10:00 P.M. Filinto Müller was trying to run the "universal capital of gaiety and carnival" with regulations fit for a convent.

But even a carnival without the traditional "fantasy" costumes and masks and with restrictions on the use of confetti was spectacle enough to a Bavarian German. From her tiny bedroom window Olga watched, delighted, as ragtag carnival groups passed by in defiance of police authority, dancing the samba down the middle of the street, wearing face paint and a minimum of clothes. The big, bulky radio Manoel dos Santos had managed to bring home played the few successful carnival songs of the year over and over again: "Querido Adão," a lively dance tune sung by Carmen Miranda, "É Bom Parar," and "A Marchinha do Grande Galo" (Dance of the Top Rooster), which made Olga laugh out loud, especially the part where the singer crooned "co-co-rico, co-co-rico." There wasn't much to do in the house on Rua Honório. Accustomed though they were to living underground since their arrival in Brazil, Olga and Prestes knew that this time it was different—they couldn't afford to take one step out of the house. Once the loudspeakers from the passing parade fell silent, the couple would lie down in their tiny room, and Olga would translate for Prestes, from the German, poems or passages from Goethe and Schiller, her favorite writers.

The house required special precautions to prevent their being seen and identified by neighbors. There were five small rooms: two sitting rooms, two bedrooms, and a kitchen. Since the garden walls were quite low and there were people living on both sides, Prestes and Olga could go to the outside lavatory only at night, crossing the garden in the shadows, having turned off all the outside lights beforehand. Their clothing—including the luxurious trousseau purchased in Paris—had been left behind in Ipanema, and improvisation was the order of the day. A length of linen purchased by Manoel's wife, dona Júlia, was transformed into an elegant dress designed and cut by Prestes and sewn by Olga.

Even living in such strict secrecy, they were not completely isolated from the world and from politics. Manoel arrived home every day with rolled newspapers under his arm containing small packets of bakery paper, which the couple opened and read avidly: messages sent by spies for the CP in prisons, police stations, and even in Filinto Müller's office. When the Prestes Column disbanded, hundreds of men had returned home to Brazil jobless. Lieutenant João Alberto, a member of the Column who decided in 1930 to side with Vargas, was appointed to the position that would later be Müller's: chief of police of the Federal District. And it fell to him, between 1932 and 1933, to place Column veterans in jobs as detectives and police officials—many of whom, still loyal to Prestes and his ideas, became informants for the CP inside the police force. From the building on Rua da Relacâo, where Captain Müller's office was located, from Santo Antônio Hill, or from the prison on Rua Frei Caneca, scribbled notes were sent to Ilvo Meirelles, who delivered them to Manoel dos Santos. Often, together with the summaries of depositions or warnings about a raid the police were planning, came notes from Prestes's friends who had no idea where to find him but knew who would. Rio's mayor, Pedro Ernesto, used these mysterious messages to offer Olga and Prestes a more secure hiding place. His proposal and those of many others, such as Virgílio de Mello Franco, a liberal congressman from Minas Gerais who offered his house to the couple several times, were rejected by Prestes, who explained his continued refusals to Olga in this way: "They're good people, but from the point of view of the authorities I just can't trust them. They could be tools of the authorities without knowing it. They may not know where we are now, but they would know where we're going."

An item in one of the newspapers Manoel brought home made Olga and Prestes very apprehensive. District Chief Lineu Costa had asked Captain Filinto Müller to investigate leaks of official reports and judicial documents regarding the insurrection. The police, obviously, were beginning to suspect that there were Communist spies within police precincts and within the special records offices established in each precinct to preserve the statements of political prisoners. It was through one of these informants, in fact, that Prestes learned that Filinto Müller was the man in charge of the combined police and military drive to find and arrest him and Olga. One of the messages smuggled to Prestes inside his daily paper reported that Getúlio Vargas had recently authorized reinforcements for the tomato heads—and that he was preparing a "fine-tooth-comb operation," with house-to-house searches. Müller knew that as a boy Prestes had lived for several years in the Boca do Mato neighborhood, near Meyer, so he decided to begin the hunt there. The informant assured Prestes that the only information the police had about the location of the safe house—provided by Barron and by a CP leader during torture sessions—was extremely vague. All they had said was that Olga and Prestes were hiding "in the vicinity of Meyer"—which would not be of much help. One last piece of news regarding the operation sounded to Prestes like some kind of prank: Müller had ordered the man in charge of the house-to-house search to take Olga's police dog, Prince, along with him as he worked, believing that the dog would help them track his owners by their scents.

Days later, an updated report arrived with information that was even more precise, and more worrying. After covering the entire neighborhood of Boca do Mato without results, the police would move on that very evening to search Meyer. Müller had divided the area into four sections, with a platoon of fifty tomato heads assigned to each. In addition to the two hundred tomato heads armed with machine guns, dozens of civil police patrolled street corners, checked local bars, and kept an eye out for suspicious activity of any kind. Müller gave express orders: they were to cover all the streets in Meyer and all the houses on those streets. Before knocking at the door of a house, soldiers should surround it to prevent anyone from escaping from the back or side doors. At the slightest suspicion that they had located the house in which Prestes and Olga were hiding, someone should fire a shot into the air, which would be the signal for all groups in the area to converge on the scene. Once it was confirmed that they had found the house, the order was to go in shooting.

Two weeks of searching Meyer produced scant results. A couple of "subversive" books had been found in one house, and on another occasion there was quite a stir when a man bolted out a back door to escape the police, but he turned out to be merely a common thief on the local wanted list. In the predawn hours of March 5, in torrential rain, fifty soldiers and three civil police commanded by José Torres Galvão (the "head jailer" who had taken Xanthaky to interrogate Ewert on Santo Antônio Hill) began searching the immediate area of Rua Honório. They started at the top of Rua En-

genho de Dentro, which was paved and flat. At around 2:00 A.M.
there was a small incident: a high-level court functionary lived in
one of the houses and he considered an invasion by troops at that
hour an infringement of his individual rights. Galvão radioed Müller, whose response was gruff: "Arrest the guy and anyone else who
objects to the searches." Every living room, bedroom, kitchen,
bathroom, and garden was rigorously examined. Old people,
women, and children were awakened so that Galvão could make
sure "the man" was not hiding in their houses. By 4:00 A.M. the
troops had made their way to the steep, unpaved end of the street.
The previous weeks' deluge had made a deep rut down the middle,
which ran with thick red mud. The soldiers had to climb the stretch
on foot; police cars that had ventured this far ended up stuck in mud
to their bumpers. At 5:00 A.M. a patrol arrived at number 279.
Repeating the maneuver they had been mechanically performing
day after day, ten soldiers surrounded the house while a small group
led by Galvão knocked loudly on the front door. Dona Júlia awoke,
alarmed, and asked through the door before releasing the latch,
"Who is it?"

From the other side Galvão replied, "The police. Open up."

She opened the door a crack and shrank back at the number of
weapons pointing in her face. One of the soldiers guarding the back
door shouted, "Galvão, someone's messing with the door back
here."

It was Prestes, still in pajamas and slippers, trying to escape.
When he heard the shout, he ducked inside and headed toward the
bedroom again, hoping to climb out the window and into the street.
There was no time. Galvão saw Prestes at the window and yelled to
the men at the front door: "Go in shooting. It's Prestes!"

An indeterminate number of soldiers and civil police shoved
dona Júlia aside and swarmed down the narrow corridor after
Prestes, their guns cocked. That was when something unexpected
occurred. A tall woman pushed her way in front of Prestes, shielding him with her body and shouting. And what came out of her
mouth was not a plea for mercy but an order: "Don't shoot! He's
unarmed!"

Olga's unexpected gesture paralyzed them. Perhaps because she
was a woman, perhaps because she yelled with such force—the fact

was that if there had been a chance of taking Prestes dead, they had missed it. Galvão fired his revolver into the air and seconds later the entire street was overrun by an army of soaking-wet men. Jullien appeared leading Prince; the dog immediately recognized his owners and began barking. Unruffled, Prestes simply asked Galvão to allow him to get dressed, but his request was turned down.

"We're taking you just as you are."

Out in the street, they tried to put the couple in separate cars, but Olga knew that would be a death sentence for Prestes. She clutched him so fiercely there was no alternative but to allow them to be transported to police headquarters together. The convoy of police cars roared through the city, waking people all along the way: sirens wailed, shots were fired into the air, while two hundred drenched soldiers swilled down bottles of cane liquor in the backs of the trucks.

The anticipated arrival of Prestes, Olga, and dona Júlia plunged headquarters into a state of uproar. Men armed with machine guns guarded all the doors as well as all roads leading to the building, and Captain Correia awaited the procession at the main entrance, surrounded by bodyguards. He had already informed Filinto Müller of Prestes's arrest, but Müller decided not to be present when his old commander was brought in. Instead, he called President Vargas with the good news and then went back to sleep.

As soon as they stepped out of the car in the inner courtyard of police headquarters, Olga and Prestes were separated. Captain Correia announced they would each be taken upstairs to give their statements. Encircled by armed guards, Prestes was ushered into a tiny elevator. As the gate closed, the two looked at each other for the last time.

12

The Police "Suicide" Barron

LIEUTENANT EUSÉBIO DE QUEIROZ FILHO, chief of the tomato heads, gave Prestes the news just minutes after he arrived at police headquarters. And he did so with a provocative smile: "You might as well know that it was the American, Victor Barron, who informed on you. But it looks like the gringo's conscience really got to him, because he ended up jumping out of the window and killing himself."

The first suspicion that Barron had not committed suicide but had been killed by the police arose from a statement made by Müller only hours later. During a press conference covering the details of the arrest of Prestes and Olga, Müller made a slip and revealed that Barron had died without divulging the address of the couple's last hideout. This confirmed the fact that despite the violence inflicted on him, the American had provided nothing more than the vague information that he had driven them "close to Meyer." Müller was precise in his disclosure: "Barron was persistent in his denials. He was a man experienced in handling difficult situations and accustomed to confronting and confusing the police.

He admitted to nothing beyond having driven Luís Carlos Prestes to the Meyer district."

If Barron had not denounced Prestes—and Prestes doubted from the beginning that he had—then why would he kill himself? Why the self-loathing? Among reporters at the press conference was a correspondent of the Associated Press wire service, who asked another as yet unanswered question: how could someone kill himself by jumping out of a second-story window that didn't even look out over the street but rather an inner patio, which effectively reduced the fall to only one story? The foreign correspondent's subsequent article in U.S. newspapers contained several more disconcerting questions. Perhaps a one-story fall could conceivably have caused Barron's death, if he had landed on the concrete and fractured his skull—but the death certificate signed by Dr. Borges de Mendonça and delivered to the U.S. embassy gave the cause of death as "a fractured rib, causing rupture of the lungs and the left kidney, accompanied by internal bleeding." Without incriminating anyone by name, the reporters commented among themselves that these were injuries typical of someone who had been severely beaten.

Prestes was incensed over the news of Barron's "suicide." As he was being booked, he was gruff with detectives and investigators, reacting to their questions with monosyllables or, more often, by simply refusing to make any response at all. When the clerk asked him his profession, he said curtly, "Captain in the army."

The clerk corrected him. "Don't you mean ex-captain?"

"No, I don't!" he replied, irritated. "I am a captain in the Brazilian army."

Surrounded by the head honchos of the Security Police—Eurico Bellens Porto, Hymalaia Virgolino, Miranda Correia, Canavarro Pereira—Prestes made it clear during his first few minutes of captivity that they would get no information out of him, a decision he resolutely maintained until the last moment of his long years in prison. When District Chief Porto asked what his role had been in the November 27 insurrection, Prestes said, "I have nothing to say with regard to that."

"But where were you on November 27?"

"I have no comment with regard to that."

"What is your connection with Mr. Harry Berger, or Arthur Ernst Ewert?"

"I have nothing to tell you. The only subject I can comment on is the Prestes Column. Everything I have to say about my recent activities, I said in my last public manifestos."

Finally, Bellens Porto handed him the last page of his "statement" to sign. Prestes again became irritated. "I'm not signing this! The only way I'll sign is if I can initial all the previous pages, so you can't slip in extra pages of things I didn't say."

It was the first time a prisoner had used that tone at police headquarters. The detectives agreed to his request. When he had initialed each page, he signed the last one and declared, disgusted, for everyone to hear, "This is all just a joke, anyway!"

The only person who didn't have the courage to confront Prestes face to face was Filinto Müller. The chief of police arrived at his office early and discreetly peeked into the room where Prestes was being interrogated by his subordinates, but did not want to be seen. Captain Müller did permit an exceptional visit by two outsiders: Majors Cordeiro de Farias and Riograndino Kruel, Column veterans who arrived at police headquarters early in the morning to talk with their ex-commander. After they had gone, Prestes remarked bitterly, "I know very well they didn't come here in solidarity, but merely to verify that it's really me."

Sitting in his office, Müller was savoring his victory. Vicente Rao, the minister of justice, stopped by with Vargas's congratulations to Müller and the men who had captured Prestes. Rao, Müller with Olga's dog, Prince, at his feet, Correia, and Galvão posed for press photographers beside the chief's desk, on top of which sat a box of material confiscated from the house on Rua Honório. After the visit, Müller composed a telegram to be sent to all state governors:

I HAVE THE HONOR OF COMMUNICATING TO YOUR
EXCELLENCY THAT THE DILIGENCE OF THE FEDERAL
DISTRICT POLICE WAS TODAY REWARDED BY THE CAPTURE
OF COMMUNIST LEADER LUÍS CARLOS PRESTES,
APPREHENDED ALONG WITH A COPIOUS ARCHIVE OF
SUBVERSIVE MATERIALS.
CORDIALLY,
FILINTO MÜLLER
CHIEF OF POLICE

Müller's use of the word "copious" to describe the amount of material accumulated by Prestes and Olga in their short time on Rua Honório was no exaggeration. There were boxes and more boxes of letters, papers, documents, manifestos, and receipts, the contents of which were eloquently summarized in one of the arrest documents:

. . . a map of the Federal District; a proclamation to members of the Twenty-second Batallion and the police affiliated with the movement; a proclamation to the workers, peasants, soldiers, students, small businessmen, and oppressed people of Pernambuco; a leaflet printed on pink paper entitled "We trim the nails of the thieves who steal from the people"; a calling card imprinted "Antônio Vilar, Lisbon"; a proclamation on pink paper entitled "We will free Harry Berger who, along with his wife, is being tortured mercilessly at police headquarters"; a proclamation printed on green paper to officers and sergeants in the army; five mimeographed sheets entitled "The Revolution has Begun!"; a circular on white paper entitled "Harry Berger, Great Fighter against Fascism and Anti-warrior"; three mimeographed sheets entitled "Central Committee Resolutions on the Communists' Task in Preparing and Realizing the National Revolution"; two typed sheets entitled "In the face of police provocations directed by the Intelligence Service and the fascist reaction of the traitorous and tyrannical government of Vargas and his accomplices, We raise high the Flag of the Struggle for the Liberation of Brazil"; a mimeographed sheet entitled "Instructions for Work with Unions and the Preparation of Strikes during the Present State of Siege"; a sheet of foolscap paper with blue-lined borders, beginning with the hand-written phrase "he recognizes a note he wrote to Berger under the pseudonym GIN"; four mimeographed sheets with the admissions made to the police by Adalberto de Andrade Fernandes; an identification document used to request a visa in the names Antônio Vilar and Maria Bergner, with two photographs in the margin, stamped by the Brazilian consulate in Buenos Aires; a Portuguese passport granted to Antônio Vilar and his wife, Maria Bergner Vilar, March 8, 1935, in Rouen, France; roughly one hundred letters in French and Portuguese, signed by "amigo Gar," "amigo Cleto," "Amiguinha," "Prado," "Mel," "Souza," "G.," "B.," and "amigo S."; a typed page entitled "Copy of report regarding Garota's responses at the last interrogation," signed "M.," in pen; two typed sheets entitled "Garota's Responses."

Not much money was found at the house on Rua Honório: a little more than 1,000 Dutch guilders and $162 U.S. A small fortune already lay in police safes—the dollars, pesos, French francs, guilders, German marks, and pounds sterling confiscated from foreigners who had been taken into custody or from various other safe houses. But it wasn't money the police were looking for. In the mass of paper found in Meyer, Filinto Müller discovered something much more valuable—pieces to a puzzle that, once solved, would allow him to charge Prestes with a crime that carried a greater penalty than any that could be imposed on him for leading the Communist insurrection. Analyzing questionnaires and reports found at Rua Honório, the police began to unearth evidence about what the press called the "red tribunal"—the process by which the leadership of the CP condemned to death and executed Miranda's young wife, Elvira Cupelo Colônio, also known as "Garota," or "Elza Fernandes."

It was never clear whether Elvira was mentally unbalanced or, as the Communist leadership concluded, simply a traitor who had betrayed them to the police. To many of the other prisoners in the House of Detention where she was interned, Elvira was simply an adolescent from the interior, overwhelmed by Rio de Janeiro and the notoriety of being married to the highest officer of the Communist Party. Maria Werneck de Castro, a lawyer accused of involvement in the rebellion and one of Elvira's cellmates in the women's wing, was shocked to hear her reveal what happened to the money she collected from militants as contributions to the Party. Laughing and scandalizing the other prisoners, Elvira said, "Maria, you know when I came to your house to pick up some money, and told you Miranda sent me? Well, the money wasn't for the Party—it was so that I could buy some new towels! But that's the same thing anyway, right? Aren't we all Communists?"

Whether she was unbalanced, unprepared, or an agent of the other side, the police tried to get as much as they could from Elvira. The House of Detention's register of bookings and releases showed one thing for certain: without any apparent explanation, Elvira Cupelo Colônio was released innumerable times, only to be arrested again two or three days later. Carmen Ghioldi, Maria Werneck de Castro, Nise da Silveira, and others took her firmly in hand and explained that the police were only letting her out so that she could lead them to other safe houses, but Elvira ignored their warnings. Every time she was released half a dozen more Communist leaders fell into Filinto Müller's hands. And since the police, with unusual generosity, allowed her regular visits to her husband in his cell in the House of Corrections, the Party began to be suspicious of him as well.

Even before Olga and Prestes were arrested, the leadership had decided to get to the bottom of the situation once and for all. On one of Elvira's releases from prison, the Party spirited her away and into the custody of Francisco Meirelles, in his house on the Guaratiba highway. Since Vallée was one of the few foreigners still at large, he was given the task of putting together a series of questions to be put to her during the subsequent inquiry. Vallée wrote them out in French, and they were delivered by hand to the other four members of the National Secretariat assigned to the case: General Secretary Lauro Reginaldo da Rocha ("Bangu"), Honório de Freitas Guimarães ("Milionário"), Adelino Deícola dos Santos ("Tampinha"), and José Lago Molares ("Brito"). Questions and answers went back and forth for two weeks, after which the leadership concluded that Elvira had effectively collaborated with the police in exchange for the promise that she and her husband would be freed and sent to his home state, Bahia, where they dreamed of living together. The result of the "inquest" was delivered to Olga and Prestes at their hideout in Meyer along with two notes from "Miranda," in which he complained and expressed concern about his wife, who hadn't visited him for many days. The Party leadership decided these notes were fakes, "undoubtedly concocted by the police to throw us off the track," said Milionário. As for Elvira's "trial," Prestes was tough. If the Party had concluded that she was in fact a traitor, "why such vacillation in carrying out the . . . decision?" he wrote in a secret note to the leadership:

I was painfully surprised by your vacillation and lack of decisiveness. This is no way to lead the Party of the Proletariat, the Party of the Revolutionary class. . . . I've already expressed my opinion with respect to what we should do. Why change the decision? Has she or has she not betrayed us?

Elvira's fate was sealed. The decision to carry out the sentence was made at a meeting attended by Milionário, Eduardo Ribeiro Xavier ("Abóbora"), Tampinha, Bangu, Manoel Severino Cavalcanti ("Gaguinho"), and Francisco Natividade Lyra ("Cabeção"). In late February Elvira was moved to a more secluded location, where Milionário, Gaguinho, Tampinha, Abóbora, and Cabeção were waiting. At dusk, as Elvira talked with the group in a small back room of the house, Cabeção cut a piece of rope from a clothesline in the garden, then came back inside and sat down next to her. In one quick move he slipped the rope around her neck and tightened it. Elvira tried to struggle to her feet, but Cabeção, an enormous man, knocked her to the ground and jumped on top of her. Once she had been subdued, the whole group—except for Abóbora, who sat in a corner of the room vomiting—participated in strangling her. The body was carried to another room, where Cabeção enlisted the help of the others to fold it in two, head to toe. The sound of the bones breaking was horrifying, but in this position the body fit inside a gunnysack. Elvira was buried in the garden under a tree.

While the suspicion that Elvira had been murdered provoked a sensation in the pro-government Brazilian press, the Rio and São Paulo newspapers accepted without question the police version of Victor Barron's death as a suicide. The story appeared on the front pages of the most important American daily newspapers, however, because the Associated Press insisted on discovering the true circumstances of his death and because of the clamor raised by Barron's mother, Edna Hill, and various U.S. intellectuals.

On March 6, Edna Hill received a telegram—collect—just one paragraph long, from the U.S. Secretary of State.

I REGRET TO INFORM YOU AMERICAN AMBASSADOR, RIO DE JANEIRO, BRAZIL, TELEGRAPHICALLY REPORTS YOUR SON, VICTOR A. BARRON, SUCCEEDED EVADING HIS GUARD AND COMMITTED SUICIDE MARCH 5, BY PLUNGING INTO PAVED AREA OF COURTYARD TWO STORIES BELOW.
CORDELL HULL
SECRETARY OF STATE

If Edna Hill had read the *New York Times* that morning, she would have learned more about the tragedy, sooner and in an even less palatable form. The *Times* ran the story pretty much as it had been released to the American press, publishing in effect the Brazilian police version:

RED BETRAYS CHIEF AND KILLS HIMSELF

RIO DE JANEIRO, March 5—Despondent because he had given the information leading to the arrest of Luís Carlos Prestes, alleged leader of the radical revolt last November, Victor Allen Barron, 27 years old, an American, committed suicide here today by throwing himself from the second floor of police headquarters.

His skull was fractured and he was rushed to an emergency hospital, where he died soon afterward.

Barron, according to the United States Embassy here, . . . arrived in Brazil last June, describing himself alternately as a radio operator and a salesman. The local police describe him as a Communist who . . . participated in the revolt by driving an automobile for the rebels, chiefly conveying Prestes from one point to another.

It was stated at the United States Embassy that he had been well treated by the police and that authorities had promised him he would be deported to the United States today provided he would divulge the hiding place of Prestes.

After hours of questioning, Barron put his finger on a map of Rio de Janeiro, pointing to the suburb of Meyer, where the alleged leader of the revolt, a former captain in the Brazilian Army, was later captured.

The arrest of Prestes was effected largely by his police dog. The police had found the dog, which they knew to be Prestes's, in the house of Harry Berger, alleged American Communist, whom they arrested in December. It led them to the house where Prestes was and leaped upon its master.

Prestes, known as the "Bearded Knight of Hope," had shaved off his whiskers while in hiding. He was found after more than 100 police, uniformed and plainclothes, had drawn a cordon around the suburb.

Reprinted at first only by the *Washington Star*, the AP story had major ramifications in the United States. Suspicion that something was wrong with it surfaced the following day in many papers, prompting a public outcry demanding that the government call for an investigation of the true cause of Barron's death. Edna Hill convinced Senator Albert Carter to request Secretary of State Hull to intervene through the American diplomatic corps in Rio. Not satisfied with this, Edna Hill wrote to President Franklin Roosevelt the same day.

Dear President Roosevelt,

Will you please investigate the cause of my son's death in Rio de Janeiro, Brazil. Somehow (I cannot believe he would take his own life, unless the punishment inflicted on him was too great to bear) I know that if he had a chance to come home, that he would have sacrificed anything to do so.

He loved his home and people.

I cannot understand why I have been told three stories concerning his death, one from the press, one from the Brazilian ambassador and the other from Albert E. Carter, Senator.

Can you find out if he has left any word for his mother? And another thing, Mr. Roosevelt, I would like to call your attention to when I received telegrams of my son's death, officially I had to pay before I could receive the message, besides being grief stricken. I also found myself in an embarrassing situation.

I am only writing this in a last hope to find out just what did happen to cause my young son's death, he was 26 years old.

I also would like to know if there was any scar on his leg as I have no chance to identify him in any way as my son.

Very respectfully yours,

Mrs. Edna Hill
1023 44th Ave.
Oakland, Calif.

The third version of the story, which Edna Hill attributed to Senator Carter, derived from the suspicions raised in the press— that there were no apparent reasons for Barron to commit suicide and that, even had he tried, it would be impossible for a fall of less than two meters to cause such serious injuries. President Roosevelt immediately assigned both problems—responding to Edna Hill's letter and to the clamor in the U.S. Congress—to Cordell Hull's desk. A commission was set up to investigate not just the true cause of Barron's death but also the American embassy's failure to protect a U.S. citizen. Chaired by attorney Charles Arthur, grandson of President Chester Arthur, the commission was full of prominent names, including Jeanette Rankin, the first woman to win a seat in the American Congress; writers Malcolm Cowley, John Dos Passos, Sherwood Anderson, Crane Brinton, Lillian Hellman, Theodore Dreiser, and Upton Sinclair; composer Aaron Copland; historian Waldo Frank; and linguist Edward Sapir, among others. The group reported to Roosevelt and to Hull, insisting that the government place a statement in Washington and New York newspapers in which the U.S. ambassador to Brazil, Hugh Gibson, was accused of collaboration with the Rio police. "We are inclined to hold Ambassador Gibson at least partially responsible for the situation leading to Mr. Barron's 'suicide,'" the commission declared in their extensive report, which concluded with some very serious accusations:

> Out of all the conflicting accounts, one fact stands out clear as crystal. Whether Barron did or did not give information which aided the police in arresting Prestes; whether Barron was murdered outright or whether he was tortured and harassed until he could no longer endure life, this much is certain: the American Embassy in Brazil, instead of performing its duty to this American citizen, instead of protecting him from police methods which smack of the medieval Inquisition and "Star Chamber," actually aided or attempted to give aid to the police of a foreign power against an American citizen. The American Embassy in Brazil stands indicted as a partner to the crime along with the brutal police of President Getúlio Vargas. Is America negotiating with a free and independent Brazil or is America engaging in a conquest? Is this the good neighbor policy in diplomacy? The American people want to know.

Congress approved a petition sponsored by Congressman Vito Marcantonio to mount a congressional commission of inquiry to investigate whether the American embassy had collaborated in the circumstances surrounding Barron's death. Less than a week later, Congress adopted Resolution 243, obliging the U.S. State Department to provide, "with the utmost urgency," the following information to Congress:

First. All facts pertaining to the death of one Victor A. Barron, an American citizen, who met his death while in the custody of the police at Rio de Janeiro, Brazil, on or about March 5, 1936.

Second. What was done by Honorable Hugh S. Gibson, American Ambassador to Brazil, to protect the American citizen, Victor A. Barron.

Third. Did Honorable Hugh S. Gibson, American Ambassador to Brazil, aid and abet in the arrest or questioning of Victor A. Barron?

Fourth. Did Honorable Hugh S. Gibson, American Ambassador to Brazil, or his agents, question said Victor A. Barron while said Victor A. Barron was in the custody of the Brazilian police for the purpose of obtaining information relating to Victor A. Barron's political activities?

Fifth. Any and all information with respect to the conduct of Honorable Hugh S. Gibson, American Ambassador to Brazil, and his agents, in connection with the arrest and death of Victor A. Barron.

Congressman Alexander Johnson of Texas, a right-winger who had tried in every way possible to obstruct the formation of the commission of inquiry to begin with, managed to convince the full House to restrict the request for information to the participation of the American embassy in Barron's death, preventing Congress from seeking the truth about the central question: Had Barron committed suicide or had he died as a result of being tortured? Even so, Congress required Secretary of State Hull to provide Congressman Sam McReynolds, chairman of the Foreign Affairs Committee of the House of Representatives, with a detailed report on the embassy's involvement in the so-called Brazilian connection of the international Communist movement. Since the investigation was limited to the involvement of Hugh Gibson and his agents, the State Department's answers were deemed satisfactory, and on March 26 the House approved a resolution sponsored by Johnson calling for the closing of the investigation.

But the U.S. decision to put the "Barron case" on ice did not relieve the international pressure on Brazil. News of Arthur and Elise Ewert's torture at the hands of Brazilian authorities was leaked to the press—the foreign press, of course, since Brazilian newspapers, without exception (including those not sympathetic to Getúlio Vargas), had become mouthpieces of the government. In their zeal to please the Vargas regime, the Brazilian media embraced anticommunism and anti-Semitism and nourished among the population a real hatred for foreigners in general, and Communists and Jews in particular. Any foreigner who wasn't a Jew became one by association. *O Globo* gave the news of Ewert's arrest a scandalous eight-column headline on the front page:

SON OF ISRAEL AND AGENT OF MOSCOW! THE EMISSARY OF
THE COMINTERN LIVED IN A GREEN BUNGALOW IN
COPACABANA, WITH MONEY AND INSTRUCTIONS FOR THE
RED REVOLUTION! HARRY BERGEN, STALIN'S
REPRESENTATIVE! APPREHENDED ALONG WITH HIM, THE
NATIONAL LIBERATION ALLIANCE FILES AND A SAFE-
CONDUCT PASS FOR ENTRY INTO GOVERNMENT BUREAUS!

Ewert had never used the name Bergen, was not a Jew, had not been arrested in Copacabana, was in fact an adversary of Stalin, and didn't have a pass for entry into a bureau of any kind—but none of that mattered. What was essential was to foster in the population the idea of a monstrous Jewish-Communist conspiracy that came from abroad—it didn't matter where—to enslave Brazil.

Over and above repeated condemnations of torture made by members of the National Congress, including the deputy from Paraná, Otávio da Silveira, and a senator from Pará, Abel Chermont— which the press, with Olympian detachment, simply ignored—a single incident between Captain Filinto Müller and a small group of Britons helped to mobilize European public opinion in defense of the Ewerts. Early in March, Marian Cameron Campbell and Christine Hastings, wives of members of the House of Commons in London, had arrived in Rio with their secretary, Richard Freeman. Disembarking at the port, the women announced to the press that they had come in the name of the democratic institutions of their country to investigate claims of torture against political prisoners, particularly foreigners, in Brazil. Advised of their arrival by reporters, Captain Müller went to the Hotel Glória to meet them and, after deciding that their trip was "sponsored by Moscow," put the two women under house arrest in the hotel, guarded by two policemen, and ordered that their terrified secretary be thrown into jail.

This situation lasted four days, until the threat of an international incident spurred Britain's ambassador to Brazil to insist that the three be released to set sail immediately on the *Arlanza,* which was about to leave for Europe.

The repercussions could not have been worse. Several weeks later the *New Statesman and Nation* printed an article entitled "A Brazilian Misadventure," in which the unfortunate tourists gave their version of the treatment of prisoners in Brazil—a version no doubt colored by what Richard Freeman had witnessed in the cells on Santo Antônio Hill and by the Ewert case.

The article stirred things up in England: a confidential telegram from the Brazilian ambassador, Régis de Oliviera, informed his foreign minister, José Carlos de Macedo Soares, that the Brazilian embassy in London had received "innumerable letters from members of Parliament and other important people regarding rumors about police abuse of a certain Arthur Ewert, ex-member of the Reichstag, and his wife." The letter-writing campaign, continued the diplomat, was apparently inspired "by a certain Minna Ewert, resident of London, who claims to be a sister of the alleged victim." Régis de Oliviera implored Macedo Soares for more detailed information about the couple. While Arthur Ewert was on the brink of madness, prisoner in a veritable cave of a cell whose ceiling was about twenty inches lower than his height, the letter from the Brazilian foreign minister in response to the request from the embassy in London was a model of lies and dissimulation:

> Arthur Ewert, or Harry Berger, and his wife, Elise Saborowsky [*sic*] Ewert, or Machla Berger, have been prisoners in Rio de Janeiro since December of last year, but any rumors that they have been victims of torture by the police authorities here are completely unfounded. The police, acting with maximum dedication, have not needed to employ violent means, much preferring more humanitarian measures, which, it may be added, are the only hope of defeating tyranny.
>
> Well aware of the nefarious work being undertaken in our country by Moscow's agents—Brazilians and foreigners alike— the Brazilian government is only concerned with defending the nation by means of all that is strong in us, upholding the law and

pursuing, in their lairs, all those who try to subvert order and attack our institutions.

The police have granted to Berger and his wife, as they have to all Communist prisoners in Brazil, full medical and judicial protection. Nevertheless, Berger has persisted in going on a hunger strike, for fear of being poisoned. He has, for this reason, lost a considerable amount of weight, leading to a natural weakening of his general condition. A medical team designated to examine him has confirmed that Berger is in perfect health and merely needs to eat properly.

Berger's wife, Elise Ewert, is also in good health; her deportation papers came through some days ago. Prestes's so-called wife, Maria Bergner Vilar, who also uses the name Olga Prestes, is also to be deported from Brazilian territory.

José Carlos de Macedo Soares
Minister of Foreign Affairs

ЛУИС КАРЛОС ПРЕСТЕС — ГЕРОЙ БРАЗИЛЬСКОГО НАРОДА

ЛАСЕРДА

This article, published in the Moscow daily *Pravda* in August 1935, reported that Prestes, recently elected to the leadership of the Comintern, was in the Soviet capital—but it was only an attempt to confuse Brazilian and British intelligence. In fact, since early that year, Prestes had been in Rio preparing for the insurrection. (*A Noite*)

Prestes and Olga left Moscow and crossed the world using false identities. After obtaining an entry visa for Brazil in Buenos Aires, they left Montevideo on the Latécoère company's hydroplane *Santos Dumont*, headed for Praia Grande in the state of São Paulo. (SMT; MAF)

Rodolfo Ghioldi. (ARG)

Experienced Comintern agent Arthur Ernst Ewert (left) and his wife, Elise (top right), left Shanghai with false U.S. passports and joined the group Moscow had sent to Brazil to help Luís Carlos Prestes organize the Communist revolt of November 27, 1935. (SMT; SMT)

On the eve of the revolt, Prestes gave a "safe-conduct" to Harry Berger. (SMT)

Until the revolt in Rio de Janeiro, Ewert's FBI file contained nothing but a 1930 letter from J. Edgar Hoover to the State Department, questioning whether the German Communist had been in the United States in 1927. (NA, D.C.)

Though the government managed to contain the revolt early on November 27, the newspaper *A Manhã* described a "national insurrection" that never happened. Below: The facade of the Third Infantry Regiment building, taken by the rebels during the first hours of November 27 and partly destroyed by government forces. (ITR; ITR)

Victor Allen Barron. A telegram from U.S. Secretary of State Cordell Hull informed Barron's mother that her son had committed suicide in Rio. (NA, D.C.; NA, D.C.)

Department of State

Washington,

March 6, 1936.

Mrs. Edna Hill,

    1023 - 44th Avenue,

        Oakland, California.

    I regret to inform you American Ambassador, Rio de Janeiro, Brazil, telegraphically reports your son, Victor A. Barron succeeded evading his guard and committed suicide March fifth by plunging into paved area of patio two stories below.

Secretary of State.

Barron, Victor A./18

EKT

FA

LA

332.113-BAARON, VICTOR A

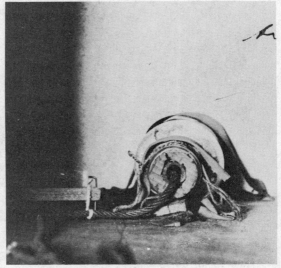

German Paul Gruber installed an explosives system in Olga and Prestes's house on Rua Barão da Torre in Ipanema to protect Party documents from the police. The failure of the system raised suspicions about Gruber's loyalty. (SMT; SMT)

When the revolt failed, the repressions began. Here, rebel soldiers are taken to the prison on the Isle of Flowers by the hundreds. (ITR)

Armed with pistols, machine guns, and rifles, the Special Police "tomato heads" sweep the streets of Rio. (ITR)

Wearing pajamas, Captain Agildo Barata, who headed the revolt at the Third Infantry Regiment, is led off to give a deposition to military police. (ITR)

Surrounded by Special Police, Prestes is taken prisoner as Filinto Müller's manhunt comes to an end. (ARG)

The fake passport in which Olga and Prestes are identified as "Maria" and "Antonio"; it was confiscated on their arrest. (SMT)

Escorted by police to make a deposition, Olga announced to reporters that she was expecting a child by Prestes: "The government is going to commit an injustice against a pregnant woman." (ITR)

Elvira Colônio, aka "Garota" (left), put to death by order of the leadership of the Communist Party on suspicion of betrayal, and her husband, "Miranda" (below), a Communist leader who became a police collaborator. (ITR; SMT)

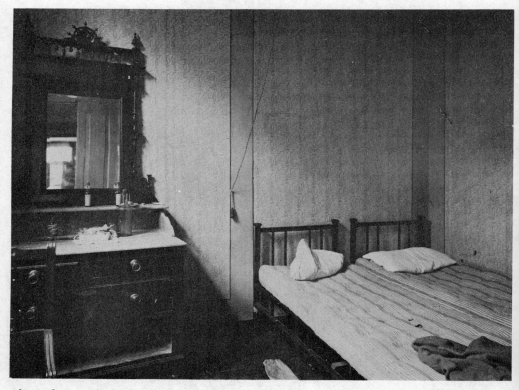

Olga and Prestes's room in the house on Rua Honório, where they were arrested in early March. (ITR)

The rebels in prison. From left to right, first row, seated: Socrates Goncalves, Alvaro de Souza, Benedito Carvalho; second row, seated: Pedroso, Agliberto Vieira, Gutman; standing: Aires, David, Ivan Ribeiro, Leivas Otero, Picasso, Rodolfo Ghioldi, Agildo Barata, Moraes Rego, unidentified, Ilvo Meirelles, unidentified. (ARG)

Filinto Müller (in bow tie) sifts through the documents found in the house on Rua Honório. (ITR)

POLICIA CIVIL DO DISTRITO FEDERAL

DELEGACIA ESPECIAL DE SEGURANÇA POLITICA E SOCIAL

DO DELEGADO

Recebi d. Delegacia de Segurança Politica e Social e por ordem de Luiz
Carlos Prestes a importancia de $ 150.00
(cento e cincoenta dollars americanos).-

Rio, 23/9/1936

Maria Prestes

Above: The last document signed by Olga as "Maria Prestes" before she was deported. Left: Prestes is interrogated at Special Police headquarters on Santo Antônio Hill. (SMT; ITR)

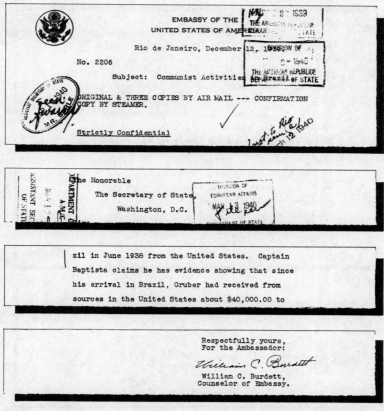

Through the Brazilian embassy in London, the British government requests information on Paul Gruber. (NA, RdJ)

EMBASSY OF THE
UNITED STATES OF AMERICA

Rio de Janeiro, December 12, 1939

No. 2206

Subject: Communist Activities

ORIGINAL & THREE COPIES BY AIR MAIL --- CONFIRMATION COPY BY STEAMER.

Strictly Confidential

The Honorable
    The Secretary of State,
        Washington, D.C.

zil in June 1938 from the United States. Captain
Baptista claims he has evidence showing that since
his arrival in Brazil, Gruber had received from
sources in the United States about $40,000.00 to

Respectfully yours,
For the Ambassador:

William C. Burdett,
Counselor of Embassy.

In 1940, after Gruber has been arrested and then released in Brazil, the American embassy in Rio reveals that he may have received $40,000 from U.S. sources. (NA, D.C.)

N? 145.   Berlim, 24 de Abril de 1936.

Confidencial.

A propaganda communista
no Brasil.

de Berlim.   Respeitosamente devo insistir, a pedido das autoridades da "Gestapo", afim que de futuro esse facto seja evitado.

Prestes.   Depois de apuradas syndicancias o serviço secreto al-
lemão informou-me ter podido identificar Maria Prestes que ahi-
se intitula esposa de Luiz Carlos Prestes.

4.   Para que Vossa Excellencia possa avaliar do tra-
balho feito é bastante indicar que a "Gestapo" consultou 25.000
photographias e 60.000 fichas até conseguir estabelecer precisa-
mente a identidade daquella mulher.

6.   Pelas informações agora obtidas, e como referi
no meu telegramma n? 40, Olga Meirelles, Olga Villar, Maria
Bergner ou Maria Prestes, citada nos jornaes brasileiros como
esposa de Luiz Carlos Prestes, pode ser identificada como sendo
Olga Benario, agente communista da III Internacional deveras
efficiente, de grande intelligencia e coragem.

            Olga Benario é de raça israelita tendo nascido
em 12 de Fevereiro de 1908, em Munich, na Baviera.   Desde o
anno de 1925 que Olga Benario é conhecida da policia allemã

de estar ou ter estado Braun no nosso paiz.

16.   Tenho procurado exercer uma severa vigilancia no
serviço de vistos em passaportes de viajantes que se destinam a
portos brasileiros.

17.   Na maioria esses individuos são judeus e se apre-
sentam como turistas exhibindo passagens de 1a. classe e certi-
ficados bancarios quasi todos concedidos pelo "Iwria Bank" desta

25.   Rogo a Vossa Excellencia levar o que precede ao
conhecimento de nossas autoridades competentes, salientando o
caracter estrictamente confidencial com o qual me foram trans-
mittidas as alludidas informações.

            Aproveito o ensejo para renovar a Vossa Excel-
lencia os protestos da minha respeitosa consideração.

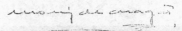

In an official letter to Itamaraty, the Brazilian ambassador in Berlin
transmits the Gestapo's information identifying the woman arrested
with Prestes as Olga Benario. (HAMFAB)

13

The Brazilian Ambassador and the Gestapo

OLGA WAS WELL AWARE that she was in danger of being deported. During her ten days at police headquarters she heard that since the failed insurrection Getúlio Vargas had sent hundreds of "undesirable aliens" back to Europe. But she also knew there was one thing in her favor: her true identity remained a secret. The police knew only her first name, which had surfaced during Rodolfo Ghioldi's interrogation. Throughout a week and a half of questioning, she had refused to give the authorities any information whatsoever and irritatingly repeated the same answers again and again.

"Name?"

"Maria Bergner Vilar."

"Nationality?"

"Brazilian."

Despite her thick accent, she said this firmly and naturally. The police pressed her.

137

"What? Brazilian?"

"Yes, Brazilian. I'm married to Luís Carlos Prestes, who is Brazilian. Therefore, I am Brazilian."

At first the press identified her as Olga Meirelles, sister of Lieutenant Sylo Meirelles, one of Prestes's comrades in the revolt. The next story confidently asserted that her real name was Olga Berger [*sic*] and that she had been born in Ostend, Belgium. She had met Prestes when she was working for the Soviet Union's trading company in Brussels, and the couple had been married in Montevideo, en route to Brazil. A "major scoop" in the daily *O Estado de São Paulo* insisted that Prestes's wife was Olga Jazikoff Pandarsky, an extremist arrested months earlier in São Paulo and deported by presidential decree.

The mystery surrounding Olga's real name and background was soon dispelled, however. The Brazilian embassy in Berlin maintained close, friendly relations with the Gestapo, and Ambassador José Joaquim Moniz de Aragão regularly passed on to his superiors in Itamaraty precious information obtained from Gestapo headquarters. Aragão's spontaneous contributions took the form of reports on the activities of the so-called international subversion in Europe. The Brazilian diplomat took particular delight in identifying those who were, as he put it, "Israelites." A few days after the arrest of Olga and Prestes, a long official letter from Aragão arrived at the Ministry of Foreign Affairs, addressed to Foreign Minister Macedo Soares and marked "confidential":

Dear Minister:

As an addendum to my official letter no. 136 of the 16th of this month, I sent Your Excellency telegram no. 40, dated the 23rd, summarizing information given to me in strictest confidence by the German secret police. Upon making this information available, the German authorities reminded me more than once of the inconvenience that would arise should the origin of said confidential communication be made public, since this could prejudice the operations of informants and expose them to reprisals from agents of the Third International. The files on Harry Berger that I obtained from the German secret police . . . were published by the majority of the newspapers in Rio and other states, complete with the disclosure of the fact that they had been furnished by the German police. Considering the absolute confidentiality requested, this event met with an unpleasant reaction here, and I confess that I was astonished to see this information reproduced in *A Noite* and *O Globo* without reference to their origin being expunged. I must respectfully insist, at the request of the German authorities of the Gestapo, that this be avoided in the future. Since it is a matter of our own interest as well, I am certain that Your Excellency will intervene in the most effective manner to comply with this request.

After first reading newspaper accounts of the arrest of Luís Carlos Prestes and a woman who, as far as I can tell, our police have until now been unable to identify positively, I contacted the Gestapo, furnishing them with several photographs from the Brazilian press of the woman who calls herself Maria Meirelles, Maria Bergner Vilar, and Maria Prestes. After an exhaustive investigation, the German secret police informed me they had been successful in identifying Maria Prestes, who calls herself Luís Carlos Prestes's wife. So that Your Excellency may have an idea of the work involved in this investigation, suffice it to say that the Gestapo consulted 25,000 photographs and 60,000 files before establishing the woman's identity.

Everything would be greatly simplified if our police would attend to my repeated requests that files and photographs be provided to me of Communist agents in custody there, as well as those who have been deported, so that the authorities here might assist in identifying them. Furthermore, in light of the assistance I have received from the Gestapo, it would be only appropriate, from my point of view, for us to comply with the Germans' request to be furnished with copies of documents confiscated from extremists in Brazil that happen to refer directly or indirectly to Communist activity in Germany. As I reported in telegram no. 40, according to available information, the Olga Meirelles, Olga Vilar, Maria Bergner, or Maria Prestes referred to in the Brazilian press as Luís Carlos Prestes's wife can be identified as Olga Benario, a Communist agent of the Third International known for her great intelligence and courage. Olga Benario, an Israelite, was born February 12, 1908, in Munich. Since 1925, she has been listed by German police as a very active and effective Communist agent. From 1926 to 1928 she worked in the Soviet commercial delegation in Berlin, the offices of which were located in the embassy proper. Her role there also included espionage of a military nature, provoking the interest of the national defense. In 1928 she was sentenced to three months' imprisonment for an armed attack on Moabit Prison on April 11 of that year, leading to the escape of Communist agent Otto Braun. After serving her time, Olga Benario fled to Russia and participated in the Fifth Congress of the Communist Youth International, which took place in Moscow between August 19 and September 18, 1928. She resided in the Soviet capital until 1920. Her relationship with Luís Carlos Prestes probably dates from the meeting of the World Congress of the Third International in Moscow in 1935.

Olga Benario has used the following names in her Communist activities:

Eva Kruger, single, born Berlin, March 12, 1908.

Olga Bergner, single, born Erfurt, April 2, 1904.

Frieda Wolf Behrendt, married, born Erfurt, July 27, 1903.

Maria Vilar or Maria Prestes, born 1908.

It is suspected here that she served as liaison agent between Arthur Ewert, alias Harry Berger, Luís Carlos Prestes, and the Soviet Trade Bureau in Montevideo, and that her duties included organizing the propaganda wing of the Communist Youth in Brazil. Considering Olga Benario's past connections with the aforementioned Otto Braun, the German secret police deemed it potentially useful to provide me with detailed information regarding Braun, reputedly a dangerous agent of Comintern propaganda. An elementary school teacher, Otto Braun was born in Ismaning, a small city near Munich, September 28, 1900, and was identified as an active Communist agent in 1921. He lived in Germany with Olga Benario from 1926 until 1928, that is until his escape from Moabit Prison in Berlin. By 1926 Braun was quite well known among German Communists not least for the courses he taught in various cities on the formation of red shock troops and lectures he gave on the role of Communist action in the class struggle toward the Soviet International revolution. Braun was arrested by German police in 1928 and charged with the crime of high treason, subsequently escaping, as I said, with the armed assistance of Olga Benario on April 11, 1928. Traveling through Belgium and Holland with false identity papers, Braun fled to Russia, where he probably rejoined

Benario. Considering these circumstances, the German secret police consider it extremely possible that he has also been active in Brazil in concert with other agents of Moscow.

Otto Braun has operated under the following aliases: Oscar Schumann, Karl Wagner, Erwin Resch, Arthur Behrendt, Hans Landeburg. Enclosed Your Excellency will find photographs in duplicate of Olga Benario and Otto Braun, as well as copies of their files, including fingerprints of both. All these documents were supplied to me by the Gestapo.

I should also inform Your Excellency that after my own inquiry at the Consular Department of this embassy, I have arrived at the conclusion that at an undetermined time Otto Braun requested from that department information about the documents necessary for, as well as the possibilities of, traveling to Brazil. This information was provided to me by the vice-consul, Mr. Carlos Meissner Júnior, after I showed him a photograph of the individual in question, and further reinforces the suspicion that Braun might very well be in Brazil at the present time.

I have tried to exercise extreme vigilance with regard to the visas of travelers destined for Brazilian ports. Most of these prospective travelers are Jews who claim to be tourists and show as evidence first-class tickets and bank certificates from the Iwria Bank in Berlin. It is interesting to note that these tickets are, in the majority of cases, for French steamships, whose first-class berths cost less than those in first or even second class on German ships. It seems strange that certain individuals, though merely shoemakers, tailors, cabinetmakers, etc., claim to be businessmen and tourists and present round-trip tickets despite the fact that there is no record of any of them returning from Brazil.

In light of this, I decided to look further into the Iwria Bank, and my investigation confirms that it is a Jewish institution, all the more suspicious for being mainly concerned with the financial and professional interests of Israelites living in Germany. This bank has without a doubt acted illegally, facilitating the flight of Jewish capital, and there is a well-founded supposition that it is also involved in the transfer of money to fund Communist propaganda, principally in Czechoslovakia and possibly other countries. I have therefore decided—and I hope to merit Your Excellency's approval of this decision—that our Consular

Department should no longer accept bank guarantees from this establishment.

I implore Your Excellency to apprise the appropriate Brazilian authorities of the above information, stressing the strictly confidential nature of all herein contained.

I would like to take this opportunity to reiterate to Your Excellency my respectful request for secrecy in dealing with this problem.

Moniz de Aragão

Macedo Soares apparently did not take seriously Aragão's repeated requests that this information not be made public. Less than twenty-four hours after the diplomat's letter arrived at Itamaraty, all the information regarding Olga's true identity and political background appeared in the *Correio da Manhã* (Rio) and the *Folha da Manhã* and *Correio Paulistano* (São Paulo). Whoever leaked the story was careful, however, to preserve Itamaraty's public image, omitting Aragão's anti-Semitic suggestions regarding immigration policy, as well as concealing the intimacy of relations between the Brazilian embassy in Berlin and the Nazi secret service. The very same day the details of Olga Benario's past were made public, she was transferred from an improvised cell at police headquarters to prison. The reverential awe of policemen at all levels for Luís Carlos Prestes seemed to extend also to the woman they believed to be his wife: in spite of threats and psychological torture, no one had touched a hair on her head. During the transfer, however, Olga feared that one of the police threats was being carried out: her interrogators had promised that if she continued refusing to collaborate, they would send her to a prison for common criminals.

Olga's fear of being placed among thieves and murderers explains the look of panic on her face as she was led into a cell that already housed many prisoners. Her fear, though, was short-lived: these women included doctors, writers, actresses, several workers, two attorneys, and, to Olga's great surprise, many women she knew well or had heard of, including her good friend Sabo, Ewert's wife. They had without exception been arrested for the same reason she had—involvement in the November 27 rebellion.

Through the bars of her cell, which was located on the second floor of a U-shaped block, Olga could see forty-eight smaller cubicles—the women's cells were larger—where nearly two hundred men were crowded together. The multitude of military were easily identifiable by their short, above-the-ears haircuts. And most of them looked as though they were under thirty years old. Olga knew these prisoners were only an insignificant portion of the total number of victims of the repression that had come crashing down on Brazil after the failed revolt her husband had led. The night before she was transferred to the House of Detention on Rua Frei Caneca, in order to frighten her a guard had read her the tally of police operations disclosed by Captain Müller to a Rio newspaper. In four months the police had made 3,250 "investigatory" arrests and 441 house searches (euphemism for raids on private homes, which generally took place at night without legal consent), and had filled the jails with over 3,000 people: 901 civilians and 2,146 soldiers. And all this within Müller's jurisdiction alone, that is, from the city of Rio de Janeiro.

The women's double-width cell was at the curve of the horseshoe, beside a small infirmary. The cell's position afforded its occupants the privilege of a view of the entire building, with the exception of the two cells located directly beneath it on the ground floor. And since the so-called hall of women had originally been two cells whose dividing wall had been torn down, it contained twice the comfort the mens' did: two low porcelain latrines and two metal sinks. Tattered curtains hung from overhead wires, allowing for privacy during use of the latrines. On the wall opposite the infirmary the women had installed a "closet"—sheets tacked to a frame made of broomsticks—the purpose of which was not so much to hold belongings as to hide a hole dug through the wall to the cell next door. Women whose husbands or boyfriends were also incarcerated in the House of Detention used this "periscope," as it was called, to exchange a few quick, furtive declarations of love after the men's fresh-air period. All cell doors faced the central yard (the inside of the horseshoe), where the men were allowed to circulate freely until 7:00 P.M., when they had to return to their cells. In this courtyard, dubbed Red Square, the prisoners held meetings, courses in Marxism, mathematics, literacy, languages, and Brazilian history, and, at the insistence of some of the rebellious lieutenants, physical education classes.

The majority of prisoners had been in the House of Detention since November, and by the time Olga arrived the prison was functioning like an individual organism. The ultimate authority among inmates was a democratically elected body called the Collective, which took the initiative in mobilizing petitions, group protests, and hunger strikes. Since most foreign prisoners, as well as some of those from other states, had no family in Rio, the Collective took charge of gathering and redistributing fairly the extra food brought by visitors: fruit, chocolate, cakes, etc.

Olga was still getting acquainted with her new cellmates when kitchen workers, accompanied by two armed guards, arrived carrying a huge kettle full of the evening's "chow"—which looked inedible—and began handing out tin plates and spoons. The activity in Red Square was over by that hour: at seven o'clock the guards ran from cell to cell, locking everyone in for the night. After dinner, Olga was startled to hear a booming voice call out from one of the cells on the second floor.

"Whether or not you think it's great, everyone to the grate! It's time for radio ANL, the Voice of Freedom!"

She would soon get used to the Brazilian way of dealing with the tragedy of imprisonment under a dictatorship. Every evening after dinner, like clockwork, the same phrase rang out, and the prison's improvised radio station was on the air. The inmates rose to their feet and sang first "The International" and then the hymn of the National Liberation Alliance, set to the tune of the national anthem:

> Alliance, Alliance,
> Let us show our will!
> Against twenty or one thousand
> Let us liberate Brazil!
>
> This song must be proclaimed,
> This voice's clamor never hushed!
> There must be liberty in Brazil,
> Won in the streets by us!

Though still feeling a bit shy that first night in detention, Olga sang along—"The International" in French and the ANL hymn in thick, accented Portuguese. Then a fat young doctor named Manuel Venâncio Campos da Paz Júnior, the official announcer of the "Voice

144

of Freedom," shimmied up the bars of his cell to broadcast the news that had arrived secretly from the outside, as well as the jokes and wisecracks that Aparício Torelli—the "Baron of Itararé," recognized today as one of the greatest Brazilian humorists of all time—had spent all day inventing in his cell. That day, in honor of Olga's arrival, the Baron had prepared a special "report" on her husband's archrival. Campos da Paz's rendition, with his own father applauding the loudest, was a big hit with the inmates:

"Attention! Your attention comrades! This news just in from the street: only minutes before going stark-raving mad, the president of the republic decided to hand down a sentence of life imprisonment to the well-known scoundrel Filinto Mule!"

As she listened, Olga scanned the audience and found a number of familiar faces—some at a distance, framed by iron bars, and others right there in her cell. She had met Campos da Paz on the beach one day with Américo Dias Leite when she had gone to pick up letters from Paris addressed to "Yvone Vilar." Though her understanding of Portuguese was limited then, she had picked up the acid tone of the question put to Dias Leite by the roly-poly physician: "Did you think you fooled us for a minute, Dias, with that story about how you went to France to study? And now, right before my eyes, I see the beautiful blue-eyed contraband you smuggled back with you. . . ."

Among her cellmates, in addition to Sabo and Carmen Ghioldi, Olga recognized the young lawyer Maria Werneck de Castro. Months before their arrest, Prestes had suggested that Olga consult Maria's husband, attorney Luís Werneck de Castro, to try to legalize her status in Brazil. At Werneck's office, Olga had spoken briefly with Maria without identifying herself as Prestes's companion. But then came the failure of the rebellion and life underground, and the chance to gain legal status had been lost.

Olga was somewhat reserved during her first days in the House of Detention. Though she knew her fellow prisoners were revolutionaries committed to the same struggle as she, she felt it best to be cautious. From the safe house in Meyer, Olga had followed at close range the growing doubts about Elvira and Miranda—and this made her especially suspicious. Maria Werneck helped break the ice by recalling their meeting of several months earlier. By the end of her first week in the prison Maria Prestes, as she was called by her fellow inmates, was a popular figure.

In early April Olga began to suspect that she was pregnant, but at first she wasn't terribly concerned. Like the rest of the women prisoners she was preoccupied with the mental anguish Sabo had brought with her from Santo Antônio Hill. One of the ways the torturers had tried to break her emotionally was to administer violent beatings punctually, every night, at 3:00 A.M. The regularity of this torture had made Sabo neurotic, so that here, in the House of Detention, where there was no physical punishment and she was among friends, the same schedule persisted. At 3:00 A.M. precisely, Sabo began shouting, pleading with them in German not to kill her, begging them to stop beating her husband. The first time this happened the whole block awoke, imagining that they were in fact hearing the screams of someone being tortured. Within minutes every prisoner was rhythmically banging his or her tin cup on the cell bars, waking the prisoners in the House of Correction, another building entirely, and bringing hundreds of soldiers armed with submachine guns, who thought a mass rebellion was in progress. In time, the prisoners became accustomed to the middle-of-the-night screams. At first Sabo's cellmates tried to shake her out of her nightmare, but it was no use; Olga was the first and only one capable of calming her. Whispering tenderly in German, she managed to get her friend back to sleep; finally, a few weeks after Olga's arrival, Sabo was able to put the trauma behind her.

Within days of her own transfer to the House of Detention, Olga witnessed a moving scene. Some of the participants in the Natal and Recife rebellions—114 men and 2 women—arrived at Rio on board the prison ship *Manaos*, having made the trip in the steamship's hold, guarded by about fifty soldiers. As heterogeneous as the rest of the prisoners, they included intellectuals, workers, peasants, students, and many young soldiers. After several days of preliminary interrogation they were brought to the House of Detention. The moment the guards opened the block's iron gate so that they could enter, the resident inmates rose to their feet in their cells and began singing: first the Brazilian national anthem, then "The International," and finally the Alliance hymn. Rodolfo Ghioldi, the prison's official orator, had been charged by the Collective with making a welcoming speech to the arriving revolutionaries as they were settled into their cells.

Ghioldi was given strict parameters: the speech had to be optimistic, even triumphant, aimed at raising the morale of men and women who had just completed a terribly long trip under horrifying conditions. Ghioldi had argued that reality didn't permit a great deal of optimism: these were the times of Hitler, Mussolini, and Filinto Müller. The leadership stood firm, refusing further discussion. He was to use his talents to come up with a speech that would lift people's spirits. Ghioldi fulfilled the task brilliantly, drawing applause and tears of emotion when, leaning from the second-floor balcony in his shorts, he proclaimed in Spanish that the days of Franco, Hitler, Vargas, and Mussolini were numbered; that Stalin's glorious Red Army would crush the Nazi-Fascist alliance like a disgusting cockroach. Those present were locked up temporarily but they had the future in their hands. The horizon was red and humanity was drawing closer to it. Ghioldi's speech was a heartfelt declaration composed with warmth and passion. Rare was the prisoner—veteran or new arrival—without tears streaming down his or her face as the multitude applauded.

Once Ghioldi had finished, close to tears himself, he withdrew to his cell. Almost immediately one of the newcomers, a balding young man with dark hair and a tense air about him, strode in and introduced himself: "It's a pleasure to meet you, Mr. Ghioldi. My name is Graciliano Ramos. Congratulations. Those were beautiful words and I was happy to hear them. But admit it, just between the two of us: You don't honestly believe a single syllable of what you just said, do you?"

As disciplined as he was, Ghioldi was obliged to lie. "You're wrong, Señor Ramos. I most definitely believe every word I said."

Ramos wasn't convinced. "I don't know your particular history, but I'm from northeastern Brazil and I know my people. They are so backward, so brutalized by poverty, that I don't believe they will ever be able to make the revolution."

Ghioldi insisted, with apparent conviction. "But Señor Ramos, the Russian peasants were much more backward than your northeasterners, and they made a revolution that's going to change the face of the earth. The revolution doesn't depend on a people's cultural level of development alone. Without those Russian peasants, backward and brutalized as they were, the Russian Revolution could never have taken place."

Graciliano Ramos left Ghioldi's cell in silence, without a word of argument.

The climate of the building changed with the arrival of the revolutionaries from the north. Not because their presence practically doubled the inmate population, but mainly because of their merrymaking and wisecracking. Even the military who had come on the *Manoas* were less demanding of discipline than those from Rio. And the northeasterners brought with them the latest marvel in communications, the "shitophone." This innovation—reportedly invented by an ingenious Marxist-Leninist sergeant from Pernambuco—was operated by holding down the chain after flushing the toilet so that the water level didn't come back up in the bowl. Two toilets in different cells, kept empty like this, miraculously became an excellent means of communication, demanding only that the users overcome their queasiness at placing their faces inside that foul-smelling hole to speak and hear what was being said at the other end. Explaining his gadget to the prisoners at top decibel level, the alleged inventor boasted, "This item is much more advanced than the telephone. If it weren't for the smell of shit you have to put up with, I would have been the one—not Alexander Graham Bell—to go down in history!"

Olga became as thoroughly a part of the Collective as if she were Brazilian. Within a week of her arrival she organized a women's chorale, which was an immediate sensation on the daily broadcast. The women sang "The International" in French, the majority of them reading the lyrics from the sheets Olga copied, and closed the program with the "Red Flag" sung in Italian:

> Avanti popolo! A la riscorsa!
> Bandiera Rossa! Bandiera Rossa!
> Bandiera Rossa che trionfera!
> E viva il comunismo per la libertà!

For the last two lines the women were joined by a chorus of some three hundred voices, a thundering roar that was well worth the punishment it often earned the members of the Collective:

Viva Lenine, abasso il re!
Viva Lenine, abasso il re!

One month after being transferred to the House of Detention, Olga announced to her cellmates that there was no longer any doubt in her mind: she was expecting a child. Her first concern was to try to get the news to Prestes. She went to see the warden, accompanied by fellow inmate Dr. Nise da Silveira, and informed him that from then on she would need the care necessary for an expectant mother. And she asked whether she could write to Prestes to tell him he was going to be a father. The warden didn't seem terribly interested in her condition and merely said that she should write her letter and that he would see what he could do to get it delivered. Following his instructions, she wrote—not one but dozens of letters, always in French and always with the closing "*la tienne.*" Letters he would never receive.

News of Olga's pregnancy transformed the prison. Everyone wanted to help lessen the difficulties of a pregnancy in captivity. The prisoners who received regular visitors began asking their relatives to bring special food and vitamins, always following the prescriptions of Nise da Silveira, whom fate had turned from a psychiatrist into a gynecologist and obstetrician.

Each contributed as he or she could. Carmen Ghioldi, who did extraordinary needlework, managed to get hold of needles and crochet thread and began producing a tiny wardrobe. Curiously, no one made boy's clothing, only girl's. Rosa Meirelles happened to mention to Olga that former gaucho Lieutenant José Gay da Cunha, an inmate of one of the ground-floor cells, was a draftsman. Rosa had introduced the two, through their respective cell bars, and Olga remembered the tall young man with a hooked nose who had waved to her from down below: "What a pleasure! So you are Maria Prestes!"

"I am. And you—you're a lieutenant from the *Tercerro* or from the *Escola*?"

In her Germanic Portuguese, *Tercerro* was the Third Infantry

Regiment, and *Escola* was the School of Aviation—and da Cunha had taken part in the uprising at the School of Aviation. Soon after this meeting he visited the infirmary, pretending he had food poisoning after the previous night's dinner. While the guard was distracted, he strayed over toward the women's cell. Olga took the opportunity to make a request: she wanted him to sketch the models of planes presently in use by the Brazilian air force, so that Carmen Ghioldi could embroider them on tiny infant shirts and bibs. Gay da Cunha drew the planes in meticulous detail on tiny pieces of paper and smuggled them to the women's cell; a few days later, a small package of infant clothing was lowered to the ground floor via the "flier," so the lieutenant could check to see that the embroidery matched the original designs.

The flier, another northeastern invention, was a system of lines and pulleys made with empty spools from Carmen Ghioldi's crochet thread, which transported notes and small, light packages between Red Square and the cells on the second floor. It was generally used to deliver messages that couldn't be transmitted by a yell or to send back "homework" from the courses in Marxism and philosophy that Olga and Rodolfo Ghioldi taught. When being used to communicate between cells on the same floor, the flier took a roundabout course, stopping at courtyard level, where someone redirected it upstairs to the cell number indicated on the note.

A clipping from the newspaper *O Globo* came to Olga via the flier with news of a hearing the previous evening before Judge Barros Barreto, during which Prestes had assumed full responsibility for the November 27 uprising, exempting all his comrades—foreigners and leaders of the Brazilian CP alike—from any participation in the organization of the revolt. Olga could see from the clipping the fear Prestes inspired in the government: Lieutenant Eusébio de Queiroz Filho, commander of the general barracks of the Special Police, described the security measures undertaken to guard the "red leader":

All approaches to Santo Antônio Hill are extremely dangerous, due to mines and electrified fencing. Three machine guns have been installed at the top of the hill, making the prisoner's escape impossible. The high voltage of the barbed wire constitutes a serious life threat to anyone who would dare attempt to circumvent the established order.

When news of her husband didn't arrive on the flier Olga would receive instructions to be in the women's "closet" at a certain time so that someone could bring her news from outside via the "periscope." She frequently had to wait hours in line, especially if the person in front of her was Valentina Bastos. Valentina was madly in love with her husband, millionaire Adolfo Barbosa Bastos ("Crybaby"), who was charged with contributing a veritable fortune to the CP coffers though he had never been the kind of activist to attend meetings. Valentina and Adolfo spent hours exchanging declarations of love through the periscope, though the only possible contact was to caress the tips of each other's fingers. In order for the two prisoners to communicate through the tiny hole between cells without attracting the guards' attention, a contrivance was devised that required the participation of almost everyone at one time or another: the entire time the periscope was in use at least one latrine had to be flushed continuously, to muffle the sound of the voices. This was dubbed "the tidal wave."

As the weeks passed, Olga's pregnancy became more evident. During one of her many visits to the notary's office for further depositions, Olga told the reporters, who were always milling around looking for news, that she was expecting a child by Luís Carlos Prestes. One fact, however, prevented her and her new-found friends from relishing her pregnancy and coming childbirth. The threat of expulsion from Brazil was becoming more and more real.

In early May, District Chief Bellens Porto, whom Filinto Müller had assigned to preside over the police investigation of the rebellion, announced that his work was coming to an end: hundreds of people—Brazilians and foreigners, civilians and military personnel—had been indicted for participating in the uprising. But his reports on three of the women in custody at the House of Detention were inconclusive. At first he said that there was no way to punish them in Brazil, since they had not been charged with any crime. "There is not sufficient evidence to indict foreigners Elise Ewert, Carmen Alfaya de Ghioldi, or Maria Bergner Prestes for any specific form of participation," he lamented in an official memo to Captain Müller. But if the law didn't prescribe any punishment for the three, so much the worse for the law. It would be unthinkable to set free the wives of the three top Communist leaders. Bellens Porto came up with an even stiffer penalty: "These women are clearly undesirable elements, whose continued presence in Brazil is unadvisable. For these reasons, begging your favor, may I remind Your Excellency of the advisability of bringing suitable expulsion proceedings against them."

14

A "Noxious" Foreigner

WHILE THE THREAT of expulsion was becoming more and more imminent an ounce of hope allowed Olga to dream of having her baby in Brazil: despite the state of siege (recently extended once more) and the undisguised sympathy of the Vargas government toward Nazi Germany, the Brazilian constitution, which was still in force, guaranteed a woman expecting a child of Brazilian paternity the right to give birth in Brazil. It didn't matter that she was still in prison, because Olga believed that one day both she and Prestes would be freed. What terrified her was the prospect of being sent back to Germany. For her—not just a Jew, but also a Communist—falling into Hitler's hands would be fatal.

Though Brazilian law apparently stood in Olga's favor, the news coming in on the flier or via the periscope was discouraging. Of all the cases of expulsion of undesirable aliens—and there were hundreds and hundreds—there was one in particular that Olga had followed closely, even before being arrested, and she had been appalled by the outcome. After holding Genny Gleizer, a seventeen-year-old Romanian Jew, for four months on the vague charge of "subversion," the Vargas government had decided to deport her, despite protests from hundreds of unions, student groups, and intellectuals both in Brazil and abroad. During the deportation proceedings several moving gestures of solidarity bore witness to sympathetic public opinion. When it was announced, for example, that if Genny were to marry a Brazilian the law would protect her from expulsion, various writers and intellectuals stepped up to volunteer. At a protest march in São Paulo calling for her release, Paulo Emílio Salles Gomes, a student, proclaimed that as soon as he left the speaker's platform he would go directly to a civil registry to find a judge willing to officiate at his marriage to the girl. He was too late. Journalist Arthur Piccinini, who had been covering the "Genny case" for the daily *A Platéia*, had already asked a justice of the peace in the Sé district of São Paulo to publish the marriage banns for his wedding. Impervious to all this, the government deported Genny Gleizer to Europe in October 1935.

Brazilian Communists knew that this could well be Olga's fate and prepared themselves for the worst. The Brazilian Committee of Red Aid International informed their counterparts in European ports of the Brazilian political situation and of the government's successive deportations of European "extremists" to their countries of origin—especially to those dominated by the Nazi-Fascist wave. Brazilian Red Aid asked the European stevedores to inspect all ships arriving from Brazil and to release from their holds any deported foreigners. The mobilization of the dockworkers, a traditionally politicized group, paralyzed European ports every time a ship from Brazil docked to load or unload cargo. When the authorities tried to stop the inspections, dockworkers in all ports simultaneously went on strike until the order to prevent searches was revoked. A single inspection of a merchant marine ship in Le Havre resulted in the release of seventeen deportees—German, Italian, Portuguese, and Polish. In the shops and on the docks of still-Republican Spain, thousands of copies of a small pamphlet inspired by the Brazilians' appeal circulated from hand to hand:

To all Comrades of the Spanish Section
of Red Aid International:

As part of a cruel and overt war against the country's anti-imperialists, the reactionary government of Brazil is deporting dozens of foreign activists. We are informing you of this so that you can be vigilant about all ships that have made stops in Brazil and expedite the disembarkation on Spanish soil of these victims of the Brazilian repression. We ask that you do everything in your power to prevent nationals of Fascist countries from arriving in their home-lands. Their wish is to disembark in Spain or France, for which we request your assistance.

Revolutionary greetings,
The São Paulo Regional Committee
of Red Aid International

The hardening of the repression in Brazil justified Red Aid's worst fears. Prestes was threatened with prosecution for directing the rebellion, ordering the murder of Elvira Colônio, and deserting from the army. The mayor of the Federal District, Pedro Ernesto, had been arrested by order of Filinto Müller. Bonfim ("Miranda"), after being informed that his wife had disappeared and probably been executed by order of the CP leadership, was even more loquacious in his revelations to the police. In April 1936, Olga was summoned to an office in the House of Detention to be confronted by Bonfim. So important were these two figures to the govern-ment's case that District Chief Bellens Porto, the man assigned by Müller to head the investigation of the rebellion, personally di-rected the session. Olga denied that she had ever met Bonfim and refused to initial the official papers stating his identity. He, on the other hand, confirmed without hesitation that Olga was the woman he had met at meetings with Prestes, Arthur Ewert, and Rodolfo Ghioldi, shamelessly adding that the police would find more infor-mation on the German woman's activities in statements he had made to District Chief Pereira. Impassive, Olga simply listened, searching for an answer to the question she had asked herself and Prestes many times before: How could this man have managed to climb to the highest post in a Communist Party? After telling her prison comrades, either in person or via the flier, about Bonfim's behavior during the confrontation, she found that others had also harbored their suspicions. Even the discreet and retiring Graciliano Ramos, who participated very little in the life of the building and instead spent hours buried in his cell scribbling notes on pads of paper, had already expressed alarm at Bonfim's unpreparedness and

155

suspicious exhibitionism: he was known to display proudly to his fellow prisoners the marks of his supposed torture.

At the end of May—by which time Olga's belly was blossoming—the government decided to commemorate the six-month anniversary of the quelling of the November revolt, referred to as the "Communist conspiracy." Commanders of the army, navy, and air force issued reports recalling various episodes and organized visits to the tombs of the men who died fighting the rebels. A notice appeared in the press that the national Rotary Club would dedicate that month's luncheon meeting, scheduled for May 27, "to the study of the problem of defending against extremism," and had invited Captain Miranda Correia, chief of security, to speak on the subject. Guests of honor at the banquet included the minister of justice, Vicente Rao; the minister of war, General João Gomes; Rear Admiral Aristides Guilhem; and chief of police Captain Filinto Müller. From this moment, the government began broadcasting their own version of events, which included the claim that the rebels had killed loyal officers and enlisted men in their beds during the early hours of November 27. Autopsies on the two dozen dead provided no indication, however, that this accusation was true.

But it wasn't the victors alone who celebrated the anniversary of the uprising. In their own way, even within prison walls, the defeated marked the date as well. The person in large part responsible for the festivities was Sergeant Júlio Alves, an excellent metal craftsman. Months before, Alves had asked a fellow prisoner from Minas Gerais to have his relatives bring more of a certain kind of cheese whenever they visited. The cheese came packed in a tin about the size of a soccer ball, made of soft metal. Alves would make one half of each sphere into a small stove and the other half into a pan to place on top, for use in the clandestine kitchens set up in many of the cells. But the sergeant really outdid himself with his newest creation. On the afternoon of May 27 the flier was in constant use, delivering to each of the forty-nine cells in the House of Detention a small package containing Alves's gift to commemorate the six-month anniversary of the revolt: a small tool sculpted from cheese tins that would open any of the locks of the cells. Each picklock tool came with a warning scribbled on the wrapping: "To be used only in cases of dire necessity. If they catch us with this, we'll all be shot! Long live the proletarian revolution!" Aparício Torelli, the "Baron Humorist of Itararé," spread the word throughout the prison that these tools, in addition to opening doors, possessed the magic power of uniting Marxists and Christians. "They were made by the unquestionably Communist Sergeant Júlio Alves and blessed by the apparently Christian Father Nascimento."

Father Nascimento was one of the most colorful characters in the prison. The first time he visited the cellblock, his left hand rose in a closed-fist salute while his right arm cradled a big basket of fruit and cheese he had brought for the inmates. Director of a center for orphans in Niterói, a town near Rio, he had been arrested as he innocently solicited from shopkeepers contributions to a fund for "the families of the unfortunate Communists arrested in November." Someone had denounced him and he was sent to the House of Detention in Rio, where the police threatened him on his arrival: "Now, Father Sonofabitch, we're going to throw you in with the Communists so you can see close up those bastards you were collecting money for."

The torment the police arranged for Father Nascimento was to make him witness torture sessions in the House of Corrections. After one of these experiences he stopped in front of Olga's cell. Staring at her blossoming belly, he fell to his knees as if in prayer and cried pathetically, "Tell me, senhora, is there a God?"

Among the charges against Father Nascimento was the crime of tuning the shortwave radio at the orphanage to transmissions from Radio Moscow and Radio Republican Spain and calling the children in after dinner to listen with him. The children got so used to the ritual that whenever he forgot to turn on the radio after dinner one of them would pull on his cassock and say, "Father, it's time for the samba!"

The samba was "The International"—the introduction to all Radio Moscow's programs in those days.

Father Nascimento held the title of most dedicated student in every one of the courses offered in the prison. He studied Marxism with Olga, philosophy with Ghioldi, Russian and English with Raphael Kemprad (a White Russian raised in Germany and imprisoned in Rio, though no one knew why), and chess, checkers, political geography, and Brazilian history with whoever was teaching. When two of the classes he was taking happened to meet at the same time, he would ask a fellow student to write a summary of the class and send it to him via the flier. There was only one course he refused to take, claiming it was "a matter of conscience"—the interminable physical education sessions imposed by the young lieutenants. Actually, it was sheer laziness on his part.

Like the majority of prisoners, Father Nascimento had a special predilection for the courses given by Rodolfo Ghioldi. Ghioldi had planned to spend his time in jail "as discreetly as possible," but he found himself bombarded with requests from inmates wanting to learn more about so-called revolutionary theory. What, they wanted to know, was meant by the term *anti-imperialist revolution*? Or *democratic revolution*? What was the worker-peasant alliance? What did it mean that the proletariat was the class that leads and the Communist Party the vanguard of the proletariat? Could he explain the aims of the Peruvian political party APRA (American Popular Revolutionary Alliance)? What could he tell them about the Mexican revolution? The flier brought Ghioldi the most detailed questions, and it soon became clear he would have to shed his intended anonymity. When the prisoners were locked up for the night, he helped them do their "homework" assignments, often sent via little notes from Olga. When they were allowed to circulate, he spoke openly to anyone who would listen about something Olga never had the heart to address. Though Ghioldi was known to hold forth on Latin America, Marxist philosophy, and the Chinese revolution, his favorite topic was the peasant movement in Brazil. Speaking passable Portuguese, he interviewed dozens of revolutionaries from rural areas and became a specialist on the subject, eventually writing a long essay on the Brazilian agrarian problem.

Blending reports about what she had witnessed in the Soviet Union with the rudiments of Marxist theory, Olga preferred to speak to the small groups that generally met in the women's cell. Gathered around her, humble cobblers sat beside army officials and lawyers such as Hermes Lima, who decades later, in 1962, would become prime minister of Brazil, and later a minister of the Supreme Court, before being stripped of this title in 1969. Olga generally lectured for a while and then dictated a series of questions, which the students were given three days to answer via the flier. The next session would be dedicated to discussing each person's homework and understanding of the topic. The students were at wildly varying levels, and even though Portuguese was not her mother tongue, she devoted some of the discussion periods to the students' grammatical errors.

The only change in the rhythm of prison life came on visiting day, which was one Sunday a month. There were those who spent three weeks preparing for the fleeting fifty minutes with their loved ones. When visiting day finally arrived, men shaved and women put on perfume and the excitement was so great that almost everyone was up and about at 5:00 A.M., even those who had no one to visit them. The festive air remained for several hours after the visitors had gone, as prisoners exchanged news—friends asking after the health of one another's relatives, proud fathers demonstrating with their hands the height of their precocious children. Then came the redistribution of cigarettes, chocolates, cheeses, and fruits. And finally an atmosphere of deep depression would descend on the prison. Little by little the groups would dwindle as inmates returned to their cells and settled down on their lumpy beds to read the same letters dozens of times over. A keen ear could hear sobbing coming from the cells of hardened revolutionaries. Visiting day was the only day of the month that the Voice of Freedom did not go on the air.

Visiting day also brought a blast of fresh air to the prison: news from outside. Thus it was learned that José Torres Galvão, the man who had arrested Olga and Prestes, had been killed by five shots from a soldier, right in the barracks of the Special Police. Less than twenty-four hours afterward, the killer, Hernani de Andrade, mysteriously committed suicide. Rumor had it the two men had argued about who should collect the one hundred contos de réis promised by Filinto Müller to the man who captured Prestes.

On another visiting day Olga learned that the government had finally decided to send her back to Germany. The Lawyers Institute had designated Dyonísio da Silveira, a lawyer from its Department of Judicial Assistance, to defend her, but da Silveira refused the assignment. For the first time, the government allowed a letter from Olga to be delivered to Prestes, and it was only then that he learned of her pregnancy. In his reply, Prestes made two recommendations: he suggested that Olga find a homeopathic doctor to treat her during the pregnancy—Prestes himself always relied on homeopathy—and that she choose Dr. Heitor Lima as her lawyer. Though "pregnant to the naked eye," as the Baron Humorist of Itararé put it, Olga was required to undergo a gynecological examination by a police-appointed physician to confirm formally her condition. And while there was no doubt that the constitution guaranteed her right to remain in the country, since she was expecting a child of Brazilian paternity, there was no lack of jurists willing to uphold the correctness of the decision by Vargas and Filinto Müller to expel her from Brazil. When reminded of the constitutional guarantee, they would say: "Yes, but we're in a state of war, aren't we?"

Hounded by the press, jurist Clóvis Bevilacqua had to bend over backward to justify the government's decision. "This issue has been studied in all its aspects with an eye to civil law. The case now being debated is another story entirely, however. Here we enter the territory of international law. The penalty, though directed at the person being expelled, will clearly affect the unborn child. Despite this, we are of course presently in a period declared to be a state of war, and the expulsion in question is a matter of public interest, which must be honored above all else."

Bevilacqua's pompous "public interest" defense of the expulsion decision was based on nothing more than the administrative dispatch signed by Demócrito de Almeida, an assistant police chief, and by Filinto Müller, both of whom considered Olga's deportation "not merely just, but necessary to the Brazilian community at large." Knowing full well that her return to Germany could mean the death of both mother and child, Bevilacqua still declared, ironically, that he saw only one valid reason to prevent Olga's expulsion: "Only for humanitarian reasons. . . . In the days when there was a death sentence, the sentence was not executed if the accused was pregnant; instead they would wait until after the child was born. For humanitarian reasons."

As prescribed by law, Olga had to give written notice of her desire to be defended by Heitor Lima, who was informed of her decision the same day in an official letter from Captain Miranda Correia.

Though a liberal without the remotest connection to the ideals of the November rebels, Lima agreed to represent Olga:

Captain Affonso de Miranda Correia
Chief of Security

Response to your letter raises three main points.

In the first place, I would like to point out that the government is facilitating the defense of those indicted for crimes against the political and social order, whereas the present state of war could legitimately have permitted the restriction of such right of defense. I want to stress this fact, which appeases the national legal conscience.

Secondly, with the exception of very special cases, it is not lawful for an attorney to refuse to represent a defendant, no matter how heinous the crime attributed to him, but rather it is imperative, urgent, and compulsory to provide legal assistance when a prisoner is being held incommunicado, wounded by general repudiation, and in a situation ripe for the infringement of those prescriptions without which no conviction would be lawful because it would not represent the logical and legal outcome resulting from the free debate between the prosecution and the defense. Furthermore, to refuse legal counsel during a period in which lawyers are not granted immunity* would be an act of cowardice.

In the third and final place, the prisoner requesting my assistance is a woman. That fact alone demands that I, steadfastly dedicated to fighting for the mitigation of female misfortune on the face of this earth, and committed to redeeming, at least in small part, the crimes of civilization against women, for which I as a man share responsibility, that fact alone, I repeat, demands that I come to the aid of the accused. In addition, I have read in the press that the defendant is preparing for the most important experience in a woman's life: the birth of a child. She is, therefore, crowned with a halo that makes her, as it were, holy. Whatever the risks of the job, then, I will confront

---

* Brazilian law normally guaranteed immunity to lawyers so that they could defend their clients without fear of prosecution. However, new laws had been introduced that removed such guarantees so that a lawyer such as Lima might be prosecuted for defending a subversive.

them, dedicating myself to my client for as long as I can find legal recourse for the fulfillment of my mission.

Sincerely,
Heitor Lima

Lima's first action, three days after agreeing to represent Olga— or Maria Prestes, as he insisted on calling her—was to enter a writ of habeas corpus with the Supreme Court. The object of this was not to press for Olga's release, which he knew the authorities would never consider, but to try to prevent the execution of the deportation decree based on the grounds provided by Captain Müller and already handed down by the minister of justice. As Heitor Lima sifted through the piles of statements and complaints relating to the rebellion, he became more and more convinced that the decision to deport Olga had been based on the personal enmity and desire for revenge of Getúlio Vargas and Filinto Müller. Enmity not toward Olga herself, whom neither of the men knew, but toward her husband and the father of her child, Luís Carlos Prestes. None of the hundreds of papers contained a single accusation against Olga for any crime she could have committed in Brazil. Nor had her extradition been requested by the Third Reich. Vargas and Müller had spontaneously made the decision to send Adolf Hitler a woman who was Jewish, Communist, and four months pregnant. As justification for this action, the Brazilian authorities quoted a three-line paragraph from the National Security Law, penned by the minister of justice only months earlier:

The Republic may expel from her national territory foreigners dangerous to public order or noxious to the interests of the country.

Careful to avoid mentioning the problem of anti-Semitism, but courageous enough to describe the president of Brazil as "a man of astonishing defects, who lacks a statesman's vision of the whole," Heitor Lima thus entered his request for habeas corpus, which ended with this assessment and plea:

What will happen if the habeas corpus is granted?
The defendant will remain in custody incommunicado. The inves-

tigation, in which the police see strong elements for conviction, will move ahead. Given the irrefutable evidence the police claim to have against the defendant, the judicial authority will convict her. Maria Prestes will thus be rendered incapable of performing any action noxious to the public order. Even convicted and imprisoned, however, she will be capable of being useful as wife and mother.

The present petition arrives neither sealed nor with duly attached accompanying documentation because the defendant finds herself utterly devoid of resources. She wears the same dress today as she was wearing when she was arrested, and what little money, personal belongings, and clothing the police seized at her residence have not as of this date been returned to her.

The petitioner thus requests that the following measures be taken by the Illustrious Supreme Court:

1) Rule on the present petition without cost to the defendant.
2) Solicit information from the minister of justice regarding the allegations contained in this formal petition, of which I enclose a copy.
3) Requisition legal files pursuant to the expulsion proceedings.
4) Order the defendant to appear for a trial hearing.
5) Have the defendant examined by a medical specialist to confirm her pregnancy.
6) Instruct the chief of police to report whether his investigation of the defendant and Luís Carlos Prestes will result in Maria Prestes herself being accused of any crimes against the social and political order.
7) Finally, grant a writ of habeas corpus to prevent the defendant from being expelled from national territory, without prejudice to the lawsuit or lawsuits pending or to be brought against her in the future.

Heitor Lima

The Supreme Court's first reaction came from its president, Minister Edmundo Lins, and was not very encouraging. His response to the request that the writ be processed without cost to the defendant was scrawled in the minister's own hand at the top of the first page of the petition:

Remit fees for official seal and return, if you wish.

E. Lins

Lima gave as good as he got. Ever the feminist, he scrawled his reply at the bottom of the document and returned it the same day:

> If masculine justice, even when exercised by a conscience of the finest carat, such as that of the distinguished president of the Supreme Court, must insist upon hampering the defense of an incarcerated woman with no material resources, at least the history of Brazilian civilization will not record in its judicial annals this disgrace: the conviction of a woman without any man raising his voice on her behalf in the "Palace of the Law." This petitioner will satisfy all court costs for the case.
>
> Heitor Lima

The court's ruling on the petition could not have been more appalling. Judge Bento de Faria, the court-designated *rapporteur* of the case, denied one by one all of the lawyer's requests. And, alleging that the institution of habeas corpus had been suspended by the state of war decreed by Getúlio Vargas, he decided simply to ignore the petition. The president of the Supreme Court voted with the *rapporteur*, as did six other judges. The three remaining judges avoided actually refusing to recognize the petition: they acknowledged that it had been submitted but refused the habeas corpus. The "Palace of the Law," as Heitor Lima had called it, had unanimously condemned Olga Benario to death.

15

Rebellion in "Red Square"

THE NEWS OF THE Supreme Court's decision exploded like a bomb among the prisoners. Red Square was deserted, and for the first weekday ever, the Voice of Freedom did not go on the air. The prison on Rua Frei Caneca was wrapped in a pall of depression greater than on the evenings after visitors left; but unlike visiting days, on the evening of June 17 tears gave way to rage. An attentive listener in the House of Detention would have heard, not weeping, but conspiratorial voices whispering in all the cells. The Collective had decided that Olga would not be removed from the prison without resistance from the inmates, and preparations were in progress.

An incident three or four days after the judiciary's decision showed that Müller was expecting some kind of reaction from the inmates. At 3:00 A.M. the prisoners were awakened by a clatter of furniture and objects falling, noises that seemed to come from beyond the infirmary, where a small chapel separated the so-called first-timers' block or House of Detention, from the House of Correction. Police reaction to the racket demonstrated Müller's vigilance. Within minutes, dozens of guards armed with machine guns occupied Red Square, tear-gas canisters hanging from their belts. Three soldiers were ordered to enter the cell of Hercolino Cascardo, Alcedo Cavalcanti, Agildo Barata, and Sebastião da Hora, members of a committee designated by the Collective to press Dr. Aloysio Neiva, director of the House of Detention, for better prison conditions. The authorities imagined these men had instigated a rebellion against Olga's removal from the prison. The inmates, for their part, believed this show of force was an attempt to isolate the leaders so that they could take Olga away without resistance from her comrades. Even though they were unarmed, Barata and Cascardo hurled themselves at the soldiers and tried to grab their weapons. To add to the confusion, the deafening *canecaço* began— hundreds of prisoners beating their tin cups against the cell bars. Filinto Müller was called at home and arrived at the House of Detention with two companies of tomato heads, who sealed off the streets around the prison complex. In the women's cell, Olga was hidden inside the closet that protected the periscope, and her cellmates stood ready to attack anyone who tried to remove her, armed with the only weapons at their disposal—fingernails and teeth. It was only after daybreak, when the troops managed to restore order in the block, that the origin of the noise that had almost provoked a tragedy was discovered—a large rat had dislodged a piece of wood on the improvised altar in the chapel, causing religious figures, censers, bottles of holy water, and a heavy wooden lectern to fall to the floor.

News of both the "rebellion" and the Supreme Court's decision reached Prestes in his cubicle on Santo Antônio Hill through the mechanism that had kept him informed of outside events since the day of his arrest, even though he was being held strictly incommunicado. Soldiers and prison guards who had been his comrades in the Column—or who simply admired the legend of the Knight of Hope—hid tiny packets of waterproof paper in his food: newspaper clippings rolled into minuscule cylinders one column wide and about the width of a cigarette. After dinner, Prestes slipped under the covers of his bed to unroll each tiny tube so he could read the news of the day. He read everything, even the advertisements, and simply stuffed the strips of newspaper under his mattress after reading them. Every two weeks when the commandant of the general barracks of the Special Police personally inspected the cell, he would find a mountain of paper under the mattress. Perhaps fearing a tongue-lashing from his illustrious prisoner, the commandant never admonished Prestes for this infraction, instead preferring to pretend that he had seen nothing. Minutes after the search, a soldier would appear to carry off the fortnight's collection of newspaper clippings.

These smuggled newspapers kept Prestes informed about his wife's health and legal position. Whenever Olga was taken out of prison to give statements to the police who were preparing the case against her, her photograph appeared in the press: always surrounded by police, always elegant—her hair tied back, the small purse that had been a gift from a friend, the same dress he had cut and that she had sewn while they were living underground in Meyer. When he read the descriptions of Olga in the press, or the exchanges between her and reporters, the Communist leader's heart tightened. From the *Correio da Manhã:*

> Smiling at the questions of the official, Olga did seem slightly upset, however, by the presence of the photographers. Calm throughout the hearing, she spoke fluent Portuguese, pausing before each answer, apparently to think. When she arrived at police headquarters, Olga was the object of general curiosity; she wore a white dress, was hatless, and her hair was parted in the middle and tied back with a ribbon. Black, low-heeled shoes, and a gray leather bag completed the modest outfit of the beautiful extremist who had operated under several different names as an agent of Moscow in various European cities.

And from the *Diário da Noite:*

> Olga Benario was interviewed by our reporter as she left District Chief Demócrito de Almeida's office. As always, she sidestepped all questions regarding her political activities and the assistance she had given to Luís Carlos Prestes. Revealing herself to be sentimental, she said, "I will bear my husband's name with honor until the last." She avoided replying to questions about the location and circumstances of

her marriage to Prestes, saying only that they had married, adding that she was 28 years old and called herself Maria Bergner at the time. Olga claimed she was being persecuted by the Brazilian authorities and characterized their behavior toward her as cruel. Finally, satisfying the curiosity of all reporters present, she remarked that "the police are about to carry out an absurd reprisal against a mother-to-be."

Prestes was not the only one concerned about the fate of mother and child. Since the day the couple was arrested in Rio, Prestes's mother, dona Leocádia, and his sister, Lígia, had been mounting a massive campaign on their behalf in Europe. On the evening of March 7, Dmitri Manuilski, the general secretary of the Third International, had made a second visit to the Prestes's apartment in Moscow, but this time instead of joining a celebration he had come as the representative of the Executive Committee of the Comintern to inform them of some terrible news: Prestes and Olga had fallen into the hands of Getúlio Vargas and Filinto Müller. Dona Leocádia, to whom it was also news that her son had married, immediately decided not to stay in the Soviet Union one day longer, and accompanied by Lígia, one of her four daughters, she left on the first train for Spain. They chose Spain because of its newly elected popular government, which would facilitate the entry of two women with Brazilian passports that were long expired and, since Brazil did not maintain diplomatic relations with the Soviet Union, could not be renewed there.

They traversed Spain organizing protests in all the provincial capitals to demand the release of political prisoners in Brazil, especially of the leader of the 1935 uprising and of all foreigners threatened with deportation. The Brazilian ambassador in Madrid, who was reluctant to grant the two women new passports, finally acceded because every afternoon a large crowd gathered in front of the embassy shouting, "Passports for Prestes's mother and sister!" The whirlwind of protest marches went on for over a month, with the legendary Dolores Ibárruri, "La Pasionaria," making appearances in many major cities.

From Spain the two women went on to France, where they found Paris plastered with enormous posters demanding Prestes's and

Olga's release. Next they headed for England, where they were guests of Lady Hastings—one of the women Filinto Müller had expelled from Brazil—and organized demonstrations in Hyde Park attended by thousands. On their first day in England, dona Leocádia and Lígia received a visit from Lord Listowel—dressed utterly in character in cutaway coat, top hat, and cane—who presented them with a corbeil of white lilies. He was one of the first, weeks later, to sign his name to a petition to Getúlio Vargas calling for the redemocratization of Brazil.

Dona Leocádia and Lígia knew, though, that to have any effect in Brazil their campaign would have to mobilize the American people. They therefore applied for U.S. visas, but their request was turned down. They returned to Paris hoping to obtain visas there, but at the American embassy they were confronted by a voluminous dossier on the desk of the ambassador. This mass of papers detailed the repercussions of their campaign in Spain, Britain, and France. The ambassador pounded the dossier in front of him and said, "You want me to give you entry visas so you can do *this* in the United States!"

Not surprisingly, the visas were denied. They were equally unsuccessful in Brussels and Geneva. There was no alternative but to continue the campaign in Europe. The "Paris Committee" for the liberation of Prestes and Olga was one of the most active, its principal leaders being André Malraux and Romain Rolland, who participated in all the street demonstrations and other protest activities. Every country in Europe had at least one committee, and Latin America, Australia, and New Zealand were also mobilized. Every piece of news arriving from Brazil was translated into French and distributed all over the world, along with pleas that institutions and individuals urge the Brazilian government to release Olga and Prestes.

Getúlio Vargas kept the prisoners in detention in a state of gruesome suspense for most of July and August. The expulsions of Elise Ewert and Carmen Ghioldi had been decreed, pending only the bureaucratic measures necessary to enforce the act. There was no official movement on Olga's case, however. The tension lasted until August 23, when a newspaper article smuggled into the prison was passed from hand to hand until it finally reached the women's cell:

Olga

The president of the republic has signed a decree by the Ministry of Justice expelling from Brazilian territory German national Maria Bergner Vilar, also known as Frieda Wolf Behrendt, Olga Bergner, Olga Meirelles, Eva Kruger, Maria Prestes, and Olga Benario, on the basis that her presence here is noxious to the country's interests and dangerous to the public order.

Days passed, and to everyone's surprise Olga remained in the House of Detention, along with Elise Ewert and Carmen Ghioldi. There was a reason for the delay: Filinto Müller feared the mobilization of Red Aid in European ports. His scheme of having vengeance on Prestes while simultaneously pleasing the Nazi regime would be frustrated should Communist dockworkers waylay the ship transporting Olga to Germany. Instead, he would remain in constant contact with the administration of the port of Rio de Janeiro and wait as long as necessary for a ship to dock in Brazil that was scheduled to return to Germany without stops along the way.

The delay permitted one last attempt to save Olga, by then in her seventh month of pregnancy. On September 15 attorney Luís Werneck de Castro, the husband of Olga's cellmate Maria Werneck, petitioned the Supreme Court once more for a writ of habeas corpus. The petition explained that Olga was in the late stages of pregnancy and asked that Vargas's decree be temporarily suspended. Werneck de Castro argued that Olga should be examined by a medical team of three, to be named by the judge in charge of granting the writ, to determine whether she was in a condition to undertake a voyage to Europe. The lawyer had two goals in mind. If the Supreme Court granted the habeas corpus, the sleepy Brazilian judiciary would move slowly enough to permit Olga to have the baby in Brazil. Deporting her afterward, Werneck imagined, with a newborn Brazilian citizen in her arms, would be an entirely different problem for the government to face. Second, he believed that even if his petition was refused it might prompt the president, who was to meet with his cabinet in a few days, to exempt Olga from the penalty imposed on her. As in the past, however, the Supreme Court refused to so much as acknowledge Werneck's request. And in the cabinet meeting attended by Filinto Müller, the subject of Olga Benario never even reached the agenda.

News that the delay in deporting Olga was the result of Captain Müller's decision to wait for a ship that would avoid European ports of call finally reached Heitor Lima. All the legal maneuvers having failed, his only remaining chance to prevent Olga from falling into Hitler's hands was to get her on a passenger ship that would make stops in Europe. The lawyer devised a new plan—the writing of a dramatic letter to the president's wife:

Her Excellency Mrs. Darcy Vargas:

Only when impelled by extraordinary circumstances would one of your fellow countrymen dare to write to you without a previous introduction. A group of Brazilian mothers today entrusted me, as Maria Prestes's attorney, with the duty of trying to obtain for my client sufficient funds to purchase a first-class passage, as well as the care, both during the voyage and at the port of embarkation, required for a person in her delicate condition, in order to ensure the life of her child.

I immediately wrote a letter to our illustrious minister of justice, requesting his assistance in the execution of my noble mission. Much as I respect Vicente Rao's intelligence, I have to bear in mind that men are incapable of understanding women and their problems. Beneath their verbal pomp and the hypocrisy of manners, men still retain their instincts which, though refined and polished after many centuries of civilization, they have manifested since the beginning of time in the company of their defenseless mates, who must submit to their every whim.

The myth that women are an enigma was invented precisely to justify the atrocities male civilization has visited upon them. There is nothing more accessible than the soul of a woman. Men pretend not to understand women in order to avoid the enormous list of things they owe them. In this case, it has fallen to me, then, to direct an appeal to the maternal feelings of the first lady of Brazil, imploring her intervention with our noble president, so that the efforts of these mothers on behalf of the unfortunate Maria Prestes might not be in vain.

Brazilian women are unsurpassed in their dedication, piety, and tolerance. They simply do not know how to hate; what they do best, and always, is to guide, assist, befriend, and forgive. In a word, what they do best is to love. I would belittle the attitude of these sublime souls if I ventured to describe it further. You, madam, experience this supreme grandeur firsthand. In the name of the Brazilian mothers who came to me for help, I urge your intervention. Brazil has become accustomed to seeing you as a tutelary figure, always ready to cooperate in humanitarian enterprises. Guileless, unpretentious, and unaffected as you are, it is not worldliness that attracts you to the places where the unfortunate are cared for, but rather a pure sentiment of human solidarity, a harmonious spirit, a keen and sympathetic heart.

I implore you to prove once again that your generosity exceeds your beauty. If you do, you will have been immensely generous.

Heitor Lima

Lima hoped that if the president's wife became involved in the case, Filinto Müller would not be able to prevent Olga from making the voyage to Europe on a passenger ship. But when there was no response whatsoever to his letter, he knew the die was cast. There was nothing to do but await the day of deportation. On September 21, 1936, Müller summoned his assistants, along with Aloysio Neiva, the director of the House of Detention, to his office on Rua da Relacão. The ship *La Coruña*, chartered by the German shipping company Hamburg-Südamerikanische Dampfschiffahrt-Gesellschaft, was to dock in the port of Rio de Janeiro before the sun rose on September 23 with one objective: to collect Olga Prestes and Elise Ewert. The steamer would remain in Rio for only one day; no other ship was scheduled in the near future to make the same trip as *La Coruña*—sailing directly to Hamburg. Two Brazilian policemen who spoke fluent German had been chosen to accompany the prisoners on their voyage. Müller informed those present that it would be their responsibility to remove the two women from the House of Detention. By force, if necessary.

Shortly after dinner Carlos Brandes, a police official, appeared at the door of the women's cell. Brandes was an ingratiating fellow who frequented Rio's society circles passing himself off as a "high-level employee" of the Ministry of Foreign Affairs. The Left claimed he was a representative of British Intelligence in Brazil. He was accompanied by two high-ranking officials from Filinto Müller's office, together with three armed guards. Closing his fingers around the bars of the women's cell, he said delicately, "Good evening. The police are aware of the fact that Olga has not been well today and so we've been sent to transfer her to a hospital better equipped to care for her than the prison infirmary. . . . If she doesn't receive better medical attention, she risks premature delivery. . . ."

The women did not let him finish his sentence. They rose to their feet and began frenetically beating their tin cups on the bars. It was either Maria Werneck de Castro or Beatriz Bandeira who yelled out to Red Square, "Everybody up! That creep Brandes is here to take Maria Prestes!"

Inside every cell, the person designated by the Collective as caretaker of the picklock—Júlio Alves's gift of May 27—sprang into action. Within minutes the cell doors were flung open and hundreds of prisoners assembled in the main courtyard. In cells where the precious key couldn't be located in the confusion, the inmates smashed their cots and used the pieces to break open the rusty locks. The prisoners swarmed out of their squalid cells like enraged animals, half-naked, each one brandishing whatever might be useful as a weapon: empty milk bottles, pieces of wood, and broken beds. Brandes tried to be forceful but stuck to the original story. He stood outside the women's cell shouting to those down below, "I didn't come here to argue with you people. I came here to do my job. If you try to prevent me from removing her you will be responsible for the consequences. Is that what you want? You want her to have a miscarriage and lose the baby so you can blame the police afterward? I'm only here to take her to the hospital!"

An even louder voice rose above the tumult. "To a hospital in Berlin, you Nazi bastard!"

By this time Brandes and his men were surrounded by prisoners from the second floor, but still he tried to negotiate, appealing to the elder Campos da Paz, "Dr. Campos da Paz, I implore you to calm your comrades and explain to them that I'm simply not capable of such a despicable act!"

The response was more shouting and insults. "Fascist son of a bitch! If you want to take Maria Prestes out of here you're going to have to kill all of us, one by one!"

His face drenched with sweat, Brandes insisted, "I give you my word of honor that this woman will be admitted immediately to a maternity ward! I guarantee it. I've already called for an ambulance to make the trip more comfortable. I cannot allow your protests to prevent me from following my express orders to transfer her to the hospital!"

Lieutenant Gay da Cunha—the man who had sketched the designs of the Brazilian air force planes for the baby's layette—gathered a group of colleagues from the School of Aviation and the Third Infantry Regiment and said, "There's no way we'll get anywhere negotiating with them. Violence is the only way. The head guard is upstairs with Brandes. If we don't grab him and his two bodyguards this thing is going to be over in minutes."

A group of prisoners climbed the iron steps to the cells on the second floor. Carrying blades made by Júlio Alves from guava paste tins, they joined the crowd that had gathered around Brandes and suddenly grabbed him and the two soldiers by the neck and dragged them back to the ground floor. The three hostages were locked in a cell and guarded by some of the more athletic officers. At a hastily called meeting of the Collective, Rodolfo Ghioldi suggested that Communist physician Valério Konder be the prisoner to conduct negotiations from that point on.

The third guard, separated from his fellow soldiers, tried to save his skin by running out the door. A group of inmates took advantage of the confusion and occupied the women's cell. Olga was stretched out on her bed, protected only by the greasy curtains hiding the periscope.

Valério Konder advised Carlos Brandes firmly, "You are free to leave. From now on the only person we will talk to is the prison director, Dr. Aloysio Neiva. Any attempt to take Maria Prestes out by force and the hostages will pay with their lives."

No one was under the illusion that the resistance could yield any real results, but they knew the disturbance gave the police the impression that they were capable of anything. The prisoners tossed everything in their cells into Red Square, yanking the iron doors off their rusty hinges and throwing them down with a deafening crash, while others banged their cups on the floor, the walls, the bars, shouting wildly, "Don't take her! Don't take her! Don't take her!"

There was only one prisoner who didn't participate. Curled up on his bed, chain-smoking, Graciliano Ramos looked as if he were going mad. Staring fixedly at the floor, grasping his head in his hands, he said over and over again, paralyzed, in a voice that was almost inaudible in the midst of all that racket, "It's not true, they're not really doing this. . . . Shipping her off to Hitler's Germany? She's a Jew. . . . She's pregnant. . . . Brazil can't do this to her. . . ."

In the middle of the night the police made it clear they were not disposed to any form of negotiation. Special Police troops armed with machine guns, tear-gas grenades, and even flamethrowers, and led by Filinto Müller, surrounded the prison complex on Rua Frei Caneca. A group of elite sharpshooters isolated the block and waited for orders to move in. The tension lasted all night long. Though armed only with wooden clubs, empty bottles, and home-made knives, the inmates continued their tough talk. "In order to get Maria Prestes out of here, you fascist dogs are going to have to kill three hundred Brazilians!"

Both sides were nervous, neither one wanting to risk taking the initiative. It was past midday when the first official communiqué came from outside. The prison director was authorized by Captain Müller to bring a proposal to the inmates: Olga Benario would leave the prison and go straight to the hospital, accompanied by a committee of prisoners to be named by the Collective. First to be consulted was Olga herself, who immediately agreed. She said that the resistance was a heroic display on the part of her Brazilian comrades but would lead to nothing. They would be massacred by the troops surrounding the building. In addition, Olga was afraid that Müller would use the situation to make Prestes his personal hostage. She was terrified that if the resistance continued they would kill him. In order to convince the most obstinate, who intended to take the rebellion to its bitter end, she made an appeal. "Let them take me to the hospital. I want to have my baby here in Brazil. . . ."

When finally—from naïveté or from simply recognizing a lost cause—the Collective accepted Müller's proposal, night had fallen. After much discussion it was agreed that the "committee" to accompany Olga to the hospital would be composed of two prisoners only, one chosen by the men and one by the women. They were Campos da Paz Júnior, because he was a doctor, and Maria Werneck de Castro, who had demonstrated great firmness during the twenty-four hours of resistance. It was agreed that the three would travel by ambulance to Gafrée Guinle maternity hospital and that Olga's escorts would leave her side only when she was back at the House of Detention.

As Maria Werneck walked downstairs besides the stretcher carrying Olga, Campos da Paz yelled up to her, "I'll go out down here and meet you at the main entrance!"

He was allowed to join the two women as planned, but before they reached the outside door Maria realized they had been tricked. Dr. Campos da Paz was dragged off by ten policemen and shoved into a van. Maria and Olga were settled into the back of an ambulance, and the procession moved out onto the main street, surrounded by dozens of policemen with machine guns and protected on all sides by jeeps full of soldiers. Maria was surprised to see they were in fact heading toward Gafrée Guinle hospital. For a few minutes she imagined that Olga might really be in danger of premature delivery and that the government had decided not to take any chances. Olga took Maria's hand and said, "Don't worry, it's going to be all right."

When the ambulance stopped, it was Maria's turn to reassure Olga. "You were right: we're at Gafrée Guinle. I know the place well."

The ambulance doors opened and Maria looked out in horror. All traffic and pedestrians had been cleared from all adjacent streets so there would be no witnesses, and the entrance to the hospital was sealed by dozens more military and police vehicles. It looked like some kind of war zone. A gargantuan cop loomed above her, a machine gun on a leather thong slung across his chest. He pointed to a police van that had pulled up behind the ambulance and ordered Maria Werneck to get in.

She resisted. "No! I'm staying with Maria Prestes. I have Dr. Brandes's word that I can stay with her and I'm not going anywhere."

Brandes himself appeared next, and Maria Werneck looked him straight in the eye. "Dr. Brandes, you know me, and not just from prison but from earlier days. You gave me your word that I would go to the hospital with her and I'm not leaving now!"

Brandes was cynical. "Yes, I did give you my word, dona Maria, but these are orders from higher up."

The giant cop smiled and motioned to the van with the tip of his machine gun. "Like I said. Get in there."

Olga squeezed Maria's hand and said, "Go on, Maria. There's no use resisting here."

After the women kissed good-bye, Maria Werneck was put into the van and the door was slammed behind her. She felt a leg nudge her in the dark and asked who was there. A deep, resonant voice replied, "It's me, Maria, Campos da Paz. They couldn't take me back to the prison because they don't want the others to find out about their scheme."

Olga never saw so much as the hospital parking lot. The military convoy continued on to the port under a fine, persistent rain. When, finally, she was taken out of the ambulance to be carried to the ship on her stretcher, she glimpsed the name of the steamer: *La Coruña*. For an instant she dared hope she was about to board a Spanish ship. But craning her neck a little further, she looked up and saw, flying from the main mast, a flag with a black swastika in the center.

16

In the Cellars of the Gestapo

TWENTY POUNDS LIGHTER than when first arrested despite being seven months pregnant, carrying only the $150 found by the police in the house on Rua Honório and a small bundle of baby clothes, Olga was moved from the stretcher to a bed in a minuscule cabin aboard *La Coruña,* where she became lost in thought until roused by a knocking at the door. The door opened and a face appeared: João Guilherme Neumann, the detective assigned by Filinto Müller to guard Olga during the voyage and deliver her to Gestapo officials in Hamburg. Neumann was forty-two, the grandson of German immigrants who grew flowers in the mountain city of Petrópolis in the state of Rio. He was a member of the political police capture squad—he had apprehended Beatriz Bandeira, one of Olga's cellmates—and had been chosen as Olga's escort because he spoke fluent German. Clearly uncomfortable, the detective told his charge he had nothing personal against her or her ideals and that he was there on a strictly professional basis.

"I'm a cop. I don't argue with orders unless they're absurd."

Neumann also brought the welcome news that they would not be traveling alone: Elise Ewert was also on her way from the House of Detention and would be installed in the cabin next to Olga's; her escort for the trip was to be Luiz Felipe Peixoto, another of Müller's men. As soon as Peixoto and Sabo arrived, *La Coruña* would weigh anchor and head for Hamburg. Before she was carried on board, Olga had heard the ship's captain, Heinrich von Appen, arguing with Brazilian and German police. The port was too noisy for her to catch much of the conversation, but Neumann explained that when the captain had seen Olga, he demanded to know how many months pregnant she was.

"Seven months," someone replied.

"Then she's not coming aboard," von Appen declared gruffly. "I have orders to transport two women prisoners and two guards, but no one said anything about one of the prisoners being seven months pregnant. This is against international law. And on my ship, I'm the one who calls the shots."

A plainclothes German policeman showed the captain his badge and put forward a very convincing argument. "Your orders are from President Vargas himself, and the prisoner is considered of maximum interest to the Gestapo. If you refuse to take her, I would suggest that you not even dock in Hamburg. Officials there will be expecting her, and if she doesn't show up it's very possible that the fate reserved for her will be assigned to you."

So Captain von Appen was not the only one to call the shots on his ship: Olga was brought on board against his will and against maritime law. Olga took advantage of Neumann's apparent sympathy to suggest that they would need to install a bell in her cabin in case she became ill during the night. Neumann agreed and explained the restrictions that would be placed on the prisoners during the voyage. During the day they could circulate in the small corridor outside the four cabins—Olga's and Sabo's in the middle and Peixoto's and Neumann's on either side. Since the cabins were at the stern of the ship and at the end of the corridor, the captain had only to close off one end, where he placed a sign in German: "This area prohibited by orders of the captain." For the next few weeks, then, the only view of the world Olga and Sabo would have was through four portholes along eleven yards of corridor.

As he left, Neumann told Olga to remain in her cabin; his orders were that the door was to be locked from the outside at night. In the absence of a bell, if she needed anything she should pound on the door.

An hour later a thunderous noise shook the whole cabin. Only then did Olga realize she had been assigned a berth right beside the ship's engines. Apparently, Sabo had arrived and *La Coruña* was preparing to weigh anchor. It was a night of insomnia and vomiting. Every half hour Olga had to rush to the sink in the tiny bathroom. In addition to the pitching and rolling of the ship and the roaring of the engines, the closeness to the engine room made the cabin a veritable oven. The only fresh air came through a tiny ventilator in the ceiling. Around daybreak the ship began to toss less and only then did she manage to get some sleep.

Olga's first day on board was spent locked in her cabin, where she was cared for by Sabo. In addition to the bell, which the captain installed that morning, Neumann managed to get her some anti-seasickness pills. From the second day on, the women were allowed to bring chairs from their cabins out into the corridor, where they sat knitting and crocheting, getting up every hour or two to stretch their legs and stare out of the portholes at the ocean. The trip was a kind of imprisonment for the policemen as well, since they had to spend the whole day walking from cabin to corridor, corridor to cabin. Olga tried to be polite, but she spoke to them only when necessary and avoided prolonged conversation. Sabo was even less communicative. Still suffering from the effects of her torture at the hands of the Brazilian and German police, she simply refused to speak to either one, except to protest at the quality of Olga's food or treatment.

Though it was obvious that Olga was reluctant to talk, Neumann insisted on approaching her, sometimes to complain about Sabo's gruffness—"She's a nasty one," he would say—or even to ask for details of her own political and personal life. On one occasion the conversation turned to talk of the deportation, and he couldn't contain his curiosity:

"But couldn't you prove that you and Captain Prestes were married?"

He was a policeman, he worked for Filinto Müller, he was cooperating with the Gestapo in Hamburg. . . . Forever hopeful, Olga tried to throw him off the track. "We were married in Marseilles, but we didn't have the papers to prove it."

Contrary to what the police had been told, *La Coruña* made one stop before Hamburg, but at another Brazilian port: on the fourth day of the voyage the ship docked at Salvador, Bahia. The port was overrun by troops—Müller had been warned and wasn't taking any chances. The ship would stay only long enough to pick up a load of piassava palm. Olga asked for permission to give a crew member money to do some shopping for her, since she had come on board with only the clothes on her back and a small bundle of baby things. Von Appen agreed, and once the ship was again on the high seas a package was delivered to her cabin: two pairs of sandals (one for her and one for Sabo), a toothbrush and toothpaste, and supplies for knitting and crocheting.

On September 30, the ship cruised past Fernando de Noronha Island, off the northern coast of Brazil. Neumann mentioned that this was where the government planned to transfer prisoners convicted of participation in the November revolt. Taking advantage of the good weather and calm seas, the captain decided to practice rescue maneuvers, during which Olga and Sabo had to remain locked in their rooms. Three days later, under a black sky, they crossed the equator. In the middle of the night Olga was awakened by the familiar sound of songs she remembered from her childhood in Munich and imagined she was dreaming. Soon she understood: a group of German sailors on the main deck was commemorating the ship's crossing back into the Northern Hemisphere, dancing and singing to the accompaniment of a harmonica. Two nights later, Olga and Sabo were allowed to leave their cabins after dinner to look out the portholes: *La Coruña* expected to catch sight of a German Zeppelin en route from Europe to South America. As soon as it appeared on the horizon, the captain had the searchlights on the main deck aimed at the sky, to salute the dirigible airship's crew and to improve his passengers' view of the craft. For several minutes the Zeppelin seemed to hover directly over the ship, performing maneuvers and flying so low that it seemed it would smash into the ship's funnels. Dashing from one porthole to another to get a better view, Olga and Sabo could see the passengers standing at the rail of the Zeppelin, elegantly dressed men and women with glasses in their hands, waving to those below.

Toward the end of the first week in October, as he skirted the island of Madeira, Captain von Appen received new warnings not to dock at European ports under any circumstances. If he did so, the wireless operators reminded him, the two women would inevitably be taken off the ship. The earlier incident at Le Havre had been blatantly exaggerated, turning the seventeen liberated deportees into "more than a hundred." Captain von Appen was also informed that he should be prepared for attempts to free Olga and Sabo in the form of pirate attacks on the high seas. At least this was what Neumann told Olga after one of his forays to the upper decks of the ship.

La Coruña was still teeming with such tales on the night of October 12, when the crew was surprised to see a ship fast approaching, her whistle sounding an SOS. Von Appen immediately switched off the engines so he could figure out what was going on. Joining his officers on the bridge, he saw that it was an enormous two-masted sailing ship, clearly not a fishing vessel. Several sailors on the mystery craft's deck were trying unsuccessfully to communicate with the Germans in Spanish. Von Appen sent for Neumann, who was belowdecks with his prisoners.

Before going up on deck, Neumann told Olga that something strange was going on: an unknown ship was stopped in front of *La Coruña* and the captain had called him to the bridge. Olga was convinced that Republican Spaniards had arrived to free her. Once on the bridge, Neumann heard someone on the other ship yelling, "Portuguese! Portuguese!" to indicate the language of the crew. After much shouting back and forth, Neumann found out what they wanted: the ship's navigation equipment had failed and they merely needed to know their latitude and longitude. Once he was back belowdecks, Neumann told Olga, "I guess it wasn't your time yet, dona Olga. It was just a Portuguese pleasure boat that had lost its way."

October 16 dawned with the German steamer in the middle of the English Channel; by nightfall the coast of Belgium was in sight. The temperature had fallen dramatically and unexpectedly, prompting Captain von Appen to authorize additional blankets for

the prisoners and their guards. The following day was spent crossing the North Sea and by dusk they were entering the River Elbe in
Germany. At 6:00 A.M. on October 18 there was a knock at Neumann's door. "Herr Neumann! Herr Neumann!"

A sailor instructed Neumann to come up to the captain's stateroom and to bring the prisoners with him. Neumann hastily woke
Olga and Sabo, called to his colleague Peixoto, and, looking out one
of the portholes, realized that the ship was docking in Hamburg.
Once in von Appen's quarters, Olga was terrified at what she saw: a
dozen black uniforms with the unmistakable swastika embroidered
on the collar of their jackets. The SS had come to meet her. Hud-
dling in blankets and wearing the sandals bought in Salvador, Olga
and Sabo were turned over to the Nazis in less than two minutes,
with no formalities whatsoever. One of the men simply identified
himself by name and rank and announced that he was there "in the
name of the Führer to collect the two criminals."

La Coruña's four passengers parted company then and there.
Neumann and Peixoto boarded a train to Berlin, where Ambassador
Moniz de Aragão handed them two tickets to Brazil on a ship from
the Lloyd's fleet and a generous stipend of £250, duly authorized by
the Chancellery in Rio de Janeiro. Olga and Sabo didn't even have a
chance to say good-bye to each other: Sabo was put in one police
van and Olga in another, and they sped off at high speed, surrounded by armed SS men, disappearing into the fog in the direction of Berlin.

It was a seven-hour trip in freezing temperatures. All Olga could
make out in the darkness were the vague profiles of soldiers, discern-
ible from the glow of their cigarettes or from the sudden flame of a
match as another was lit. With her hands manacled beside her legs
to iron rings on the van's metal bench, Olga began having muscle
cramps after a half hour, but she thought it better to say nothing and
endure the pain. A little after midday, in heavy rain, and with the
temperature still falling, the van arrived in Berlin. The doors were
flung open and Olga recognized where she was: at 15 Barnimstrasse, the Gestapo's dreaded women's prison, a four-story
construction more than a hundred years old, through whose doors
her heroine Rosa Luxemburg had passed two decades earlier. Notified by their eager colleague Moniz de Aragão, the Gestapo was

well prepared to receive her and had arranged for a welcoming committee at least as impressive as the one at the port: a woman barber was waiting in the prison infirmary, scissors in hand. Olga was directed to a chair, still handcuffed, and informed by a prison official, "We're going to give you a little haircut to avoid the spread of lice. They're very common, you know, in Jews and Communists."

Olga was then handed a striped uniform, obviously worn before by some extremely fat prisoner. She felt ridiculous: as thin as a rail, potbellied, her hair chopped off at the scalp, and wearing something that fit her like a potato sack. Walking with difficulty because of the weight of her stomach, her body aching from the long trip in the van, she was led to the very depths of the gray building. The farther they went, the more encouraging were the sounds she heard: voices and babies crying. She tried to console herself—"At least I won't be the only mother in this hell." Her cell was a cubicle two yards square with a rough cement floor, a thin mattress on a slab of concrete, a meager flannel blanket—"I should have tried to bring one from the ship," she thought—a sink, and a hole in the floor. Standing on tiptoe, she was able to peer through a small barred window into an interior courtyard. Before she had even finished examining the cell, the iron door opened behind her. A military doctor had been sent to certify the state of her pregnancy. After a cursory examination throughout which the doctor showed an air of nausea, he proclaimed, "Your health is excellent and you should go into labor within four weeks."

Even before *La Coruña* docked in Hamburg, a Communist sailor arriving in France on a Brazilian cargo ship had delivered by hand to Lígia and dona Leocádia a letter informing them of what had happened to Olga. This was their first news, both that Olga was pregnant and that she had been deported. Horrified, they tried to mobilize the liberation committees, Workers' Central, and the French Communist Party in an attempt to pull the two women off the ship should it dock somewhere before its final destination. Despite the vigilance at French and Spanish ports, *La Coruña* cruised along the European coast unnoticed. Dona Leocádia did manage to arrange for a lawyer to be in Hamburg to try to contact

Olga or Elise, but he wasn't able to so much as see the ship. Access to all piers was forbidden by the Gestapo, and no one could enter or leave the area that day without passing an SS checkpoint. Prestes's mother and sister were not about to give up. They decided to go to Germany themselves, accompanied by a group of British women. On November 11 they arrived at Gestapo headquarters on Prinz Albrechtstrasse, where they were informed that Olga was well and that the baby had not yet been born. Their insistent requests to visit the prisoner were denied; the Nazis' only concession was to permit them to leave a package of food and clothing at the reception desk of the prison on Barnimstrasse. The package was delivered to Olga without the slightest indication of who had sent it, but since a newly arrived inmate had told her about the campaign her mother-in-law and sister-in-law were organizing in France and England, she deduced the origin of the gifts.

Lígia and dona Leocádia returned to France with nothing more than a vague promise from the Germans that they would be advised by the Red Cross when the baby was born. Desperate, dona Leocádia knocked on every possible door, repeating the same lament to anyone who would listen: "The Nazis locked up my son, and now they want to kill my daughter-in-law and my unborn grandchild."

Realizing that in Paris the chances of receiving word from Germany were limited, the Prestes women decided to go to Geneva, headquarters of the International Red Cross and the League of Nations. They were greeted coolly at the League of Nations and came away with only a promise that telegrams would be sent to the Brazilian government—telegrams that merely inquired after Prestes's legal situation, no protests of any kind. Repeating their appeal to the Red Cross, they were promised that representatives of the agency in Germany would work energetically so that at least news of the child's birth would reach the two women.

Despite the awful conditions in the Berlin prison, Olga hadn't lost her spirit. Citing international and German law, she demanded the right to receive newspapers on a regular basis. Since the law didn't stipulate what sort of newspapers, the request was granted: every morning a copy of *Volkischer Beobachter*, the official paper of the Nazi Party, was delivered to Olga. It contained nothing but reports on the "Jewish-Bolshevik conspiracy" and the virtues of Adolf Hitler's National Socialism. The reports that mattered to Olga—news about the fate of Communists in the European countries that were resisting the Fascists—came to her by word of mouth from the dozens and dozens of new political prisoners arriving at Barnimstrasse every week. When Olga asked, insistently, what crime she stood accused of, she was informed by the prison administration that no formal complaint had been lodged against her. The statute of limitations had run out on the charges relating to the armed raid on Moabit Prison, and the case involving her alleged complicity with Otto in espionage had been closed for lack of evidence. Olga found the lack of any new charges far from reassuring, however; on the contrary, it meant she would not be released in the near future. Prisoners who had not been indicted had no reason to appoint a lawyer and nothing to defend themselves from. Olga knew very well that the crimes for which she really had been incarcerated would never be invalidated under nazism: being a Jew and a Communist.

In the predawn hours of November 27, 1936, exactly one year after the frustrated Brazilian rebellion, Olga woke to find her mattress soaking wet and realized that her water had broken. She climbed out of bed, felt around for her tin drinking cup, and banged it against the iron door a few times—the previously arranged code for when childbirth seemed imminent. Just as the sun was breaking through the icy fog that enveloped the prison, Olga gave birth to a girl. Her name, Anita Leocádia, had been chosen months before: Anita in memory of the Brazilian heroine Anita Garibaldi, wife of Giuseppe Garibaldi, the revolutionary forger of the unification of Italy; and Leocádia in honor of the mother-in-law Olga had never met but had learned to love and respect through Prestes—and who was now crisscrossing Europe to mobilize committees for her release. The baby was wrapped in the infant clothes made by Olga's cellmates in Brazil—some of them so big they were used as blankets for little Anita Leocádia.

Despite the adverse circumstances of Olga's pregnancy, the baby had been born surprisingly plump and healthy. The prison matron informed Olga that with the birth of the child her rations would increase: in addition to the two bowls of watery pea soup she received daily, for the next six months she would be given a cup of milk and a bowl of oatmeal. But this was accompanied by a frightening warning. "Prison rules dictate that the infants be separated from their mothers after six months and sent to state orphanages," the matron began. "But we're going to make an exception in your case. We are aware that there are people in France and England using your name to campaign against the Reich. To prove that this is a humanitarian regime, we're going to let the baby stay with you for as long as you can breast-feed her."

While this news threw Olga into a panic, there was a ray of hope in it as well: the concession made by the Nazis would buy dona Leocádia and Lígia more time to intensify their campaign for the freedom of both mother and child. How long Olga could keep Anita with her, meanwhile, would depend entirely on her body: she would have to get sufficient nutrition from her meager rations to produce milk—a lot of milk, for a long time.

It was not until early February, when Anita was more than two months old, that the Red Cross informed dona Leocádia and Lígia of her birth. The agency also told them that Olga had received the two letters dona Leocádia had written from Geneva and that correspondence between them had finally been authorized, though it would be subject to censorship by the Gestapo and would have to be written in German. In the meantime, the women were informed, Anita was at risk: she would be taken away as soon as her mother's milk ran out. Tucked inside the envelope with the letter from the Red Cross was a smaller envelope, stamped with the Nazi eagle of the censorship service, containing a note from Olga to her mother-in-law, whom she had begun to refer to as "mother":

Berlin, 1/31/37

Dear Mother,

I have just received your letters of January 1 and 9. You can't imagine the joy they brought me.

First, I want to let you know that you're a grandmother. Little Anita Leocádia was born on November 27. She's a healthy girl, 8 lbs. 5 oz. at birth, and has black hair and blue eyes. She's doing well and her smile alone takes me away from this terrible place. I'm doing all I can to make sure Anita has everything she needs. I'm breast-feeding her, and intend to do so for as long as possible.

At present I am being held under "protective custody" in the infirmary of a women's prison. There were complications with the birth and I was seriously ill, but I'm fine now.

You asked how often you can write to me. According to prison rules, I'm allowed to receive a letter every 10 days. I'll be happy to keep you informed about my daughter's development! Please write to me whenever you can and tell me what you know about Carlos's situation. I have not had word from him since September 23, that is, since the day I was expelled from Brazil. I wrote to him after the little one was born but still haven't received a reply. I'd like you to send me a picture of Carlos in one of your next letters, because I have none with me here.

Dear mother, I wait impatiently to hear from you. With my best wishes for your health . . .

A kiss from your daughter,

Olga

The campaign in France was widened to call for Prestes's release in Brazil as well as Olga's and Anita's in Germany. Dona Leocádia and Lígia joined forces with another brave woman, Minna Ewert, who was traveling all over Europe working for the freedom of Arthur and Elise Ewert, her brother and sister-in-law. Minna managed to send a telegram to President Roosevelt denouncing Ewert's torture in Brazilian prisons and calling for U.S. government intervention.

Prestes's mother and sister focused on the primary concern of Olga's health: she had to be supplied with substantial nourishment so she would be able to breast-feed the child long enough to give the campaign for their freedom time to grow. Every other week dona Leocádia and Lígia sent Olga a fat package weighing some forty-five pounds, containing food, chocolate, and clothing. German import duties cost two or three times the value of the items in the package. As far as they could tell from the infrequent letters they received, only half the packages got to her, but even so their trouble yielded results: Olga was recuperating and had abundant milk. Dona Leocádia and Lígia also pressed on with the campaign, never accepting for a minute the idea of separating mother and daughter, always calling for Olga's release as well as the child's, reminding people that she was innocent and that no formal charges had been brought against her. In addition, they had to find a way to get Prestes the news that he was the father of a little girl.

Back in Rio, Heráclito Fontoura Sobral Pinto, a lawyer and Christian activist, had taken it upon himself to defend Prestes and Arthur Ewert before the National Security Tribunal, an extrajudicial court created specifically to try those involved in the November 1935 insurrection. Sobral wangled a visit to the prison to inform Prestes of his initiative but was angrily rebuffed. Prestes rejected his offer, claiming Sobral was a man of bourgeois mentality who lacked both the capacity and the real desire to defend him and who was incapable of understanding Communist thought. When the lawyer insisted that he only wanted to help, Prestes's answer was a threat: "Any initiative you make on my behalf without my consent will cost you dearly: I will denounce you internationally as an imposter!"

The illustrious prisoner's reaction did not intimidate Sobral Pinto. While it was true that he was an intransigent anti-Communist, the idea of defending a Communist blended perfectly with the thought of St. Augustine: "Love the sinner but hate the sin." He explained it this way to his friends: "I know that communism denies and offends God, but I also know that Communists are the way they are because they are sinners." A decidedly persistent man, Sobral appealed to one of the very few people who had influence on the prisoner: his mother. Just a few weeks after the harsh words of their first meeting, Prestes received a letter from Paris in which dona Leocádia asked him to trust Sobral Pinto. Apparently this maternal advice had an impact on the son's behavior.

The lawyer's first move was to denounce the dictatorship's treatment of Arthur Ewert, focusing public attention on the case. Early in 1937, a Rio newspaper had published a police notice about a citizen of the southern city of Curitiba named Mansur Karan, who had been sent to prison for beating a horse to death. Sobral Pinto tried to save Ewert's life by pointing to the judge's decision to convict Karan and referring to an article in the animal protection laws stipulating that "all animals in the country shall be wards of the state." If the laws regarding the treatment of human beings were not sufficient to prevent the torture of the German prisoner, he argued, Ewert should at least be guaranteed protection under the laws providing for the humane treatment of animals.

Thanks to Sobral Pinto's intervention, Prestes began receiving letters from his mother and sister. Though both had been writing to him regularly since his imprisonment, the police had not let him see a single one. A letter from his mother in Paris, dated March 6, 1937, was his first news of Anita Leocádia's birth:

My dear son,

I hope with all my heart that you are still well and strong in body and spirit. I have received nothing from you, though I've sent letter after letter to the prison where you've been incarcerated since March 1936. I have no way of knowing whether you received them. Today I decided to write to you again, hoping for better results this time, that is, hoping these lines will reach you, bringing you our love and longing, but even more importantly the wonderful news we have just received. You have a little daughter, born on November 27 in the hospital of a women's prison in Berlin, and our dear Olga named her Anita Leocádia, in honor of the Brazilian heroine Anita Garibaldi and as a kindness to your mother. What an admirable creature your wife is, and how worthy of you. We congratulate you effusively on this wonderful event. After all the crises we've been through and the terrible uncertainty about the fate of heroic Olga and the precious child she carried in her womb, you can well imagine the indescribable emotion that flooded over us and the enormous joy that filled our hearts when we heard the happy news. We are all indebted to our heroic Olga, whose calm and patience in the face of terrible mental suffering made this wonderful event possible. I'm enclosing a letter from her—the only one I've received, though I write three times a month, as allowed by prison rules—so you can share in some of the details of the birth of your little daughter. Through the intermediary of friends, I have already sent you a small sum of money, warm clothing, etc. You can rest easy, because we will also take good care of these two dear creatures over here and do everything in our power to make sure they lack for nothing. We (Lígia and I) are just finishing a little handmade layette and very soon we will send it to our sweet Anita. I've already sent Olga the picture she asked for. . . .

Well, my dear son, I'll close now, since this letter is already too long, but first I want to remind you to write to Olga if you can—she is so worried because she hasn't heard from you. Send the letter to me and I'll make sure she gets it. Your sisters send their love, and kiss you with immense affection. With warm hugs, great longing, and my most ardent prayers for your precious health,

Your devoted mother,
Leocádia Prestes

17

Dona Leocádia Takes On the Gestapo

THE NEWS THAT HE WAS a father, that Olga was alive, and that his mother and sisters were well filled Prestes with hope at a time when he found himself facing condemnation by the National Security Tribunal. Sitting in his cubicle, he read and reread dozens of times over the letters from his wife and mother. When Sobral Pinto told him he had authorization to answer Olga's letter, he asked for one favor. Aware that his letters would be censored, first by Filinto Müller's men and then by the Gestapo in Berlin, Prestes asked his lawyer to buy him a German grammar book and dictionary: "At least then the Nazis here in Brazil will have to arrange for a translator in order to censor my letters."

Armed with only these two books and the rudiments of German he had learned from Olga, he wrote to his wife in her native language. Weeks later he received the first reply—a short note that, after being screened by the Nazis, had been sent to the Red Cross in Geneva and then on to dona Leocádia in France, who sent it to Sobral Pinto's office in Rio, until finally it reached Prestes in his cell:

Berlin, April 1937

Dear Karli,

Before anything else, I want to tell you about our little girl, who is already more than four months old. Physically, she is a mixture of the two of us. She has dark hair like yours, and your mouth and hands. Her eyes are big and blue, though not as light as mine—hers are a kind of violet-blue. She has a soft, white complexion, with beautiful rosy cheeks. How I wish you could see her. But the prettiest thing about her is her smile. A smile so pretty it makes you forget everything bad in this world. I imagine how you would play with her, pulling her funny tufts of hair.

Mother sent me a picture of you. I spend hours with our little Anita Leocádia on my lap staring at your picture as if I were beside you. It's already been over a year since we were separated, but I will find the strength to wait for the happy day when we will be together again.

Your Olga

It was not until two months later, in June, that Olga received news of her husband again, in a letter from dona Leocádia. And it was bad news: on May 8 Prestes had been convicted by the National Security Tribunal and sentenced to sixteen years and eight months in prison; Arthur Ewert was given thirteen years. Judge Barros Barreto imposed so many obstructions to the presence of the prisoners' lawyers in the closed courtroom that Prestes asked Sobral Pinto to let him speak in his own defense. His speech was a bill of indictment aimed more at the population at large than at the body of jurors sitting there with the obvious charge to convict him. Dona Leocádia reported that even after sentencing Prestes would remain in custody under the same severe restrictions. Objects for personal use brought to the prison by Sobral Pinto were rigorously searched. "Luís Carlos Prestes's handkerchiefs are shaken out and held up to the light, the waistbands of his shorts are stretched out inch by inch so the police can be sure no note, no tiny steel saw, has been concealed in them by his mother," the tireless lawyer complained. "A bar of soap was cut in half, chocolate bars broken into bits, ties turned inside out, and the lining of a cashmere suit was almost torn open at the seams."

193

Olga

Worried that Anita might be sent to a Nazi orphanage, dona Leocádia also wrote to Olga saying that she had decided to return to Berlin to work for their release. The news Prestes received during these months was no better, with the exception of another letter from his wife, who had had to wait not ten days but thirty to write to him again:

May 12, 1937

Carlos,

I can't find the words to say how happy I was to get your letter of March 16. Dear one: I must tell you all about little Anita. You know, I look at this tiny being and see in a certain way my own life reflected there. There are new marvels to be discovered in her every day, and every day she becomes more deeply embedded in my heart. What a beautiful thing that she gets her nourishment from me, that I can give her the best of my vital forces, the strength that I possess. She likes to lie in her little bed with her legs in the air, and sometimes she grabs hold of her tiny feet. When someone approaches, you have to see how her whole face lights up. The happiest of all are her blue eyes, so clear and bright. It's amazing how many expressions such a tiny being can have. Joy, annoyance, hunger, fatigue, everything is reflected in her face. For her part, she knows perfectly well when I come near whether I'm happy or sad. When I want to nurse her, all I have to do is take her in my arms and she opens her little mouth like a famished bird. And when she needs a break, she lets go of the breast, smiles up at me, and then leans her head down to take some more. If the milk doesn't come fast enough she gets impatient and pounds me with her little hand. Ah, how I would love for her to be able to yank at one of your curls, as she always does to mine.

Oh, I could tell you so many things. How we do exercises, for example, and how we sing—but I'll save that for the next letter. There's a tree in the courtyard with a family of birds nesting in it. The young ones just hatched. If only you could see them. . . . They fly off and come back with insects and other things to eat. I spend hours watching them and thinking of us. Ah, only human beings are capable of tearing a family apart the way they have ours.

An immense ocean separates us, but I feel you very close.

Your Olga

Prestes's mother returned to Germany sometime in July 1937, this time accompanied by two British lawyers, May Miles and Kathleen Kimber. Faced with the strictness of Barnimstrasse, where Olga was not even informed that her mother-in-law was in the country, they directed their inquiries to Gestapo headquarters. The secret police refused even to discuss the idea of Olga's release. As for the fate of her daughter, they insisted that this question could be taken up only "with her relatives" and were unwilling to consider dona Leocádia as kin because there was no piece of paper to prove that Olga and Prestes were married. Without this proof, the German government would not recognize the marriage, or the fact of any family relationship between dona Leocádia and Olga or Anita. Gestapo officials declared that there was only one person in a legal position to negotiate mother and daughter's interests and that was Olga's mother, Eugenie Gutmann Benario, since Leo, her compassionate father, had died. And every time they mentioned Eugenie, they stressed that she was "a good German."

Dona Leocádia couldn't understand this: How could a Jew be "a good German" in the eyes of the Gestapo? With this doubt in mind, she and Lígia decided to make the trip to Munich. It was a long and difficult journey for a woman of sixty-three, but she was determined. Her British friends weren't sure it would be worth such an effort, considering the intransigence of the police, but dona Leocádia insisted: "If dona Eugenie is the only person who can do something for my daughter-in-law, I'm going."

After spending an entire night on the train, the four arrived at the elegant house on Karlplatz. When a maid ushered them into the living room, dona Leocádia was surprised at the luxuriousness of the furniture, carpets, and objets d'art. Olga's mother finally appeared, listened to her Brazilian visitor for a few minutes, then interrupted before dona Leocádia had finished speaking: "I simply won't allow this subject to be discussed in my home! Olga is no longer my daughter! I'd like you all to please leave, at once!"

Perplexed, dona Leocádia reiterated that both Olga's and Anita's lives were in Eugenie's hands. She pointed to a framed photograph of Olga as an adolescent and made one more attempt: "Only you can save the life of this wonderful girl, your own daughter! Please, don't do this!"

Eugenie was unambiguous: "That *was* my daughter. I have nothing to do with the Communist you say is in prison in Berlin!"

Since it was clear that dona Leocádia was determined to make her change her mind, Eugenie called her son Otto, Olga's older brother by eight years, explained the situation, and asked him to convince the guests to leave.

Otto Benario was curt. He declared that he was a lawyer, then continued, "My mother has already told you that we are not willing to so much as discuss this subject in our house, so please be on your way."

Crushed, dona Leocádia saw no alternative but to return to France. In Paris she and Lígia decided to hire a lawyer to study the legal aspects of the case. They chose François Drujon, one of France's most famous jurists. Drujon wasn't even a liberal—his conservative leanings were, in fact, well known—but, moved by dona Leocádia's campaign, he not only accepted the case but charged nothing for his services. His first initiative was to travel to Berlin to sound out the Gestapo regarding the possible solutions to the situation. Drujon managed to do something dona Leocádia and Lígia had not been allowed to do: he was granted an official meeting with the Gestapo and given authorization to visit Anita in prison. He was not permitted to see her mother, but he spent several minutes with the baby as she lay in her cradle during the prisoners' exercise period in the courtyard. The Gestapo promised Drujon that Anita would be turned over to her paternal grandmother if he furnished an official document from Brazil in which Prestes assumed paternity for the child. Instead of requiring a marriage certificate, they would accept his statement and concede kinship between dona Leocádia and Anita. The Germans offered no hope at all when it came to Olga, merely saying that "her case is very complicated." The absurd legal grounds applied thus far to her situation remained in effect and were sufficient to keep her incarcerated indefinitely, with no right to defend herself. As there were no legal charges against her, Olga was under a kind of permanent preventive custody. News of Drujon's progress with the Gestapo relieved some of the Prestes women's anxiety: if they could actually manage to get the child out of the Gestapo's grasp, half the job would be done. Then they could step up the campaign and try to arrange for some other form of expulsion or exile for the mother. So the next move was to ask Sobral Pinto to visit Prestes in prison and have him sign a declaration of paternity; with that, Anita's release would be assured. At least that was what Lígia and dona Leocádia imagined. But it wasn't as simple as it seemed.

A few weeks after Anita Leocádia was born, Olga's legendary daring had manifested itself once more. She obtained authorization from the Gestapo to petition the Brazilian embassy in Berlin to register the newborn as a Brazilian citizen. As justification, she invoked the paternity of Luís Carlos Prestes and her own status as a "Brazilian":

Berlin, December 9, 1936

To the Brazilian Embassy in Berlin:

As a citizen of the republic of Brazil, I write to request the registration of the birth of Anita Leocádia Prestes, born 11/27/36 in Berlin, daughter of Captain Luís Carlos Prestes and his wife Olga Benario Prestes.

In addition, I would like to know if you could inform me of the whereabouts of my mother-in-law, Mrs. Leocádia Prestes, and, if possible, her address.

Please direct your reply to O. Benario Prestes, Geheime Staatspolizei [Gestapo], no. 2428/36—II 1 A 1.

Respectfully,
O. Benario Prestes

The day Olga received authorization to send her petition, the Gestapo also requested information from the Brazilian embassy regarding the precise date of the arrest and separation of Olga and Prestes in Rio de Janeiro, as a way of confirming or disproving Prestes's alleged paternity of Anita. Though both letters arrived at the embassy almost simultaneously, the treatment given to each revealed once more Ambassador Moniz de Aragão's subservience to the Gestapo. Their request was transmitted to Brazil within hours, in a telegram signed by the ambassador himself:

MONDAY—20 HRS. 16—POLICE HERE URGENTLY
REQUEST INFORMATION FROM BRAZILIAN AUTHORITIES
REGARDING EXACT DATE OF ARRESTS OF OLGA BENARIO
AND LUIS CARLOS PRESTES. THIS REQUEST AIMED AT
ESTABLISHING THE PATERNITY OF A FEMALE CHILD BORN
TO OLGA HERE NOVEMBER 27 LAST, IT BEING
INDISPENSABLE TO DETERMINE UNTIL WHAT DATE
PRESTES AND OLGA COULD HAVE HAD RELATIONS. THE
CHILD IS PRESENTLY WITH HER MOTHER IN HOSPITAL AT
THE WOMEN'S PRISON IN BERLIN. WE ALSO REQUEST A
PHOTOGRAPH AND ANY INFORMATION REGARDING THE
WOMAN WHO WAS SEEN FLEEING WHEN EWERT WAS TAKEN
INTO CUSTODY, SO THAT POSSIBLY SHE CAN BE IDENTIFIED
HERE. I IMPLORE YOUR URGENT RESPONSE.
MONIZ DE ARAGÃO

To please the Gestapo, the servile diplomat implored urgency. It took him almost two weeks to send a vague and disinterested letter to Olga, even though the fate of an infant hung in the balance:

Geheime Staatspolizei [Gestapo]
Prinz Albrechtstrasse 8
Berlin
Ref. 2428/36—II 1 A 1 Berlin, December 21, 1936

To Olga Benario:

In response to your letter of the ninth of this month, the Consular Department of the Brazilian embassy in Berlin hereby informs you that your petition to register the birth of your daughter has been forwarded to the Ministry of Foreign Affairs in Rio de Janeiro, which office will issue a finding in this matter. As soon as we receive the Ministry's decision we shall forward you the same.

Mrs. Leocádia Prestes is unknown here; thus it is impossible for us to inform you of her address.

The Brazilian embassy was lying when it said on December 21 that Olga's request had been forwarded to Rio. It was not until eight days later (three weeks after receiving Olga's petition) that Moniz de Aragão sent a letter, not a telegram. Brazil's ambassador to Germany seemed to know exactly for whom he worked. Once at Itamaraty, the case received much the same treatment, reflecting the same double standard. The Chancellery responded one week later, by telegram, to the Gestapo's request, stating that (1) Prestes and Olga were arrested on March 5, 1936, and had lived together until that date; and (2) the police had identified the woman seen fleeing the scene of Ewert's arrest as the same Olga Benario.

A response to Olga's petition was not forthcoming. The Ministry of Foreign Affairs ignored the matter entirely.

The Vargas regime as a whole seemed to be unsatisfied with the penalties already imposed on Prestes and Olga. The behavior of the authorities demonstrated that they fully intended the "crimes" of the parents to be visited upon their child. When Sobral Pinto attempted to bring a notary public to Prestes's cell so that he could sign the declaration of paternity, he was informed that a special authorization was required from the Ministry of Justice. And the newly appointed minister of justice was none other than José Carlos de Macedo Soares, the same man who had headed the Ministry of Foreign Affairs when Olga was deported. Macedo Soares appointed Odette de Carvalho e Souza, his cabinet chief, "to settle the matter." Carvalho e Souza was a sanctimonious woman who was fascinated by the extreme Right and who delighted in publishing tedious and interminable "studies of spiritual, political, and social problems connected to bolshevism"—among which was a bold treatise on "the alliance between the Communists of 1935 and the 'outlaws' of the northeast." Availing herself of all the powers of her office, dona Odette tried in every way possible to prevent the notary public from witnessing Prestes's declaration of paternity. Not even the efforts of the recently appointed director of the prison, Carlos Lassance, a lawyer who was in favor of allowing the document to be signed, managed to remove the obstruction. The despair and rage of Olga, dona Leocádia, Lígia, Prestes, and Sobral Pinto deepened. At any moment the Gestapo might decree that breast-feeding had come to an end and Anita would simply vanish. Despite the fact that negotiations had begun in early July, by mid-September Sobral Pinto had no solution or information for dona Leocádia:

Olga

Rio, September 18, 1937

The Esteemed Senhora Leocádia Prestes:

It is not neglect or indifference that has prevented my writing to you, but sheer lack of time. To increase my work output in the last weeks I have regularly given up two hours usually reserved for sleep. And to make matters worse, today I am without a typist.

Dr. Lassance and I spent all day yesterday attempting, so far in vain, to get a notary public into the prison where your son is being held to witness his declaration of paternity of his daughter, Anita Leocádia. We were met with only ill will and fear. Everyone is afraid of becoming a victim of the kind of campaign already being waged against me, alleging that I am a representative of the Comintern, a soldier of Stalin, etc. I imagine you are already well aware of the lies told about your humble attorney, ever a loyal disciple of Jesus Christ, who has always, until this moment, placed his obedience to religious conscience above personal convenience.

Given the impossibility of sending you the above-mentioned declaration by tomorow's air mail, which I hope to be able to do by Thursday, I am forwarding to you today the official documents attesting to the fact that no charges have been proven here against Olga Benario Prestes. I had these documents translated and certified at the German consulate.

I must furthermore communicate another sad piece of news: I was unsuccessful in my petition to the Superior Military Tribunal, which upheld the original court ruling. I will make another attempt. Perhaps we will be more fortunate this time.

Some of your son's supporters appear not to be satisfied with my performance in the case. They want me to accept one or more assistants to be named by Luís Carlos Prestes. In my next letter, when I have a typist at my disposal, I will go into this episode in detail and all the pain it has caused me. Meanwhile, I console myself with your son's public declarations that "After all this time surrounded by the worms of the Special Police, finally a human being has appeared." That human being is me. Later in his oral defense he added: "Mr. Sobral Pinto practices advocacy as though it were a priestly mission." What more can I ask for from my *ex officio* client? From the judges and the administration I would ask a whole lot more, since they have not so far taken heed of what I have been demanding: justice.

Unable to continue for lack of time, I send the solemn declaration of my highest esteem.

Sobral Pinto

The torment lasted for several days more. Finally, on September
21, 1937, thanks to Sobral Pinto's persistence, a notary public was
ushered into Prestes's cell to draw up the paternity document.
Sobral Pinto sent the papers to the Gestapo in Berlin the same day.

Odette de Carvalho e Souza had lost the battle by a matter of
days: on September 30 a certain "Cohen Plan" was made public,
allegedly the groundwork for a new Communist revolution. The
government attributed the plan to the Comintern, but it had actually been invented by the right-winger Captain Olympio Mourão
Filho, an *integralista* officer and future originator of the 1964 military coup. This farce was used to justify a new and dramatic political
hardening: on the morning of October 1, Getúlio Vargas—until
then a constitutional president, elected by Congress with a mandate until 1938—decreed a new state of war. And on November 10
Brazil's *Estado Novo* (New State) was announced, formally institut-
ing the Vargas dictatorship. Had Odette de Carvalho e Souza managed to obstruct the signing of the paternity declaration just a few
days more, dona Leocádia's careful plan would certainly have failed.
One of the first victims of the extension of the state of war was prison
director Carlos Lassance, reduced on October 1 from jailer to
jailed.

The paternity document was delivered to the Gestapo, but it was
months before dona Leocádia was relieved of her anxiety. A German lawyer—a Social Democrat and friend of dona Leocádia's
French lawyer, François Drujon—volunteered to serve as intermediary between the Prestes family in Paris and the Gestapo in
Berlin: welcome help for Lígia and dona Leocádia, who could not
afford to travel to Berlin every week. The German authorities
procrastinated for three months before determining the child's fate
in mid-January, when Drujon received news from his German colleague: Olga's milk had run out, and Anita's grandmother and aunt
had until the end of the month to collect the child from the prison.
Nothing else had changed: only the child would be released; they

would not be allowed even to visit her mother. As welcome as it was, this news hit hard. Neither of the Prestes women could conceive of taking Anita away and leaving Olga there, alone, in prison. But what was the alternative? Should they take the chance of leaving the child in the hands of the Nazis for a little longer?

On January 19, 1938, Drujon accompanied dona Leocádia and Lígia to the women's prison on Barnimstrasse. The formalities were minimal. A doctor asked them to sign a receipt at the bottom of a certificate of health he had written, stapled to which were two photographs of the child they had never seen:

PRISON MEDICAL CERTIFICATE

Today I have once again carefully examined Anita, daughter of O. Benario Prestes. A female child of almost 14 months, Anita shows exceptionally good physical development. She is 30½ inches tall and weighs 26.2 pounds. She has been walking since 13 months and has all her incisors, both upper and lower. The mucous membranes present a rosy color. Internal organs and bodily functions are completely normal.

Berlin, January 19, 1938

Without further ado, the prison matron turned over the child to her Brazilian relatives. Anita was wearing a white woolen hat, one of the only pieces of clothing left from the batch made by Carmen Ghioldi in prison in Brazil. Pressed by Drujon to let the women see Olga, the authorities were adamant. Gestapo officials finally agreed to let dona Leocádia scribble a quick note, which was thrown into a wastepaper basket as soon as they were out the door. As they got into the waiting taxi outside the main entrance, it was clear that Anita had become a popular prisoner in Barnimstrasse. Dozens of prison officers waved from the windows, calling, *"Auf Wiedersehen, Anita! Auf Wiedersehen!"*

Dona Leocádia and Lígia were overwhelmed by conflicting feelings: elation that they had secured the child's freedom, and fear that the authorities might yet create new obstructions to their leaving the country. Trembling, they refused Drujon's invitation to celebrate Anita's liberation: from the prison they went directly to the train station.

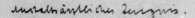

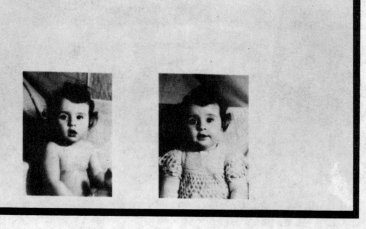

The certificate attesting to Anita's health, signed by a doctor in Berlin's
Barnimstrasse prison before she was turned over to her grandmother. (IML)

The campaign for Anita and
Olga's release, led by
Prestes's mother, dona
Leocádia (right), mobilized
support all over Europe.
Wall posters in Paris
denounced both Hitler and
Getúlio Vargas. (IML; ITR)

The cell where Olga was kept in solitary confinement at the Lichtenburg concentration camp: its security door, the concrete slab that served as a bed, and the barred window. (NMO)

The subterranean tunnels of Lichtenburg, which led to the rows of solitary-confinement cells. (IML)

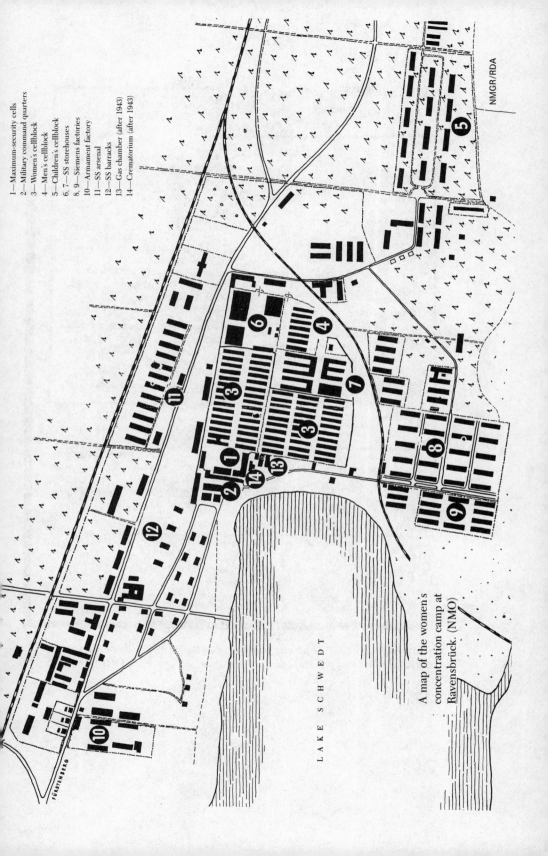

1—Maximum-security cells
2—Military command quarters
3—Women's cellblock
4—Men's cellblock
5—Children's cellblock
6, 7—SS storehouses
8, 9—Siemens factories
10—Armament factory
11—SS arsenal
12—SS barracks
13—Gas chamber (after 1943)
14—Crematorium (after 1943)

NMGR/RDA

LAKE SCHWEDT

FÜRSTENBERG

A map of the women's
concentration camp at
Ravensbrück. (NMO)

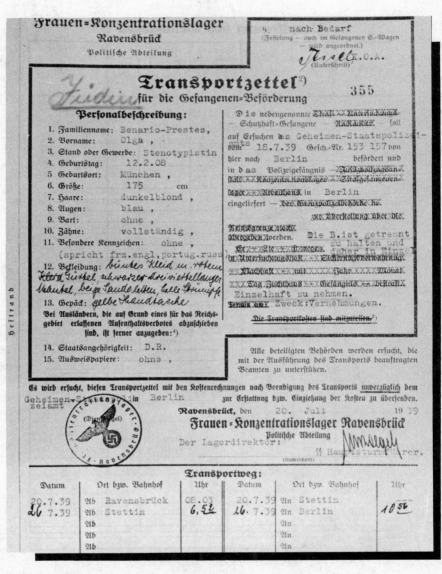

Olga's transport documents for her transfer from Ravensbrück to Berlin for interrogation. At the top is the handwritten notation "Jewess." (DCEG)

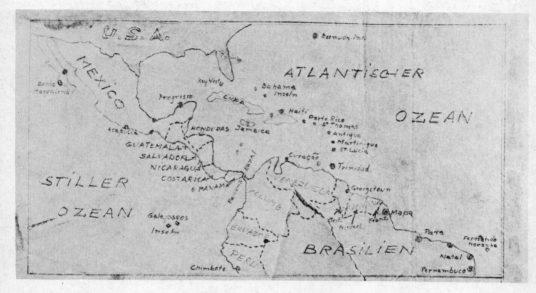

A page from the atlas Olga made to explain the war to the "antisocials." (NMO)

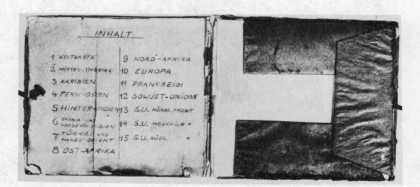

The cover and index to the atlas, which was about the size of a pack of cigarettes so it could be secretly circulated. (NMO)

A view of the women's concentration camp at Ravensbrück. (IML)

Jews, Communists, and "antisocials" at forced labor in the camp. (IML)

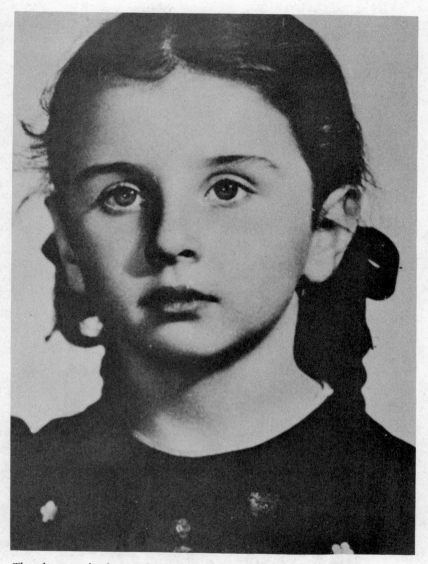

The photograph of Anita that Lígia and dona Leocádia sent to Olga at Ravensbrück in 1941, when the child was living with them in Mexico. (IML)

Heinrich Himmler, head of the SS, visiting Ravensbrück. (NMO)

The *Prügelbock*, an instrument of torture used by the Nazis to punish Ravensbrück prisoners. (NMO)

The interior of the gas chamber at Bernburg where Olga was executed early in 1942. (BSA)

Irmfried Eberl, the doctor assigned by the SS to direct the extermination camp at Bernburg. (BSA)

Nurse Kathe Hackbarth, who led Olga to the gas chamber. (BSA)

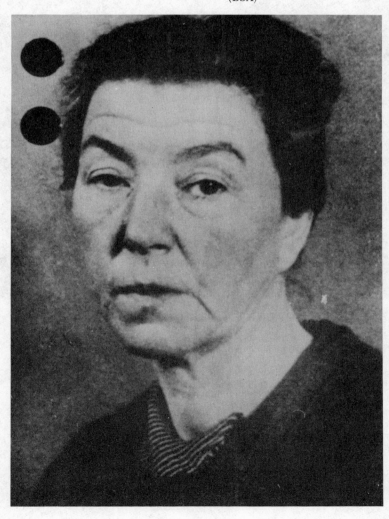

The Bernburg psychiatric hospital, which was transformed into a Nazi extermination camp. (BSA)

A portrait of Olga Benario pregnant, made by Cândido Portinari. (ITR)

A portrait of Olga
made by Di Cavalcanti
for the Communist
Party fund-raising
campaign in 1945.
(ITR)

Rio de Janeiro, 1945:
Prestes is one of the first
prisoners released under
the amnesty that
followed the defeat of
the Nazis in Europe.
(ITR)

Released under the amnesty, Arthur Ewert is welcomed in Germany by his sister Minna and by Wilhelm Pieck (standing), soon to be the first president of the German Democratic Republic. Ravaged by torture in Brazil, Ewert never regained his sanity. (IML)

São Paulo, July 15, 1945: Prestes waves to the crowd as he arrives at the rally in Pacaembu stadium. Departing for Rio that evening, he received the news that Olga was dead. (ITR)

18

With Sabo in the Nazi Fortress

OLGA WAS PLAYING peekaboo with Anita under the sheets when the matron opened the cell door and strode in, accompanied by three armed guards. She got straight to the point. "Dress the girl in something warm and give her other clothes to the guards. We've come to take her away."

In one leap, Olga threw herself on top of her daughter, clutching Anita to her chest and searching wildly for a place to hide her. She shrank back into a corner of the cell, shielding the child. Frightened, Anita began screaming loudly. Olga cried desperately, "Never! You can't do this! This is an unspeakable crime! Get out of here! You'll have to kill me to take my daughter!"

Indifferent, the matron spoke directly to the guards. "Collect the child's things. Let's get her out of here immediately. By force, if necessary."

The mother's loud weeping added to the baby's shrieking, as Olga crouched over her daughter in a corner of the cubicle. "This is a crime! A crime against an innocent baby! No! You can't take her

203

away from me! She hasn't done anything, how can you punish a tiny baby! Don't do this!"

The matron ordered the guards to pull Anita from her mother's arms. "Get the child out of here. This idiot is making a scene. She's known for at least a year that when her milk ran out the girl would be transferred to an orphanage."

Two of the guards roughly held Olga's arms from behind, while the third grabbed Anita. Olga tried to struggle free of the men, kicking their legs and attempting to bite their hands. One of them hit her on the back of the head and threw her to the bed. Then they were gone, locking the door behind them and fleeing down the hall with Anita. Olga's screams, as she flung her whole body at the thick wooden door, echoed through the building. "Murderers! Nazi dogs! Monsters! My baby, my baby! Hitler's going to kill a one-year-old baby! Murderers! Murderers!"

Olga pounded the door, screaming and cursing for a very long time. When all she had left for a voice was a hoarse squeak, she collapsed on the cement floor and remained there, unmoving, her eyes wide, as if in a trance. Many hours later she began to digest the horror she had just lived through. When her mind cleared, her body hurt all over, as if she had been beaten. She dragged herself to the bed and flopped down on her back with her eyes open until daylight began seeping through the barred window of her cell.

Olga spent several more weeks in Berlin. The food the guards brought once a day was sent back untouched. Three times during this period she was brought to Gestapo headquarters on Prinz Albrechtstrasse for interrogation. The police no longer asked her about Neukölln or the raid to liberate Otto Braun. Their questions were aimed at the imaginary "Jewish-Soviet connection" that aspired to bring down the Reich, the origin of the funds that financed the frustrated rebellion in Brazil, the supposed links between the Iwria Bank and the "gang of Communist Jews running around the world preaching revolution." But Olga didn't utter a word that would help them confirm any diabolical conspiracy against Hitler.

Little by little she recuperated. She began eating again and finding activities to keep her mind busy so she wouldn't go mad. As the days passed, she convinced herself that she must fight against becoming weakened physically and emotionally. "I can't give up," she told herself dozens of times, pacing the cell. "I must still help liberate my country, my daughter, and Carlos. I can't give up." Isolated from the other prisoners as punishment for her "hysterical outburst" the day they took Anita, Olga sculpted a miniature chess set from small chunks of bread. The black pieces were the color of rye and the white ones had a smear of toothpaste on top. An outsider would not have been able to distinguish between a pawn and a king, but Olga spent hours and hours trying to checkmate herself. The board consisted of some lines scratched on the cement with the handle of her metal cup, the dark squares tinted with orange rinds.

For approximately a month Olga lived alone with this exquisite form of torture—the brutal certainty that Anita was in a Nazi orphanage, if she was still alive. This particular hell, at least, had an end to it; at last Olga received a letter from Prestes's mother, by then in Paris. Anita was safe and sound with dona Leocádia! Her mother-in-law's short note gave Olga new life. She started to exercise again and to dream of freedom. The day they gave her authorization to resume letter writing, she wrote to dona Leocádia and Anita. Recalling her own days of political agitation in Paris, she suggested places for her mother-in-law to take the child:

> . . . I think it would be a good idea to stroll through the Jardin des Plantes, which is lovely in all seasons. It's a bit far, but the trip is interesting and well worth the money, especially if you get a good seat. Years ago when I first visited the place I remember really enjoying the beautiful arrangement of all the different species of plants. Another great attraction were the greenhouses crammed full of tropical and semitropical plants, though it was hard to bear the suffocating heat and humidity inside for very long. And if you really want to see something marvelous, visit the aquatic plants named Victoria Regia. . . .

Since the prison rationed the number of lines she was allowed to write, Olga saved words for a longer letter to Prestes—the first since Anita had been taken away:

Berlin, February 1938

Carlos,

I can tell you that, together with March 5, 1936, January 21, 1938, was the darkest day of my life. Confronted with events like these, one must either succumb or become more hardened. And you know that for me only the second alternative is possible. I am lucky—and it is a great help to me—to be able to distinguish between the insignificance of one's own problems and the events of our time. But in the midst of all this, there is some good: all my love and affection would be no substitute for what the little one needs from life outside prison. Lígia wrote telling me how Anita plays with her handbag, with the box of powder, the telephone, and the doorknob, that she walks all around the house, that she had breakfast in the dining car of a train. All this sounds to me like a fairy tale from long ago. . . .

I asked Lígia to take a picture of Anita's smile to send you— people say her smile is enchanting. And it is our little one's sweet smile that holds within it a breath of happiness for her parents.

Your Olga

Before Olga was informed that she was being transferred from Barnimstrasse, notice of the impending move had already arrived at her new address: the concentration camp at Lichtenburg, located on the outskirts of the city of Prettin, a hundred kilometers south of Berlin and halfway to the Czech border. The bearer of the news was Elise Ewert, who had spent three months at Barnimstrasse, where someone had told her she was being sent to Lichtenburg and that her companion in the Brazilian fiasco would soon follow. News of Olga's impending arrival spread through the camp quickly. Her participation in the raid to free Otto Braun, her rapid rise in Moscow, the failed rebellion in Brazil, and the separation from her daughter had made Olga Benario Prestes a heroine. There wasn't a single prison or resistance movement in Germany, or an anti-Fascist movement in other European countries, that wasn't familiar with her story in detail, and to welcome such a famous prisoner, the women of Lichtenburg secretly decided to organize a party to commemorate her arrival. For days they saved the best tidbits from food packages relatives brought from outside. "We have to give Olga a little joy and pleasure when she gets here," said Charlotte Henschel, one of the organizers of the reception.

But the party never took place. In early March Olga was escorted out of Barnimstrasse and put in a secret police vehicle, with no indication of where she was being taken. In addition to listing name, parentage, date of birth, etc., her transport papers contained the typed warning "Communist. Highly dangerous prisoner, detained on the authority of the Gestapo command." At the top, written in red pencil, was the indispensable warning "*Jüdin.*" Above and beyond being a dangerous Communist, she was a Jew. Four hours after leaving Berlin, Olga emerged from the Gestapo transport van under tight security to see the towering walls of the fortress of Lichtenburg, a monumental complex built by Napoleon's troops on the banks of the river Elbe. The place was terrifying: the enormous arch of the main entrance was framed by haughty lions in relief. Under the barred windows, pointed iron talons sprang from the brick as a permanent warning to those who might venture an escape. Along the top of the walls were curled rolls of electrified barbed wire.

Escorted down hallways with stone floors and low vaulted ceilings, Olga had the impression that she was being led into a catacomb. Every dozen steps or so another iron door was opened and noisily closed behind her until finally they arrived at a long, dark tunnel with two dozen windowless doors symmetrically placed on either side. As they stopped in front of one of these massive wooden doors, a soldier ordered, "Enter."

It was a solitary cell ten feet by five feet, protected by double doors, the external one made of wood and the internal one of iron. A small window about six feet above the floor looked out on a straight corridor, from which a dim light emanated. Horizontal and vertical bars covered the entire opening. The bed was a five-foot-long block of concrete. Less than a foot below the window was a rectangular hole in the wall—as if a brick had been left out during construction —through which Olga would receive her daily ration of food and water. A hole in the cement floor served as a latrine. On the bed were two light blankets. Other than that, the cell was barren.

Without a word the guards locked both doors and disappeared. Olga spent the first half hour calmly inspecting the room and debating where to etch her chessboard. She decided the ideal place would be on the bed itself, so she wouldn't have to spend the day with her back hunched over the floor. Under the blanket she methodically scratched sixty-four little boxes on the concrete slab with the buckle of her shoe. Without orange peel to darken half the squares, she marked them each with an X instead and then carefully removed the tiny chess pieces made of bread from the bag she had brought along with her from Berlin.

Those first days in solitary confinement were terrible: she didn't know whether she would be allowed to continue writing to her husband and mother-in-law and had not the slightest idea what type of prison Lichtenburg was—a concentration camp for Jews, a political prison, or a jail for common criminals. To lessen the despair and longing for her daughter and husband, Olga did exercises and played game after game of chess. And so that the absolute isolation wouldn't cause her to lose all sense of time, she checked off the day every morning by making a small mark on the wall with her buckle.

After the sixth day she received a surprise visitor. In the middle of the morning, around the time her ration of soup and bread was usually thrust through the hole in the wall, the doors of the cell silently opened and, much to her amazement, in slipped a smiling Gertrud Fruschulz, an old friend from Neukölln, whom Olga hadn't seen since 1928. The door was locked from the outside, and Gertrud explained the unexpected visit. Some of the food that the women had been saving for the "welcoming party" had been used to bribe a guard to permit a secret visit from one of the other prisoners. Since Gertrud was an old friend, she had been chosen to be the person to spend a few minutes with Olga and to bring her information about the prison. Though the doors were so thick that it was impossible for anyone outside the cell to hear anything that went on inside, fear of being caught prompted the visitor to whisper in Olga's ear.

Gertrud gave Olga some of the gifts that had been saved for the party: crackers, a piece of cheese, a little jam, and two chocolate bars. She had also brought a sheet of paper with dozens of tiny messages from the other prisoners. Olga was anxious to know what was going on in Germany, but the news was not very encouraging: Hitler was continuing to enlarge the Reich's territory, and internally the police were ceaselessly hunting down Jews and Communists. Gertrud was clearly alarmed, fearing that the indifference of France and England to the Nazi phenomenon would make those countries easy fodder for Hitler's apparently insatiable appetite. One fact in particular panicked Olga: the support of the majority of the German people for the Führer, who had been in power since 1933, was indisputable. His rallies attracted multitudes, crowds larger than had ever before been seen in public squares. Gertrud also told Olga a little about the fortress of Lichtenburg: over five hundred women were incarcerated there, Jews, Communists, and Social Democrats mixed together. Olga's friend Elise Ewert was one of them—after spending several weeks in solitary confinement she had been assigned to load coal into the stove in the central mess hall.

Olga recounted how Anita had been rescued by her paternal grandmother and was safe in Paris. She summarized her interrogations in Berlin, described Prestes's and Ewert's imprisonment in Brazil, complained that she received hot food only every three days and that since she had arrived she had not seen the light of day. Olga was suddenly jolted out of her narrative by three knocks at the door. Her friend was calm. "It's just that damned guard telling me our time is up. I have to go."

"Thank you for the visit and the gifts. Tell my friends not to worry: now that my daughter is safe, I'm fine. I could endure a long time in here."

The door opened, and as silently as she had appeared Gertrud Fruschulz disappeared down the dark hallway. As famished as she was, Olga was more interested in the notes from outside than in the jam and chocolate. Some twenty different hands had filled every space on the paper. The messages contained nothing special, mainly greetings, words of courage and comfort. What concerned her were the signatures—ample proof of the devastation wrought on the Left by the Nazis. Olga recognized the majority of signatures on the paper—every one of them outstanding militants from Berlin and other German cities, many of whom had been her comrades during the previous decade in Neukölln. Shaken by this realization, Olga lost her appetite and simply left the hastily wrapped gifts sitting in a corner of the cell.

The following two weeks went by without any news from outside.

Every day Olga anxiously awaited the moment rations arrived, hoping that Gertrud would return, but soon realized it would be a while before she saw her friend again. She spent her days doing calisthenics, playing chess, or just walking back and forth in her cell. In addition to keeping her body moving, exercise lessened the risk of rheumatism in that icy place, and helped tire her out so she could fall asleep earlier. Sleep became a great form of relief until she was let out of solitary confinement in early April.

Olga left her cubicle the same way she had entered: without a word of explanation for why she had been isolated or why she was now being assigned to a collective cell. Her first wish was to see Sabo. In the prison courtyard, where the prisoners were made to gather every morning to hear an unpalatable political sermon from the prison director, the women greeted her with as much festivity as possible under the circumstances. Everyone wanted to see her, to embrace her, to hear all about the rebellion in Brazil and about her daughter. When Olga insisted she had to see Sabo, the person they brought her bore little resemblance to the friend she once knew—a tubercular woman weighing less than ninety pounds with a distant, opaque, sickly look about her. The disease had not exempted her from forced labor—and the elegant and fragile hands of Arthur Ewert's delicate wife were covered with a crust of coarse skin cracked from the cold.

Olga's sadness at seeing her friend in this state was dispelled only at lunchtime when she was called to the prison command office and given a small envelope containing two letters from her mother-in-law and one from her husband. The one from Prestes was short and included passages from two Brazilian poems to soothe her longing for Brazil. The letters from dona Leocádia, meanwhile, came from farther away than Olga expected. Prestes's mother and sister feared being caught up in the war that was beginning to seem inevitable after Hitler's annexation of Austria and the Sudetenland (which had taken place while Olga was in solitary confinement). Targeted by the Right in all the countries they had traveled through during the campaign for the release of Olga and Anita, dona Leocádia and Lígia had been advised to leave Europe and so had taken Anita to Mexico. Along with the letters, Olga was given permission to reply. She wrote a letter to her mother-in-law and a short note to Prestes:

Prettin, April 1938

Dear Carlos,

. . . I have to admit that it costs me a great deal—an enormous effort—to try not to think about our daughter too much, but it's the only way to bear the pain. My longing for her is so great that I find myself getting angry at these arms that once held her and these hands that once caressed her.

The poems you sent are marvelous, and so is what you wanted to say to me through them. It makes me very happy to know that the best human feelings exist in all people, and that we only express them differently because of the particular characteristics of the culture we come from.

I translated the poems into German. "As velhas arvores" [The Old Trees] meshes so perfectly with many of the thoughts I've been having these last months. Only a great inner maturity could permit one to say: "We want to grow old smiling, as strong old trees grow old. . . ."

Your Olga

In the year she spent at Lichtenburg, Olga was taken to Berlin half a dozen times for interrogations. Every time the Gestapo needed to confirm information about Comintern activities in America, Olga was transported to the Gestapo headquarters on Prinz Albrechtstrasse. Whether or not she possessed the information in question, Olga refused to say anything at all to her interrogators, so they frequently resorted to torture. But neither blows, whippings, nor threats of a firing squad produced results. Above and beyond her resolute silence, the Gestapo police were irritated by the permanent air of superiority that Olga maintained during interrogation. "Jewish cow" was the mildest form of address they reserved for her. Though mass extermination had not yet begun, anti-Semitism was the official policy of the nation, and the arrest and persecution of Jews was growing. Among other prohibitions, "interracial" marriages had not been allowed for the previous three years, and Jews were not allowed to hold public office or to be schoolteachers at any level. If Jews were the primary victims of the Nazis, then in Hitler's Germany it was so much worse to be a Communist as well. In addition to these two offenses, Olga was a woman—of which she was publicly and permanently proud.

During the second half of 1938, after three months without any news of Prestes or her daughter, Olga began to fear that something terrible had happened. She knew that Brazil was still in a state of war and that in such circumstances it would not be difficult for Filinto Müller to make good his frustrated plan to kill Prestes. Olga's dread was finally dispelled in mid-September when she was presented with a packet of four letters from Prestes and dona Leocádia, which prison officials had left languishing in a file all that time. Along with her news, dona Leocádia sent a real treasure— which perhaps explains the guards' decision to withhold the letters: a photograph of Anita, smiling broadly and wearing an enormous bow in her hair. Olga wrote to her husband the same day:

Prettin, 9/15/38

My dear Carlos,

At last I received your precious lines of May 30, June 14 and 27, and July 27, as well as a letter dated August 31 from Mother. Little by little I am beginning to revive, after the heavy weight of having no news of you for the last three months. And what strength and warmth your letters exude! The fact that we exist and that we are irrevocably united is our inexhaustible fountain of strength and hope, every single day. Which is why just a few lines can mean so much and can loosen the armor which the instinct for self-preservation uses to shield our hearts.

Mother wrote that you had talked with Dr. Sobral Pinto. I was glad to hear this and to know that you're in good health, but what really makes me happy is that you showed him the picture of Anita.

I often think about your desire to live in the virgin forest again. I must say that the past years have taught me that nothing is impossible, and I imagine I'll go on thinking that for a long, long time. These are facts, and we're used to counting on them and living with them. You also mentioned the *"enfant gâté"* [spoiled child]. Look, it's a good thing I didn't change as much as you wanted me to, or else everything would have been much harder for me. I was very glad to hear your observations about what you've been reading, but I won't go into it any more than that because I don't want this letter to be withheld for exceeding the permitted number of lines. You ask about my health—

212

I'm all right. As for the rest, I've been studying a lot of French and English with an excellent partner.

On September 2 they finally allowed me to send Mother the tie I made for you. I hope you get it, because maybe it will bring you all the love I can't and don't want to express in these letters. And lastly, I must confess that I pinned pictures of Anita and you to my door just as you did of Anita and me—and I spend a lot of time gazing at them. But to have only this, and after such a long time, is very little.

My dear Karli, I kiss you with all my love.

Your Olga

Between the forced labor by day and her earlier solitary confinement, the months at Lichtenburg seemed interminable. Olga's insistence on the political organization of prisoners prompted prison officials to move her constantly from cell to cell and from one block to another. She had barely spent two weeks quartered with the "undesirable Jews"—thieves, beggars, and prostitutes—when she was moved in with the "bourgeois Jews"—wives of Jewish merchants and small businessmen whose property had been confiscated by the Reich for violating the racial laws. But Olga never had the chance to spend so much as a day in the block for political prisoners, whether Jewish or not. On one occasion, when she was bold enough to ask to be transferred there, the response from the official on duty was a burst of laughter: "You're here to be punished, not rewarded!"

The Lichtenburg winter was an additional cruelty. Located in a low, flat region on the banks of the Elbe, the fortress's cellars were frequently flooded by the freezing waters of the river, and pneumonia and tuberculosis were rife. Sabo's health was worsening, but the guards, aware of the close friendship between the two, insisted on keeping them apart, so that sometimes months passed without their seeing each other. A few weeks after the end of the winter of 1938–39, newly arrived prisoners brought terrible news: Hitler had occupied Czechoslovakia. Each new onslaught of Nazi troops left an inevitable trail of violence and persecution of Jews, Communists, Socialists, and Social Democrats, and overcrowding of prisons and concentration camps. Lichtenburg, with a capacity for a maximum of a thousand prisoners, was holding almost four times that number. Around this time word from outside brought news that part of the Lichtenburg population would be transferred 250 kilometers northward. On the outskirts of the small city of Furstenberg, on the shores of Lake Schwedt, construction of a concentration camp for women in Ravensbrück was almost completed. The dimensions of the new camp gave a terrifying indication of Hitler's plans: Ravensbrück would have accommodations for forty-five thousand women.

19

Slavery at Ravensbrück

THE CONVOY OF fifteen blue buses, their windows protected by iron bars, left Lichtenburg after the night's rations had been distributed and only arrived in Ravensbrück the following morning. Guarded by combat vehicles and military trucks, the convoy headed north, skirted Berlin, and continued on without a stop. Crowded onto the buses' wooden benches, small cloth bundles of personal belongings on their laps, sat 859 German prisoners and 7 Austrians. Within days, their places in Lichtenburg would be filled by Czech women arrested after the Nazi invasion. The noisy convoy awakened the population of the small and placid sixteenth-century city of Furstenberg, rumbled a few kilometers farther along a dirt road beside Lake Schwedt, and finally arrived at the new concentration camp for women.

The Nazis had been revamping the country's prison system since 1936 in preparation for the war. They closed down existing prison camps—with the exception of Dachau and Lichtenburg—and began construction of new *Konzentrationslager*, concentration camps for Jews, political enemies, and other "undesirables." These *KZ*, as they were called, were built with more "modern" concepts in mind: prisoners would be used productively to help the Reich's economy.

In the weeks immediately following *Kristallnacht* (the Night of Broken Glass, when at Nazi instigation Jewish homes, shops, and synagogues were vandalized or destroyed), the number of Jews and Communists in custody in Germany rose to sixty thousand. Construction on the camp at Ravensbrück had begun a few months earlier, toward the end of 1938, with five hundred men and women prisoners from Sachsenhausen concentration camp as laborers. Using the project model initially adopted for the construction of Buchenwald, the prisoners worked at Ravensbrück until April 1939, when two convoys of inmates arrived. The first came from Burgenland, Austria, with almost a thousand women—Jews, gypsies, and Jehovah's Witnesses. The second came from the women's prison at Lichtenburg.

After spending a year in a place as foreboding as the Lichtenburg fortress, Olga was surprised by the bucolic look of Ravensbrück. The entrance to the camp was tucked between a thicket of poplars and the tip of Lake Schwedt. To the left, on a small rise, stood the brick buildings that would house the camp commandant, chief of security, head administrator, officials of the Gestapo, and SS doctors and nurses; beside them, lined up side by side, were six rows of barracks for a battalion of six hundred SS troops divided into four combat companies and sixteen shock troop platoons. Just the other side of the troops' quarters stood a dozen large storage sheds for weaponry and other supplies. On a flat clearing five hundred meters beyond, to the right of the entrance, was the concentration camp itself: sixty enormous wooden blocks sitting symmetrically side by side and five small sheds, also made of wood, where male prisoners, who were eventually to pass through Ravensbrück, would be housed. Farther to the right of the camp, sheltered by the lake and a small clump of trees, stood twenty brick structures where the Siemens company was installing sewing machines for prisoners to produce goods for the Nazi war effort. At the very back of the camp area were thirteen wooden cellblocks designated for children. On the path between the main gate and the women's blocks stood the bunker, the only two-story building, also made of brick, where maximum-security and solitary cells were located.

From where she got off the bus, Olga could see, beyond the curve of the lake and the thicket of trees encircling the Siemens buildings, the points of the roofs and chimneys of the village of Ravensbrück, home to fifty-odd families. Surrounding the entire camp, from the lakeshore to the trees that circled the SS barracks, were huge rolls of barbed wire and a wooden sign every hundred meters with a skull and crossbones and the warning "Danger! High Voltage!" Like the majority of the other concentration camps, Ravensbrück had been built in a secluded area. And, as with other camps, the locale was chosen for its easy access by road and rail to the large population centers of the country. To transport goods produced in the Siemens factory inside the camp, the prisoners of Sachsenhausen had constructed a small branch line through the area, linking it to the Oranienburg/Neustrelitz railway line, whose tracks ran directly behind the camp officials' brick houses.

Guarded by soldiers armed with rifles, the nine hundred or so prisoners from Olga's convoy were led to the camp's main courtyard and lined up in formation. An SS official called out name after name, and each woman was given the uniform adopted throughout the country for concentration camps—gray and blue striped skirt, jacket, and turban-shaped cap—and an armband with a numbered triangle. Each woman was identified by her number; the color of the triangle corresponded to the classification of the prisoner. Red triangles were for those who had been arrested for security reasons—in the majority of cases for political reasons; blue triangles were for foreigners, immigrants, and refugees; purple triangles were for Jehovah's Witnesses, nuns, and the religious in general; green for thieves and common criminals; and black for "undesirables" or "antisocials," that is, gypsies, homosexuals, and the mentally ill. In addition, Jews received a second, inverted yellow triangle that was placed just below the other one, so that the two formed a Star of David. Olga was not surprised to be issued the black "antisocial" triangle along with the yellow Jewish one. It would have been an illusion to think that there in Ravensbrück, where discipline and strictness were more rigid that she had encountered anywhere else, she would be allowed to be quartered with the other Communists.

Hours later, Olga was housed in block 11 with over a hundred

Austrians and thirty Germans. The sickening smell made it clear
that the first order of business would be to impose rigorous discipline regarding personal hygiene: the place reeked of feces and
urine. Designated by the Gestapo as the prisoner responsible for
the Jewish "antisocial" block, Olga realized that she would never
succeed in imposing order unless she did so immediately. At six that
evening, after the camp siren announced the curfew, she called the
prisoners together for a talk. Heads and bodies popped out from the
hundreds of rough-hewn bunks placed side by side down the long
corridor. Half naked, their hair matted and wild, most of the women
looked as though they hadn't seen water for a very long time. Olga
was stern. "If we don't take care of our own bodies, the Nazis will be
able to do anything they want with us. We're all in the same boat
here, and if we want to be treated with dignity, we must first behave
like human beings and not like animals. I was chosen to be responsible for this block, and things are going to change around here
starting first thing tomorrow morning."

From the back of the room a voice called out in protest: "Go roll
in shit, you commie!"

The women exploded with laughter. Olga was not intimidated,
though she knew many of them were delinquents and criminals.
She walked between the rows of bunks to where the shout had
come from and said, "As long as I'm in charge here no one will be
denounced to the SS. We will resolve our problems among ourselves. Now I want to know who yelled out. Whoever swore at me
must come forward and discuss her objections, face to face, in front
of everyone."

There was a tense silence. A woman with red hair clipped to
almost nothing came out from under the covers. "It was me. I'm
sorry. I was just kidding. I don't have anything against you. Just tell
us what we have to do tomorrow morning and I'll be the first one out
of bed."

Without a word in reply, Olga returned to her place and continued the sermon. "First thing tomorrow we are going to do a general
cleaning of the block. We'll get up an hour before wake-up call so
we have enough time to do the job properly. After that, we'll begin a
new routine: compulsory daily showers, regardless of the weather."

Olga could see from the general reaction that the women had

accepted her leadership. They talked animatedly for a few more minutes until the second siren, which signaled absolute silence in the entire camp: it was 8:30 P.M. Within two weeks, block 11 was a changed place. Instead of the suffocating stench of the day she had arrived, Olga could smell the green eucalyptus logs used in construction. Since there was little protest about the daily bathing and cleaning, she decided to press a bit further and proposed that the women get up yet half an hour earlier each day to do exercises. And she did so by appealing to their vanity. "We have no full-length mirror here, but we can see ourselves well enough in each other to know that we're ugly and out of shape. Since they're not likely to give us rouge and lipstick, we have to do what we can on our own to be ready for our freedom. When we walk out of here, we have to be slender for our boyfriends and husbands. And, in a concentration camp, the only way to do this is to exercise."

In spite of her convincing argument, many of the women rejected Olga's proposal, reminding her that the Nazis already forced them into the exercise of working all day. To avoid problems, it was agreed that only those who wanted to would exercise—those who preferred to sleep a little longer could stay in bed. The group that opted for calisthenics was so noisy, however, that the others weren't able to stay asleep. Within days all the women had been won over to morning exercise.

As the weeks passed, Olga began worrying again about the lack of news from her family. At the end of July, when two soldiers appeared in block 11 to escort her to the commandant's quarters, Olga imagined that some letters had arrived for her. This was not the case: she was being summoned for yet another round of interrogation in Berlin. The guards handed over her bundle of clothes and ordered her to be ready to leave within minutes. The warning in her file that she was to be treated as a "highly dangerous prisoner" prompted the commandant, Fritz Suhren, to assign Olga a special escort of six soldiers and two Gestapo agents. Six weeks passed without her discovering a single reason that would justify bringing her that distance: the Gestapo merely repeated the same questions as before—and, as before, obtained nothing. But this time they showed her some photographs of prisoners and wanted suspects, which again elicited no more valuable information than anything else had done. Being back in Barnimstrasse, where she had spent a year with Anita, stirred Olga's longing for her husband and daughter. She managed to get permission to write a short note to her mother-in-law in Mexico:

Berlin, August 1939

Dear Mother, dear Lígia,

When you write to me, please send the letters to my old address—Federal Secret Police, Berlin, always noting "Division II A Prinz Albrechtstrasse 1" at the bottom.

I am alone again with only my thoughts and my immense longing for all of you. The days seem endless. But don't worry, I won't let my spirits sag. What can you tell me about Carlos? It has been six months now since I last heard from him, and this has worried me greatly: Why did he stop writing? Is he ill? Mother dear, don't hide anything from me. If something has happened, please let me know.

Tell my darling Anita that her mother thinks about her all the time and that every night when I go to sleep I imagine how good it would be to grab her little hands and to kiss her sweet face.

Hugs to all, and all my love,

Olga

On the way back from Berlin, Olga was taken to Potsdam for several days of additional interrogation and arrived in Ravensbrück only in early October. The concentration camp was a changed place. Shortly after her departure for Berlin, four hundred new prisoners had arrived—they were either newly arrested or had come from other camps. Among them was her friend Sabo, whose health had deteriorated even further. More recently, the German army had invaded Poland, carrying out the most brutal attack against Jews since the rise of Hitler. This invasion marked the beginning of what would become World War II. The initial results of the violence could be seen at Ravensbrück, which received more than a thousand women who had been taken prisoner in Poland. With Olga's prolonged absence and the arrival of new "antisocial" inmates, block 11 had deteriorated into complete bedlam. Several weeks and many arguments later, however, Olga had managed to reestablish the obligatory daily cleanup and showers; attracting the women to exercise sessions took longer and for a good reason: Siemens had completed the installation of its factory inside the camp and the women had to work up to twelve hours a day, which meant they didn't have much energy for early-morning calisthenics.

All prisoners were required to work in the Siemens factory, regardless of classification, age, or state of health. Siemens had a contract with the German government to pay the camp thirty pfennigs per day per woman, without providing any remuneration to the women themselves. Companies that preferred to preserve their international image and not install factories inside concentration camps were not left out of the deal: the SS took charge of transporting prisoners to the place of work. The Bayerische Motoren Werke, which produced BMW cars, "borrowed" 220 workers from Buchenwald; lens company Zeiss-Ikon "hired" 900 men from the Flossenburg camp; Krupp metallurgy, 500 prisoners from Buchenwald; the Daimler-Benz company, manufacturer of luxurious Mercedes-Benz cars, 110 inmates from Sachsenhausen; Volkswagen, 650 workers from Neuengamme. There was even a company mysteriously called Silva Poltwerke GmbH (Silva is a typically Brazilian name, as common in Brazil as Smith is in the United States), which rented 2,000 women from Ravensbrück. In fact, Olga's camp supplied more slave labor than any other. In all, 37,500 women—Jews, Communists, socialists, Social Democrats, gypsies, and Jehovah's Witnesses— were transported out of Ravensbrück between 1938 and 1945 to work without pay for large German companies.

In 1946, when Siemens officials were summoned to testify at the Nuremberg war crimes trials, they justified their presence in concentration camps with cold irony as a kind of philanthropy: "After all, during the coldest months of the year we always allowed the prisoners to use leftover materials, such as insulation paper and cleaning rags, to supplement their insufficient clothing." Siemens production at Ravensbrück was almost exclusively dedicated to the war effort. A middle-sized textile company made the uniforms the SS purchased for all prisoners in camps throughout Germany and in the occupied territories. The greatest percentage of Ravensbrück inmates, however, performed manual labor in the military equipment factory at the camp, which produced everything from relays for arms parts to special triggers and electronic mechanisms for submarines, field telephones and delayed action detonators for bombs, and parts for the deadly V-2 rockets invented by Werner von Braun.

Well aware that the prisoners were exhausted by their long hours at Siemens, Olga insisted on the exercise sessions, though many of the "antisocials" refused to trade any of their morning sleep for the daily exercises she organized. Olga also tried to give small groups of women some basic notions about the political issues that had led to the war. She did this in complete secrecy of course, since, if discovered, such daring would lead to serious punishment. At one of these furtive seminars Olga was given some sad news from a young Polish woman: Elise Ewert, her dear Sabo, had died three days earlier. The tuberculosis had returned with the winter, doubly virulent, and her body simply was unable to endure the illness and the forced labor. Friends who had been with her at the end reported that her last words had been agonizing and delirious. "Arthur, Arthur," she babbled, "they're coming to torture us again. . . . The shocks are going to start again, Arthur. . . ." The physical scars left by Filinto Müller's police had disappeared from Sabo's body, but her days in prison in Rio were engraved on her memory until the very end.

In early January 1940, the population at Ravensbrück—by then almost 3,000 women—unexpectedly doubled. An additional 2,940 women arrived from Poland, Austria, Czechoslovakia, and various cities in Germany. A few weeks after this new influx, it was announced that Ravensbrück would be visited by one of the most illustrious personalities of the Reich, Heinrich Himmler himself. SS officials prepared to receive their leader with great pomp—the only man higher than Himmler was Adolf Hitler. The three days before Himmler's arrival were wearisome for the inmates, who were obliged to clear the snow from camp roads, repaint any stained areas on cell walls, sweep the courtyards, etc. A group of officials spent the day looking for anything out of place, any smidgen of coal lost in a corner, and demanded, whips in hand, that the women sweep the whole place again. Unfortunately for the prisoners, there was a snowstorm the night before Himmler's visit, so the commandant himself appeared at dawn and ordered the women to clear the courtyards and paths between the blocks all over again.

Finally, surrounded by military vehicles and preceded by a motorcycle escort, Himmler arrived in a Daimler-Benz convertible with the top closed. For security reasons, all 6,000 prisoners were restricted to their quarters, with doors locked and with orders not to make any noise during the visit. Himmler was greeted at the camp entrance by the ranking SS officials and led to the central courtyard, which faced the prisoners' block, to review the troops. At the call for "Attention!" the soldiers stood rigidly before their commander. Decked out in full-dress uniform, an ankle-length gray overcoat around his shoulders and holding his leather gloves in his left hand, Himmler strode back and forth in front of the battalion standing in impeccable formation. The silence was so complete that all that could be heard was the wind whistling through the trees and the hard clip of the Nazi commander's boots. When only two platoons remained to be inspected, a bellowing voice rang out from one of the blocks, a voice from deep down in the chest, in sonorous German: "Heinrich Himmler, you are nothing but a pederast killer!"

Uncontrollable laughter rocked the fifteen blocks of prisoners. Tensely, Himmler went on with his review of the last group of men, while two platoons of shock troops broke ranks and ran, confused, from block to block, banging the butts of their rifles on the wooden walls and shouting, "Silence, you Jewish cows! Silence!" and "We're going to shoot you, you scum!" and "Silence! The first one to utter a word will be shot immediately!"

The SS command was seized with hysteria. No one, much less a Jew, "a biologically inferior being," could insult with impunity the Reichsführer SS Heinrich Himmler, commissioner for the integration of the annexed regions and high chief of the *Schutzstaffeln*, Hitler's feared SS. Furious, Himmler cut short his visit to Ravensbrück, leaving express orders that the women be harshly punished: whippings, collective penalties, withholding of food, whatever— such insolence must be answered with severity. Himmler's instructions were acted upon the same day. The brick building containing eighty solitary cells was opened—until then solitary confinement had been applied only in rare and extreme cases, such as physical attacks on SS officials—and the commandant ordered that eighty women be chosen at the discretion of the shock troops, whose duty it was to select them for exemplary punishment. One of those chosen from among the "antisocials" in block 11 was, naturally, Olga Benario. She was assigned a cell in the east wing of the ground floor of the bunker, which was built half underground and thus subject to permanent dampness. The rest of the camp's punishment was relatively light: three days without food. At mealtimes, each prisoner received only a mug of water.

The next thirty days were horrific for Olga. It was an extremely hard winter, with the temperature frequently dipping well below zero. All she had for warmth were a few cotton blankets and some pages from the *Volkischer Beobachter,* the Nazi Party newspaper, which she wrapped around her feet. The east side of the building was so damp that one of the walls was covered with a green slime, as if not even moss could grow in that dismal place. Olga didn't know whether it was just another general form of revenge against her by the SS or if they actually suspected she was responsible for the insult to Himmler—which she wasn't. For whatever reason, she was regularly whipped during her period of confinement. Without warning, the SS would walk into the cell carrying a *Prügelbock*—a modified sawhorse with a slatted concave board across the top and leather straps with buckles attached to each leg. Placed facedown, with her stomach over the convex part and her wrists and ankles secured in the leather straps, she was subjected to endless sessions during which her back, buttocks, and legs were whipped until she was nearly unconscious. Sometimes after the beatings she was left tied to the horse for the rest of the day. When the soldiers came back to take her off, they would whip her again for good measure.

When released from the bunker, physically debilitated and even thinner than before, Olga was obliged to return to work at the Siemens factory. At night, back in overcrowded block 11, she noticed that half the women there were new to her, probably transferred just before the insult to Himmler. The Nazi troop advances of the previous months provoked the frightening realization by May 1940 that Hitler's control of all of Europe was inevitable. Since early that year, not only Poland, but Denmark, Norway, Luxemburg, Holland, and Belgium had fallen under control of the Reich. Hitler was preparing to attack the next and most precious of all targets: France. In her conversations with fellow inmates—largely simple, rustic women with no political background—Olga tried to boost morale by insisting that there was one country in Europe that would surely stop the German advance: the Soviet Union. The "classes" she taught interested these "undesirables" not so much for political reasons but simply because the majority of them understood clearly that they were in Ravensbrück as victims of the regime that intended to dominate the world. Their freedom depended upon the defeat of nazism, and so they needed to understand what nazism was and how it might be buried, as they were promised it would be by this tireless German prisoner who remained active and determined, even after having been tortured, separated from her husband and daughter, and having lost her best friend.

Olga decided it would be a help to have illustrations for her lessons in international politics. With a pencil stolen from the Siemens office by a Dutch prisoner and with pieces of light cardboard torn from the production charts in the factory, she applied all her skill to sketching maps of the regions in conflict. First she painstakingly drew from memory a world map, which took several days to complete. In order to have enough light to work, Olga woke extra early and sat at the window, a board on her lap for a table. Once the world map was finished, she began working on others, detailing the war areas country by country, region by region. After working in secret for weeks, Olga proudly showed her prison companions an entire atlas, with fifteen individual maps, a hard cover, and even an index. There was only one problem: to be circulated among the women and easily hidden under a pillow or clothing, the atlas had to be in miniature, not much bigger than a pack of cigarettes, which meant that on the most detailed maps one centimeter was equivalent to hundreds of kilometers. With that treasure in her hand, Olga began giving daily classes, explaining the political side of the war. Starting from Moscow, she drew several circles around the Soviet Union and assured her friends that the idea of taking the Russian capital was a dream the Nazis would never realize.

At some point one of the prisoners—it was never discovered who—informed against Olga. The practice of denouncing fellow inmates was not uncommon in the camps. In exchange for an extra ration or a blanket, many people informed the authorities of any infringements of the rules. Olga was called to the SS command office and instructed to hand over the atlas, which was safely tucked away inside inmate Tilde Klose's blouse in the Communist block. The atlas was saved, but Olga suffered three more weeks in solitary confinement and several whippings.

Such brutal punishment did not intimidate her. On the contrary, the greater the cruelty of the SS, the more resolved was Olga to continue agitating within the camp. Some weeks after her time in solitary confinement she decided to produce a clandestine play. The script was written by the women themselves, under Olga's direction, and after several rehearsals they decided they were ready to play to an audience. Just as the show was ending, the block was raided by a squadron of SS troops. Actresses and spectators alike were roughly dragged outside and made to spend the entire night standing in the middle of the main courtyard. The following morning they had to go straight to work in the Siemens factory, without a minute's sleep. When she ran across some women from her block who had managed to hide and avoid being punished, Olga still had the spirit to quip, "Next time we'll have to write a better play. Maybe then the SS will let us stage it in peace."

20

The Final Journey

MONTHS PASSED without the prisoners at Ravensbrück hearing anything from the outside world. Only as 1940 drew to a close did Olga learn that Hitler's troops had marched on Paris and later taken Hungary and Romania. This terrible news, brought by a group of newly arrived prisoners, seemed to contradict the optimism Olga was trying to instill in her fellow inmates; at a secret meeting to bring the war atlas up to date, Olga was compelled to recognize that the Nazis already controlled eleven countries, holding under their power almost two million square kilometers of invaded territory. The widening of the war was also responsible for the lack of information about her husband and daughter. In recent months she had received only one letter from her mother-in-law, with a new photograph of Anita, and one letter from Prestes.

By the end of spring 1941, Ravensbrück was no longer exclusively a concentration camp for women. In addition to the eight thousand prisoners already quartered there, three hundred men were transferred from Dachau and assigned to two cellblocks, until then unoccupied, behind the women's blocks. Within weeks they were joined by a hundred Jewish Poles from prisons in Warsaw. Around this time Olga contracted an unidentified virus that almost killed her. And since she was now working outside carrying logs, her friends mounted something called "Operation Thermometer" so that she would be transferred back to the Siemens factory, where she could at least work sitting down. The SS had ruled that changes in work assignments for health reasons could be made only with written authorization from the camp's head doctor, Herta Oberheuser. Emmy Handke, an old friend of Olga's from Neukölln days, came up with a solution: with the help of Ilsa Jolansky, a Czech prisoner who was a specialist in forging signatures, she fabricated a certificate from Dr. Oberheuser. Well aware that Operation Thermometer—so called because the certificate stated that Olga was suffering from a high fever—could cost them weeks in solitary confinement and countless whippings on the *Prügelbock*, they went ahead with the plan anyway. Olga carried the fake document in her pocket for several weeks, until the virus passed and she went back to work hauling logs.

During her time in the factory, Olga met a German militant Communist named Margarete Buber-Neumann, who had come very close to being her companion in adventure and adversity in Brazil, and who had been at Ravensbrück since the previous year. Margarete, who was married to fellow Communist Heinz Neumann, vaguely remembered having seen Olga in the lobby of the Hotel Lux in Moscow several months after the 1928 raid on Moabit Prison. In 1935 the Comintern assigned the Buber-Neumanns to move to Brazil along with the Ghioldis, the Ewerts, the Vallées, the Grubers, Victor Barron, and Olga herself, in preparation for the Communist revolt. Before the couple was to leave for South America they spent several weeks at a military training camp outside Moscow. But on the eve of their departure they were ordered to remain in Moscow. The couple's disagreements with several Comintern leaders, explained Margarete, had prevented their leaving and probably saved their lives.

Both women realized the enormity of what had just been said: How could someone in Ravensbrück say her life had been saved? The prisoners' situation worsened by the day. A high wall near the arsenal at the entrance to the camp had been designated for executions, and one day five women were shot by a firing squad for utterly trivial reasons, such as stealing a bottle of milk from the infirmary or talking back to the guards. All five were Jews as well as Communists. The terror beginning to seize the camp grew even more intense when news circulated that a team of doctors had come to perform genetic experiments on the prisoners. Drs. Otto Grawitz, Karl Gebhardt, Martin Schuhmann, and husband-and-wife team Klaus and Gerda Weyand-Sonntag had been holed up for several days in interminable conferences. In addition, it was rumored that the two brick buildings being built next to the bunker by recently arrived prisoners from Dachau were to be a gas chamber and crematorium. Hitler would soon publicly announce the "Final Solution" to what he considered the "Jewish Problem." October found Ravensbrück in a state of absolute panic.

It was during this fearful time that Charlotte Henschel—a German prisoner who had been with Olga in Lichtenburg—was taken to the camp infirmary with suspected tuberculosis. Within days, Lina Bertam, another prisoner, came down with the disease as well, and a third prisoner a week later. As the number of tuberculosis victims grew, so did the suspicion that the bacillus was being disseminated deliberately by the doctors as part of some kind of experiment. Risking summary execution, Olga and Kate Leichner, a militant Austrian Social Democrat arrested in Vienna during the Nazi occupation, tiptoed silently between the blocks to the window of the infirmary every night to bring the sick prisoners pieces of bread and margarine robbed from the Siemens canteen, and sometimes even classic poems scribbled on scraps of paper. Just a few weeks later approximately twenty women had been diagnosed as having tuberculosis. Once the epidemic reached these proportions, patients began to disappear from the infirmary, to the despair of those left behind. Finally, prison authorities made an official announcement that the women removed from the infirmary were all victims of some "incurable illness" and that the doctors had mercifully decided to "practice euthanasia" to cut short their suffering. To further justify the decision, the camp commandant posted a copy of a government declaration that "certain physicians, previously authorized for this express purpose, may grant to the incurably ill, after a clinical analysis, a merciful death." This was the legalization of extermination.

Charlotte Henschel, who miraculously survived Ravensbrück

and nazism, observed at close hand the macabre ritual surrounding the "merciful death" granted to the tubercular women removed from the camp infirmary. One day they came to get Anne-Marie Zadek, a Polish prisoner who had been in the bed beside her. As she was led into the next room, Anne-Marie asked Charlotte to write to her mother in Warsaw to tell her of her fate. Later in the day, noticing that the door had been left unguarded, Charlotte decided to visit Anne-Marie to read her the letter. Charlotte almost passed out at what she found: her friend had died from having some substance introduced into a vein; her head was shaved and her gold teeth yanked out. Her face was frozen in a mask of terror.

Before long, medical experiments were being conducted openly on both male and female prisoners of Ravensbrück. Karl Gebhart, a close friend and the personal physician to Heinrich Himmler, was chosen by the SS high commander to carry out experiments to "observe the development of the tetanus and staphylococcus bacilli and venereal disease in women." Injections were given in the lower legs of women chosen at random, causing infections that sometimes attacked even the bones. Often the bacilli were reapplied by Dr. Gebhart's assistants—the doctor himself only administered the initial injections and appeared from time to time to follow the course of the experiment—by introducing infected shards of glass or wood into the wounds. Since, according to the doctors, the use of anesthetics might "compromise the scientific nature of the experiments," these procedures were carried out without any kind of anesthesia. Without exception, the evolution of the disease was merely "observed," never treated. The women chosen as guinea pigs were executed once the experiment was concluded.

Male prisoners were reserved for the Nazi doctors' "genetic experiments": some had their testicles exposed to the effects of X rays for twenty or thirty minutes and then were sent back to work. Two weeks later they were summoned once more to the infirmary, where their testicles were removed for examination. Afterward, one of the doctors "granted them a merciful death." The insanity knew no limits. A group of orthopedists came from Berlin specifically to choose from among the women prisoners appropriate guinea pigs for limb or bone transplant experiments: a leg, an arm, or a collarbone would be removed from one woman's body and transplanted to another's, just for the purpose of observing the degree of rejection. The compulsory donor was eliminated immediately after surgery. The receiver survived a few more days or weeks. Ravensbrück had been transformed into a laboratory of monstrosities similar to the one at Auschwitz, where Josef Mengele conducted his experiments.

The perversions announced as medical research were not the only Nazi madness. At first, executions at Ravensbrück were carried out on an individual basis only. At the beginning of winter 1942, the systematic elimination of Jews and Communists began. Dr. Fritz Mennecke was transferred to the camp. Rumor had it that Mennecke's job was to decide which prisoners might still be useful as part of the work force for the Reich's war effort—Hitler was preparing for his "final attack" on the Soviet Union—and which should be sent to the gas chamber and crematorium. From that moment on, one doctor held complete power over eight thousand women and five hundred men. Drs. Gerda Weyand-Sonntag and Herta Oberheuser were assigned to help Mennecke in his deliberations.

The removal of the first batch of prisoners after Dr. Mennecke's arrival left those who remained behind in a state of confusion: Had the women selected been transferred to other work camps or sent to the gas chamber? This question remained unanswered until a week later, when a truck brought the women's clothing back to the camp. A plan was devised to learn where the prisoners were being taken: several of the transferees were given pencil and paper and asked to record the name of every place they could identify along the way and stuff the small scraps of paper into the hems of their skirts when they arrived at their final destination. Once the clothes were returned to the camp, it would be possible to pinpoint exactly where they had been taken. The first truck to return after the scheme was put into action did not completely clarify the women's fate. The notes found in their skirt hems repeated the same name: Bernburg. But what did that mean?

Located some one hundred kilometers southwest of Berlin, Bernburg was a small city of forty thousand inhabitants, divided by the river Saale. In 1942 almost the entire population worked either for Solvay, a Belgian potassium company, or at two or three factories producing cement, alkalies, and light agricultural tools. The most imposing building in the city, after the hundred-year-old Lutheran church, was a large, dark, red-brick construction that had, since the beginning of the century, housed the Landes-Heil und Pfleg-ansalt, a provincial hospital for the mentally ill, which served patients from the area between the larger cities of Leipzig and Magdeburg. In the autumn of 1939, the serenity of the place was shattered by a decision made in Berlin. On Himmler's instructions, six of the psychiatric hospital's fifteen five-story blocks became the "property of the Reich"—an unconvincing attempt to camouflage the SS activities that were to take place there. A concrete wall was hastily constructed to separate the rest of the hospital from the requisitioned area, which was immediately occupied by 150 soldiers and officials of the SS, under the direction of Dr. Irmfried Eberl and head nurse Kathe Hackbarth.

Dr. Eberl's secret was the underground construction of large rooms with walls and floors covered in white tile and with shower heads hanging from the ceilings. At first glance, these seemed to be communal baths, but they were the testing ground of one more macabre Nazi invention: the first gas chamber for mass execution.

The gas chamber's first victims were to be a group of non-Jewish Germans. A few months before the hospital was taken over by the SS, Hitler had sent a group of twenty pilots from the Condor Legion to Spain to fight beside Franco's Fascist forces. The pilots had refused to bomb Republican targets and instead landed their Junkers and gave themselves up to General Hugo Sperrle, who sent them back to Germany as deserters. When Irmfried Eberl informed the SS high command that the Bernburg gas chamber was ready for testing, Himmler proposed that the first victims be "the cowards from the Condor Legion." The experiments worked like a dream: the pilots were executed without bullets, blood, or screams. The imaginative Dr. Eberl even came up with a way of disposing of the bodies: right beside the gas chamber, accessible by an underground corridor, he had constructed an oil-operated oven. A gruesome billow of smoke issued from the chimneys of the hospital the afternoon of the test and hung over Bernburg. When the war ended in 1945, no fewer than thirty thousand Jews, Communists, socialists, and Social Democrats had been executed in Eberl's cellar. And it was the success of the experiment at Bernburg that led the Reich to set up similar extermination camps in Grafeneck, Brandenburg, Schloss, Harthein, Sonnenstein, and Hadamar, receiving prisoners from Buchenwald, Flossenburg, Mauthausen, Dachau, Sachsenhausen, and Gross Rosen.

Early in February 1942, shortly before Olga's thirty-fourth birthday, the women were gathered in Ravensbrück's central courtyard to hear the announcement over camp loudspeakers of who would be "transferred to other concentration camps." Prisoners were called in alphabetical order rather than by number, and those whose names were read were instructed to form a group at one side. One hundred and fifty names had already been called when the disembodied voice rang out, "Olga Benario Prestes."

Olga's friends Tilde Klose, Ruth Grunspun, Irene Langer, and Rosa Menzer were also listed. When Olga returned to block 11 to collect her small bundle of personal belongings, she found two old Jewish women weeping and praying feverishly in Yiddish. Squatting beside the two, whom she had met soon after arriving at Ravensbrück, she said soothingly, "Don't cry. We're just being moved to a different camp, where life will surely be better. The war will be over soon, the Nazis will be defeated, and then we'll have peace. Be calm and strong, we'll celebrate the peace together."

After settling them into their bunks, Olga glanced out of the window and saw four blue buses belonging to Gekrat, a Berlin charity that specialized in transporting the poor and in recent years had rendered services to the SS and the Gestapo. At 8:00 P.M. the camp loudspeakers sounded their last warning: "Prisoners listed in today's call have thirty minutes to collect their things and appear before the official waiting by the buses."

Half an hour—enough time to write a letter to her husband and daughter.

Ten days later, when the truck returned to Ravensbrück with the clothing of the women who had been taken that night, Emmy Handke ran to find Olga's dress. She felt impatiently along the hem until finally she found a tiny scrap of paper on which was written one word: Bernburg.

São Paulo,

JULY 1945

ON THE AFTERNOON of Sunday, July 15, 1945, after lunching at the home of young Party militants Tuba and Hirsch Schor, the leadership of the Brazilian CP made a final check on preparations for the rally scheduled to begin within minutes at the Pacaembu soccer stadium. This would be the first mass gathering of Communists in São Paulo since the National Liberation Alliance was outlawed in 1935. Wearing a dark suit, clean shaven, and feeling fit, Luís Carlos Prestes—general secretary of the Party since the 1943 clandestine "Conference of Mantiqueira," the Second National Conference of the CP—ushered his comrades into the small living room to listen to Milton Cayres de Brito and Diogenes de Arruda Camara report on a very different street demonstration that had taken place the previous evening. As a warning to the CP, the Catholic Church had organized a "novena to Our Lady," attracting thousands of faithful into the streets to worship the image of Nossa Senhora Aparecida (Our Lady of Apparitions), the patron saint of Brazil. After the procession, which had been organized by Cardinal Carlos Carmelo de Vasconcellos Motta, the crowd had gathered in front of the Cathedral da Sé to repeat in unison the words pronounced by a bishop: "I swear to be faithful to the Church, and to repudiate and fight communism!"

It was no surprise to the Communist leadership that the most conservative sectors of the Church had reacted in this way. Brazil had, after all, experienced a veritable maelstrom of political transformation during the previous three months. In early April, when Soviet Marshals Tobulkhin and Malinovsky liberated Vienna and Bratislava from the Germans and 150,000 Nazi soldiers were surrounded by the First and Fourth American Armies in the industrial basin of the Ruhr valley, the shock waves of the war's turnaround began to reach Brazil.

Ambassador Pereira de Souza, Brazil's representative in Washington, handed the Soviet ambassador, Andrei Gromyko, a ten-line note in which the Brazilian government requested the reopening of diplomatic relations with the Soviet Union. Internally, the about-face was even more dramatic. The Brazilian government had declared its intention to discontinue telephone tapping, which had been going on for ten years, and women, students, workers, and liberal professionals were organizing protests all over the country to demand immediate amnesty for political prisoners and exiles. In all the demonstrations, the Brazilian flag was seen waving beside the red flag's hammer and sickle, without police harassment. Some politicians resolved not to wait for an amnesty to be decreed and returned from exile in Argentina, entering Brazil unhindered. Prestes sent a cable from prison to President Vargas complimenting him on the reestablishment of relations "with the heroic Soviet people," and demanding that he decree political amnesty, "even if it is necessary to exclude my personal case." The thaw had begun.

In January 1942 Vargas had broken relations with the Axis powers and on August 22, 1942, had declared war on Germany and Italy. The return to Brazil of the first members of a contingent of 25,000 soldiers sent to fight fascism in Italy brought new ferment to the campaign for national redemocratization. Five hundred officers and enlisted men had died defending freedom, and the population demanded "out of respect for the memory of our martyrs" that Brazil make a break from its vestiges of authoritarianism once and for all. Factory worker Veriano Jelén, wounded on the Italian front, was one of the first to return to Brazil; at a press conference on his arrival at the port of Rio de Janeiro he demanded direct presidential elections.

"The American soldiers in Italy participated in U.S. presidential elections, voting from their tanks and trenches. Seeing this first-hand, our men couldn't understand or accept the fact that they are denied this right. We cannot maintain a regime here in Brazil like the one we fought against with our very blood in Italy."

Vargas promised to hold elections for his successor before the end of the year. His minister of war, the same General Eurico Dutra who had directed the siege against Agildo Barata's rebels at the Third Infantry Regiment ten years earlier, declared himself a government party candidate for the presidency and included in his platform an unbelievable notion: the legalization of the Communist Party. Realizing that Vargas was beginning to yield, the opposition pressed harder and began to fight for more than just the right to participate in presidential elections. Street demonstrations called for amnesty and for an elected assembly.

On April 18, Getúlio Vargas signed a decree granting amnesty to all political prisoners. Even before the act was made public in the *Diário Oficial,* the first six beneficiaries of the measure were released from prison. Luís Carlos Prestes, Captain Trifino Correia, and Lieutenant Ivan Ribeiro walked out of the House of Detention and Carlos Marighella, Captain Agildo Barata, and Lieutenant Antônio Bento Tourinho were taken from Ilha Grande to Rio de Janeiro by boat. As the nation's most important political prisoner, Prestes received special treatment: Column veteran Orlando Leite Ribeiro, with whom he had lived in exile in Argentina and who now served the Vargas government as a civil servant in Itamaraty, was sent to inform Prestes of the signing of the decree. Ribeiro took Prestes to the home of writer Leôncio Basbaum. On the way there, Prestes asked for news of Olga and his friend Arthur Ewert, who was also to be released under the amnesty but who would probably not be able to enjoy his freedom: ravaged by torture, Ewert would be checked into a Rio psychiatric clinic.

No one had any information about Olga. Prestes asked the international news services to help him find her in the concentration camps liberated by the Allies. One of the Brazilian troop commanders in Italy, Major Emygdio Miranda, an ex-officer of the

Prestes Column, was assigned to try to find Olga and bring her back to Brazil.

In his first statement to the press, Prestes expressed his gratitude to General Lázaro Cárdenas, the former president of Mexico, for the hospitality afforded Anita and dona Leocádia, who had died two years earlier, her son still in prison. At the time of her death, Cárdenas had offered himself as hostage so that Luís Carlos Prestes might be temporarily released from prison to attend his mother's funeral in Mexico, but the Vargas government never so much as considered the proposal. Nonetheless, when a reporter asked Prestes about his relations with Vargas, Prestes gave the first indication that he intended to place political considerations above personal issues, declaring, "Mr. Vargas has given proof of his good intentions."

Those who had followed closely the fortunes of the clandestine Communist Party during the last years did not find Prestes's words surprising. Early in 1938, after the frustrated *integralista* putsch manifested itself in the attempt on Guanabara Palace by Plínio Salgado's "green shirts," the Communist newspaper *A Classe Operária* (The Working Class) had formally supported the Vargas regime's reaction to the right-wing coup. Vargas's decision of 1942 to send Brazilian troops to fight the Nazis had also contributed to reducing the CP's hostility toward him. Still, the man with such kind words for the president was Luís Carlos Prestes, who had been victimized by the Vargas repression—not only had he spent ten years of his life in prison, but above all the dictator had handed over his wife and unborn daughter to the Nazis. The first negative reaction to Prestes's support of Vargas came from none other than his former lawyer, Sobral Pinto, who condemned "any national alliance with Getúlio Vargas along the lines suggested by Carlos Prestes." Sobral Pinto was a hard-liner and pessimistic: "Strengthening Getúlio Vargas's authority in any way or on any pretext is tantamount to setting the scene for a civil war without precedent on the American continent."

A few weeks later, when Prestes made his first public appearance at a rally at the Vasco da Gama soccer stadium in Rio before eighty thousand people, his support for the government was even clearer:

The opposition demands that Vargas abandon his post so that domestic peace can be maintained. But is this really the democratic road to order, peace, and national unity? On the contrary, wouldn't Getúlio Vargas be correct in asserting that it is his duty to maintain order by leading the country to free and honest elections and surrendering power to whomever the nation elects? Stepping down now would be a kind of desertion and betrayal that would in no way contribute to national unity: instead it would awaken new hope among the Fascists and reactionaries, making things more difficult and increasing the threat of coups and of civil war. Just as in August 1942 the Brazilian people turned to Getúlio Vargas in the hope that the leader of the popular movement of 1930 would address himself to fighting to the death the Nazi aggressors, our people now expect him, influential as he is by virtue of the victory of our armies in Italy, to institute truly free and honest elections. This is his duty as a man and as a citizen. Despite all the political divergences separating us from His Excellency, against whose government we have struggled, our weapons in hand, we have no right to doubt the patriotism of our nation's leader.

In spite of publicly defending the legalization of the CP, the government could not rein in the anticommunism that had grown over the long years of the dictatorship. Two days later, General Dutra fired Major Amilcar Dutra de Menezes from his position as head of the Department of Press and Propaganda (DIP) for having lent the Party sound equipment for Prestes to address the assembled crowd. But this was the smallest repercussion of the Vasco rally. Prestes's support of Vargas cost him dearly within the CP itself. A group of Party intellectuals in São Paulo, headed by Jorge Amado (who was dubbed "the Rasputin of the Correct Line"), declared itself opposed to the direction of the leadership. In a manifesto distributed to the press, several writers rebelled against the Prestes decision, stating that "the dictatorship was in a state of utter decay, and Luís Carlos Prestes's praise for Vargas gave him the kind of powerful credibility he needed more than ever." The *Vanguarda Socialista*, edited by Trotskyite intellectual Mario Pedrosa, was cruelly ironic about the fact that Vargas had been responsible for Olga's deportation to the Gestapo, suggesting that CP militants should instead ask the president of the republic: "Getúlio Vargas, why did you send Olga Benario Prestes to Hitler?"

Indifferent to accusations and polemics, Prestes was preparing for the big rally at Pacaembu in São Paulo. Planning had begun weeks in advance. There were committees of engineers, professors, dentists, textile workers, metalworkers, cabdrivers, street sweepers. During the week preceding July 15, spontaneous demonstrations were held in several neighborhoods inviting people to attend the mass meeting at Pacaembu. At each one, the closing speech fell to a political leader, worker, or Party intellectual. The organization seemed faultless: people were to gather at various points, continue to Praça Buenos Aires, and then proceed in parade formation to the gates of the stadium. From Tuba and Hirsch Schor's home in Bela Vista, Prestes could see groups already moving up Avenida Nove de Julho toward the stadium.

A little past three o'clock Prestes decided it was time to leave. Traveling in an open car, he was saluted all along the way by demonstrators heading for the stadium. When Prestes arrived at Pacaembu, the enormous crowd gave him a standing ovation—it was estimated that the stadium with a capacity for 60,000 spectators was jammed with more than 100,000 people, filling the grass as well as the stands. Waiting for the Communist leader on the speakers' platform were General Miguel Costa, journalist and National Democratic Union representative Júlio de Mesquita Filho, Chilean Communist senator and poet Pablo Neruda, Captains Agildo Barata and Trifino Correia, and Commander Roberto Sissón. For two hours, delegates from provincial interior cities and other states as well as various categories of professionals paraded on the track. One group circled the entire stadium holding a Brazilian flag by its corners and asking for contributions for the families of victims of the Brazilian battle cruiser *Bahia*, which had sunk at the end of the war. Coins and crumpled bills rained down from the stands. Opening speakers for the rally included Miguel Costa and state secretary of the CP, Mário Scott. After the singing of the Chilean national anthem, the microphone was passed to Pablo Neruda. Rather than make a speech, Neruda recited a poem he had written in honor of Prestes, the last verses of which especially touched the audience:

I request today a great silence of volcanoes and rivers.
A great silence of homelands and plain folk.
I request silence in America, from the snowy peaks to the prairies.

Silence: let the Captain of the People speak.
Silence: that Brazil may speak through his mouth.

Visibly moved, the crowd gathered at Pacaembu couldn't stop
applauding. Neruda good-humoredly returned to the podium and
repeated the last line of the poem: "Silence: that Brazil may speak
through his mouth."

The Brazilian national anthem was then played and Prestes spoke
for an hour and a half. He gave a long analysis of the world situation,
the defeat of fascism and its consequences for Brazilian life. He
reminded those gathered that the National Liberation Alliance had
lasted only three months, referred to the 1935 defeat and to the
"infamous brutality used against us by Filinto Müller's Fascist-
leaning police," spoke at length on Brazil's current economic crisis,
and though not once mentioning Vargas by name, returned to the
point that had provoked so much controversy—the Communist
support for the president:

> We have struggled and we will continue to struggle for national
> unity. The government has for some time been yielding to our de-
> mands for democracy and has thus changed direction from the past
> years' assault on the independence and liberation of our people.
> During that time we knew how to raise our weapons in defense of
> democracy; so now will we defend ourselves, supporting the govern-
> ment in its defense of order and seeking out the agents of disorder—
> all those who preach deliverance by way of coups or civil war in the
> name of democracy, but who are in truth no more than instruments of
> Fascist provocation.

Night had fallen by the time Prestes left Pacaembu for Roosevelt
Station, where he would board a train for Rio. Surrounded by
friends, he was preparing to climb the steps to the sleeping car
when a young man pushed his way through the crowd of people
who had come to say good-bye. "Captain Prestes! Captain Prestes!
Just a minute, don't board the train!"

At first there was concern that the man was going to attack the
Communist leader, but he then identified himself. "I'm a reporter
for United Press wire service. We asked our European branch

offices to find out anything they could about Olga Benario, and have just received this telegram from our correspondent in Berlin."

Uneasy, Prestes took the paper and read it with a furrowed brow, before the silent stares of his friends. Then he raised his head and said just three words, "Olga is dead."

It was a short cable, with few details:

BERLIN—ALLIED AUTHORITIES HAVE JUST INFORMED US THAT AMONG THE 200 WOMEN EXECUTED IN THE GAS CHAMBER IN THE GERMAN CITY OF BERNBURG AT EASTER 1942 WAS ONE OLGA BENARIO PRESTES, WIFE OF BRAZILIAN COMMUNIST LEADER LUIS CARLOS PRESTES.

Prestes boarded the train, which had already started to move down the track, walked the rows of seats in silence, sat down, and read the cable once more before folding it and placing it in the pocket of his overcoat.

Only years later would Prestes receive Olga's last letter to him and their daughter. It was written while still at Ravensbrück, the night she was put on the bus to Bernburg:

Dear Ones,

Tomorrow I will need all my strength and all my courage. For this reason, I will not be able to think about the things that torment my heart, things dearer to me than my own life. And for this reason, I'm saying good-bye to you now. It's utterly impossible for me to imagine, my dear daughter, that I will never see you again, never squeeze you in my eager arms. I wanted so to be able to comb your hair, to braid your braids— ah, no, you have had them cut. But I think you look better with your hair loose anyway, a little bit messy. Above all else, I'm going to make you strong. You should wear sandals or go barefoot, running outdoors with me. Your grandmother won't like this at first, but before long she'll understand. You must respect her and love her all your life, as your father and I do. Every morning we'll do our exercises. . . . You see? I've already gone back to dreaming, as I do every night, forgetting that this is to

241

say good-bye. And now, when I'm reminded of this, the idea that I will never again be able to hold your warm little body is like death to me.

Carlos, dear Carlos, my love: Will I have to relinquish forever everything good you have given me? Even though I will never have you near me again, it would be a comfort just to have your eyes see me once more. And I want so to see your smile. I want both of you, so much, so much. But what I'd like most is to be able to live one happy day, the three of us together, as I have imagined thousands of times. Can it be possible that I'll never see how proud and happy our daughter makes you feel?

Dear Anita, dear husband. I'm crying under the blankets so that no one will hear me, because it seems that today I don't have the strength to endure something so terrible. Which is precisely why I'm struggling to say good-bye to you now, so I don't have to do it during the last and most difficult hours. After tonight, I want simply to live for whatever brief future I have left. You are the one who taught me, dearest one, what strength of will means, especially when it springs from sources like ours. I have struggled for the just and the good, for the betterment of the world. I promise you now, as I say farewell, that until the last instant I will give you no reason to be ashamed of me. Please understand: preparing for death doesn't mean giving up but rather knowing how to confront it when it arrives. So many things could still happen in the meantime. . . . I will remain firm and determined to live until the last moment. Now I must go to sleep, so tomorrow I can be strong. I kiss you both for the last time.

Olga

Epilogue

Olga Benario Prestes lent her name to streets in seven cities and to ninety-one schools, factories, and workers' brigades in the German Democratic Republic. There is also a street named after her in Riberão Preto, a city in the state of São Paulo.

Luís Carlos Prestes broke with the Central Committee of the Brazilian Communist Party in 1980 and three months later was discharged from his position as general secretary. Supported only by friends, he died nearly penniless in 1990.

Anita Leocádia Prestes lives with her aunt *Lígia Prestes* in Rio de Janeiro, where she is a university professor. She too severed her connections to the Communist Party.

Granted amnesty in 1945, *Arthur Ewert* was taken a year later to the Soviet-occupied zone of Germany. He died in 1959 in the German Democratic Republic without regaining his sanity.

Otto Braun returned to the USSR in 1939. Ten years later he moved to East Germany, where he worked as a translator at the Marxist-Leninist Institute until his death.

Rodolfo Ghioldi died in July 1985 in Buenos Aires.

Agildo Barata left the Brazilian CP in 1957. Ten years later the government stripped him of his military rank. He died in 1969 at the age of sixty-three in Rio.

After receiving amnesty in 1945, *Antônio Maciel Bonfim ("Miranda")* fell into complete political obscurity. He died of tuberculosis in Brazil.

Sobral Pinto is a lawyer in Rio de Janeiro.

Miguel Costa died in December 1959.

Filinto Müller died in July 1973, in an airplane crash at Orly Airport in France. He was a senator for the Arena Party and majority leader in the Senate at the time.

Ambassador *José Joaquim Moniz de Aragão* retired from the diplomatic service in 1952, and died at the age of eighty-seven in 1974 in Rio.

Nazi doctor *Irmfried Eberl* and nurse *Kathe Hackbarth* were executed by troops liberating the extermination camp of Bernburg.

There is scant information regarding the fate of the militant Communist Youth who participated in the raid on Moabit Prison. *Rudi König* died in Spain fighting with the International Brigade. *Margot Ring* was executed in a gas chamber in the concentration camp at Dachau. Arrested by the Gestapo, *Erich Jazosch* spent several years in prison and finally died in a gas chamber in 1943. *Erick Bombach* was shot to death by SS troops. *Klara Seleheim* died in the "March of Death" at the concentration camp at Sachsenhausen.

The women's camp at Ravensbrück was liberated by the Forty-ninth Infantry Division of the Red Army on April 30, 1945, eight days after the German surrender.

Bibliography

In addition to the works listed below, the author made extensive use of newspapers and periodicals published in Brazil, East Germany, France, Switzerland, Great Britain, and the United States.

Almeida, Angela Mendes de. *A República de Weimar e a ascenção do nazismo*. São Paulo: Editora Brasiliense, 1982.

————. "Les rapports entre communistes et social-démocrates à la veille de l'ascension du fascism: la politique de la 'Troisiéme Période' et la these du 'social-fascisme.'" Ph.D. diss., University of Paris, 1980.

Amado, Jorge. *O Cavaleiro da Esperança*. Rio de Janeiro: Record, 1979.

Angelucci, Angelo. *Todos os aviões do mundo*. São Paulo: Editora Melhoramentos, 1982.

Barata, Agildo. *Vida de um revolucionário*. São Paulo: Editora Alfa-Omega, 1978.

Basbaum, Leôncio. *Uma vida em seis tempos*. São Paulo: Editora Alfa-Omega, 1978.

————. *História Sincera da República—De 1930 a 1960*. São Paulo: Editora Alfa-Omega, 1981.

Beloch, Israel, and Alzira Alves de Abreu. *Dicionário Histórico-Biográfico Brasileiro 1930–1983*. Vols. 1–4. Rio de Janeiro: Getúlio Vargas Foundation, 1985.

Bosi, Ecléa. *Memória e Sociedade: Lembranças de Velhos*. São Paulo: T. A. Queiroz Editor, 1983.

Buber-Neumann, Margarete. *La Révolution Mondiale—L'histoire du Komintern (1919–1943), racontée par l'un de ses principaux témoins*. Paris: Casterman, 1971.

Camargo, Aspásia, and Walder de Góes. *Meio século de combates: diálogo com Cordeiro de Farias*. Rio de Janeiro: Editora Nova Fronteira, 1981.

Campos da Paz Júnior, Manuel Venâncio. "Depoimento autobiográfico. Unpublished ms., 1959.

Carvalho, Ferdinando de. *Lembrai-vos de 35*. Rio de Janeiro: Biblioteca do Exército Editora, 1981.

Cavalcanti, Paulo. *O caso eu conto, como o caso foi (Da Coluna Prestes à queda de Arraes)*. São Paulo: Editora Alfa-Omega, 1978.

Chaves Neto, Elias. *Minha vida e as lutas de meu tempo*. São Paulo: Editora Alfa-Omega, 1978.

Costa, Octávio. *Trinta Anos Depois da Volta*. Rio de Janeiro: Editora Expressão e Cultura, 1975.

Davies, R. E. *A History of the World's Airlines*. New York: AMS Press, 1967.

Deakin, F. W., and G. R. Storry. *The Case of Richard Sorge*. London: Chatto & Windus, 1966.

Dehillotte, Pierre. *Gestapo*. Porto Alegre: Livraria do Globo, 1940.

Dines, Alberto. *Morte no Paraíso—A tragédia de Stefan Zweig*. Rio de Janeiro: Editora Nova Fronteira, 1981.

Dulles, John W. F. *Brazilian Communism 1935–1945*. Austin: University of Texas Press, 1983.

————. *Anarchists and Communists in Brazil (1900–1935)*. Austin: University of Texas Press, 1973.

Ehrt, Adolf. *Révolte Armée*. Berlin-Leipzig: Éditions Eckart, 1933.

Fest, Joachim. *Hitler*. Translated by Richard and Clara Winston. New York: Harcourt Brace Jovanovich, 1974.

Forjaz, Maria Cecília Spina. *Tenentismo e Aliança Liberal (1927–1930)*. São Paulo: Livraria Editora Polis, 1978.

Gama, A. B. *Columna Prestes—2 annos de revolução*. Salvador: Officinas Gráphicas de Fonseca Filho, 1927.

Guimarães, Renato Cupertino. "Depoimento tomado a Luís Carlos Prestes, em Moscou." Unpublished ms., 1971.

Haferkorn, Katja. *Geschichte Der Deutschen Arbeiterbewegung Biographisches Lexikon*. Berlin: Dietz Verlag, 1970.

————. *Kämpfer für das deutsche und das brasilianische Volk—Arthur Ewert*. Berlin: Dietz Verlag, 1968.

Henriques, Affonso. *Vargas, o maquiavélico*. São Paulo: Palácio do Livro, 1961.

Hermlin, Stephan. *Die Erste Reihe*. Berlin: Verlag Neues Leben, 1975.

Hernandez, Leila Maria Gonçalves Leite. "Movimentos Político-Ideológicos no Brasil: ANL e AIB." Master's thesis, University of São Paulo, 1979.

Kojevnikova, Tamara, and Marina Popovitch. *A Vida—um vôo eterno*. Moscow: Molodaia Gvardia, 1978.

Konder, Leandro. *Barão de Itararé*. São Paulo: Editora Brasiliense, 1983.

Labrousse, Pierre. *Repertoire des traversées aériennes de l'Atlantique Sud par l'Aéropostale et Air France—1930/1940*. Paris: Atéliers Jean-Marie Pierre, 1974.

Landucci, Ítalo. *Cenas e episódios da Coluna Prestes*. São Paulo: Editora Brasiliense, 1947.

Laqueur, Walter Z. *Weimar: A Cultural History (1918–1933)*. New York: Putnam, 1976.

Lazitch, Branko, and M. D. Drachicovitch. *Biographical Dictionary of the Comintern*. Stanford: The Hoover Institution Press, 1973.

Lima, Heitor Ferreira. *Caminhos Percorridos*. São Paulo: Editora Brasiliense, 1982.

Lima, Lourenço Moreira. *A Coluna Prestes—Marchas e Combates*. São Paulo: Editora Alfa-Omega, 1979.

Macaulay, Neill. *The Prestes Column: Revolution in Brazil*. New York: New Viewpoints, 1974.

Maffei, Eduardo. *A morte do sapateiro—A saga dos anos 30*. São Paulo: Editora Brasiliense, 1982.

Mooney, Michael M. *The Hindenburg*. New York: Dodd, Mead, 1972.

Moraes, Dênis de, and Francisco Viana. *Prestes: lutas e autocríticas*. Petrópolis: Editora Vozes, 1982.

Müller, Charlotte. *Die Klempnerkolonne in Ravensbrück—Erinnerungen des Häftlings Nr. 10787*. Berlin: Dietz Verlag Berlin, 1983.

Nasser, David. *Falta alguém em Nuremberg*. Rio de Janeiro: Edições do Povo, 1947.

Niemeyer, Oscar, et al. *Prestes Hoje*. Rio de Janeiro: Codecri, 1983.

Pacheco, Eliézer. *O Partido Communista Brasileiro—1922–1964*. São Paulo: Editora Alfa-Omega, 1984.

Parra, Amanda. "Olga Benario e a revolução brasileira." Paper presented to the Association of Women, Rome, 1978.

Pincher, Chapman. *Too Secret, Too Long*. New York: St. Martin's Press, 1985.

Pinto, Herondino Pereira. *Nos subterrâneos do Estado Novo*. Rio de Janeiro: 1950.

Porto, Eurico Bellens. *A insurreição de 27 de novembro—Relatório*. Rio de Janeiro: Imprensa Nacional, 1936.

Quintella, Ary. *Sobral Pinto: por que defendo os Communistas*. Belo Horizonte: Editora Communicação, 1979.

Ramos, Graciliano. *Memórias do Cárcere*. Rio de Janeiro: Livraria José Olympio Editora, 1953.

Rodrigues, Leôncio Martins. *O Brasil Republicano*. Vol. X of História Geral da Civilização Brasileira. São Paulo: Difel, 1981.

Santa Rosa, Virgínio. *O Sentido do Tenentismo*. São Paulo: Editora Alfa-Omega, 1976.

Schiese, Ruddolf. *Olga Benario Prestes 1908–1942*. Berlin: Lichtenburger Lesenefte, n.d.

Segatto, José Antonio, José Paulo Nétto, José Ramos Néto, Paulo César de Azevedo, and Vladimir Sachetta. *PCB—Memória Fotográfica—1922–1982*. São Paulo: Editora Brasiliense, 1982.

Silva, Hélio. *1935, A Revolta Vermelha*. Rio de Janeiro: Editora Civilização Brasileira, 1969.

———. *1926, A Grande Marcha*. Rio de Janeiro: Editora Civilização Brasileira, 1971.

———. *1937, Todos os golpes se parecem*. Rio de Janeiro: Editora Civilização Brasileira, 1970.

———. *Vargas*. Porto Alegre: L&PM Editores, 1980.

Sodre, Nelson Werneck. *A Coluna Prestes—Análise e Depoimentos*. Rio de Janeiro: Editora Civilização Brasileira, 1980.

———. *Contribuição à História do PCB*. São Paulo: Global Editora, 1984.

Stalin, Joseph. *Problems of Leninism*. Translated from the 11th Russian edition. Moscow: 1942.

Steiner, Jean Francois. *Treblinka*. Translated by Helen Weaver. New York: Simon & Schuster, 1967.

Valtin, Jan. *Out of the Night*. New York: Alliance Book Corp., 1941.

Vergolino, Honorato Himalaya. *Denúncia dos co-réus da revolução de 27 novembro de 1935, apresentado ao Tribunal de Segurança Nacional*. Rio de Janeiro: Imprensa Nacional, 1936.

Vinhas, Moisés. *O Partidão—A luta por um partido de massas—1922–1974*. São Paulo: Editora Hucitec, 1982.

Werner, Ruth. *Olga Benario*. Berlin: Verlag Neues Leben, 1962.

Zörner, G., et al. *Frauen-KZ Ravensbrück*. Berlin: VEB Deutscher Verlag der Wissenschaften, 1977.

Sources

INSTITUTIONS

The Archives of the Lemos de Brito Prison (Rua Frei Caneca), Rio de Janeiro.

The Archives of Rodolfo Ghioldi (private collection). (ARG)

The Bernburg State Archives, Bernburg, East Germany. (BSA)

The British Library, Newspaper Archives, Colindale, London.

The Committee of Anti-Fascist Resistance, East Berlin.

The Center for Research and Documentation for Contemporary History of Brazil—The Getúlio Vargas Foundation, Rio de Janeiro. (CHB)

Documentation Center of East Germany, East Berlin. (DCEG)

Documents' Department, Abril Publishers, São Paulo.

Historical Archives of the Brazilian Workers' Movement—The Giangiacomo Feltrinelli Foundation, Milan.

The Historical Archives of the Ministry of Foreign Affairs of Brazil, Rio de Janeiro. (HAMFAB)

"Iconographia," Text Research ("Sight and Sound"), São Paulo. (ITR)

Institute for Marxism-Leninism—Central Party Archives, East Berlin. (IML)

The Edgard Leuenroth Archives—"Unicamp," Campinas, São Paulo.

The Mário de Andrade Municipal Library, São Paulo.

Musée Air France, Paris. (MAF)

National Archives, Rio de Janeiro. (NA, RdJ)

National Archives, Washington, D.C. (NA, D.C.)

The National Library, Rio de Janeiro.

National Memorial Organization, Ravensbrück, East Germany. (NMO)

SOURCES

The President Kennedy Municipal Library, São Paulo.
Public Records Office, London.
The Hermínio Sacchetta Archives, São Paulo.
The Society of Former Ravensbrück Deportees, Paris.
The State Archives of Saõ Paulo, São Paulo.
Superior Military Tribunal, Brazil (SMT)
Supreme Federal Tribunal, Brazil.
Yad Vashem—"Martyrs' and Heroes' Remembrance Authority," Jerusalem.

PERSONS INTERVIEWED BY THE AUTHOR

Zuleika Alambert
Milton Cayres de Brito
Maria Werneck de Castro
Manoel Batista Cavalcanti
José Gay da Cunha
Carmen Ghioldi
Rodolfo Ghioldi
Emmy Handke
Ilze Hunger
Gabor Lewin
Herta Lewin
Dora Mantay

Klaus Martin
Celestino Paraventi
Anna Pikarski
Anita Leocádia Prestes
Lígia Prestes
Luís Carlos Prestes
Wilfried Rupert
Beatriz Bandeira Ryff*
Tuba Schor
Kurt Seibt
Anni Sindermann
Helmut F. Spate

* Interview given to Paulo César de Azevedo.

Index